UNCTAD/ITE/EDS/5

UNITED NATIONS CONFERENCE ON TRADE AND DEVELOPMENT
Geneva

INTERNATIONAL ACCOUNTING and REPORTING ISSUES

1998 Review

**Report by the Secretariat of the
United Nations Conference on Trade and Development**

**UNITED NATIONS
New York and Geneva, 1999**

NOTE

Symbols of United Nations documents are composed of capital letters combined with figures. Mention of such a symbol indicates a reference to a United Nations document.

The designations employed and the presentation of the material in this publication do not imply the expression of any opinion whatsoever on the part of the Secretariat of the United Nations concerning the legal status of any country, territory, city or area, or of its authorities or concerning the delimitation of its frontiers or boundaries.

Material in this publication may be freely quoted or reprinted, but acknowledgement is requested, together with a reference to the document number. A copy of the publication containing the quotation or reprint should be sent to the UNCTAD secretariat.

PER
UNI
ST/CTC
I5I

UNCTAD/ITE/EDS/5

UNITED NATIONS PUBLICATION
Sales No. E. 99.II.D.5
ISBN 92-1-112444-1

PREFACE

The Intergovernmental Working Group of Experts on International Standards of Accounting and Reporting (ISAR) was created by the Economic and Social Council of the United Nations in 1982 to promote the harmonisation of national accounting and reporting standards. In 1993, the servicing of ISAR was transferred from the Former Centre on Transnational Corporations in New York to the United Nations Conference on Trade and Development (UNCTAD) in Geneva. ISAR provides an international forum where experts from developing countries, emerging markets and economies in transition, as well as national, regional and international standard-setters, meet to discuss accounting and reporting issues from a global perspective. To date, ISAR has held 15 sessions. The fifteenth session took place in Geneva from 13 to15 February 1998, and was attended by a total of 148 experts from 62 countries, including experts from developed and developing countries and countries with economies in transition, 10 professional associations and seven international organizations.

This review contains the proceedings of the fifteenth session, the objective of which was to assess recent developments in the area of environmental accounting and to provide new guidance. The discussions focused on environmental financial accounting and reporting at the corporate level. ISAR had before it not only the main document, a position paper, but also two background papers containing the results of two years of research. The position paper is included in this volume as chapter I, and the two background papers are contained in chapters II and III. The paper contained in chapter IV was presented to ISAR during its fourteenth session; revisions were requested and it was reviewed very briefly during the fifteenth session. Summaries of the relevant discussions of the experts are also included in chapters I and III.

Since the late 1980s, ISAR has been working on issues relating to environmental accounting and has undertaken a number of surveys at the national as well as the enterprise level which were designed to assess deficiencies in environmental disclosure and to develop detailed guidance to remedy them. In 1995, ISAR reviewed developments at the national standard-setting level and discovered that, although considerable research was already under way at the national level, a significant effort was still required to study and identify the most appropriate guidance for Governments, enterprises and other interested parties. It concluded that it was important to provide such guidance promptly, since without it, differences would arise and member States would find themselves in the position of having to reconcile their independent standards and procedures with those of other member States.

During two days of intense discussions, the main document, "Environmental financial accounting and reporting at the corporate level" (TD/B/COM.2/ISAR/2), was reviewed section by section. The discussion initially addressed the questions of how to define environmental costs, when to capitalize environmental costs, what constitutes an "obligation" in the environmental context, when to recognize an environmental liability, and how to treat recoveries. While there is a clear understanding of what constitutes a legal obligation, if one is to capture the essence of environmental liabilities, one must go beyond this narrow legal category. The debate thus focused on "constructive" and "equitable" obligations. Constructive obligations are business-type obligations arising from a business policy or practice rather than from a law. Some experts considered equitable obligations (right and moral things to do) as a subset of constructive obligations, but a number of experts considered that not all equitable obligations were constructive ones. The representative of the World Bank gave the example of a transnational corporation which often accounted for and reported its environmental liabilities arising from legal obligations in developed countries but was silent on such liabilities when they arose in developing countries where there was no legislation. ISAR's decision to retain and explain the concept of equitable obligations is not only valuable accounting guidance for enterprises but also expands the area of social responsibility in a very clear way. The term "equitable obligation" closes a loophole that has allowed enterprises to report liabilities only when they have no choice but to do so. On the basis of the documentation provided by the secretariat and its own discussions, ISAR formulated specific guidance to Governments, enterprises and other parties interested in accounting for and reporting environmental costs and liabilities. The guidance was issued in the form of a position paper, for copies of which the secretariat has so far received over 75 requests from transnational corporations and environmental groups. ISAR recommended that the paper should be published in several languages and disseminated at regional workshops. The paper has been translated into six languages, and workshops have been held in Brazil, Egypt and Thailand with the help of funds from the World Bank and co-operation from the United Nations Environment Programme (UNEP).

Two resource persons, one from the Association of Chartered Certified Accountants (ACCA) and the other from Ellipson AG, brought ISAR up to date with research work on environmental performance indicators which could be linked to financial performance indicators. ISAR noted that there was no consensus on the use of environmental performance indicators. Often companies within an industry reported their performance using different environmental indicators, and they did not necessarily use the same indicators from year to year. ISAR recommended that UNCTAD should invite other relevant organizations, such as the International Organization for Standardization and UNEP, to take part in this research and report the results.

Experts also reacted to the remarks of the Secretary-General of UNCTAD on the Asian crisis; experts from Bangladesh, China, Cyprus, India, Jordan, Lebanon, Pakistan and Thailand requested that UNCTAD should undertake together with the Asian countries a research project on the recent Asian financial crisis from the perspective of accounting and auditing, to identify areas where there was room for improvement in accounting and auditing systems and to draw lessons for the prevention of future crises. Subsequently, a study of 85 of the largest banks and enterprises in Asia was undertaken and is near completion.

ISAR also noted the importance of developing a global curriculum for the education of professional accountants, which could serve as a benchmark and cut the time and cost of negotiating mutual recognition agreements. The experts recommended that UNCTAD should continue its work on the development of a global curriculum, as well as on other requirements for the qualification of professional accountants, in co-operation with relevant bodies such as the International Federation of Accountants (IFAC), the Arab Society of Certified Accountants (ASCA) and ACCA. ISAR put this topic on its provisional agenda for the sixteenth session, due to be held in February 1999.

UNCTAD would like to thank the resource persons from the Canadian Institute of Chartered Accountants (CICA), ACCA and Ellipson, for their excellent contributions to the research of ISAR. It would also like to thank the World Bank for financial assistance, UNEP, the Brazilian Social and Economic Development National Bank, the University of São Paulo in Brazil and ASCA for their commitment and support in disseminating ISAR's work on environmental accounting.

Rubens Ricupero
Secretary-General of UNCTAD
Geneva, December 1998

EXECUTIVE SUMMARY

The 1998 review of International Accounting and Reporting Issues contains the proceedings of the fifteenth session of the Intergovernmental Working Group of Experts on International Standards for Accounting and Reporting (ISAR) held in February 1998 in Geneva. The main item on the agenda was how to deal appropriately with environmental costs and liabilities. While most of the discussions and conclusions were within the domain of the traditional accounting framework, the experts went further and examined the relationship between environmental and financial performance.

Chapter I deals with accounting and financial reporting for environmental costs and liabilities, focusing on the duty of management to report the financial implications of their stewardship of the environmental resources linked to their enterprise's activities. The chapter will help enterprises, regulators and standard-setting bodies to account for environmental transactions and events in financial statements and associated notes. Precise definitions are given of terms such as environment, asset, liability, contingent liability, environmental costs, environmental assets, environmental liabilities, capitalization, obligation, legal obligation and constructive obligation. Also, specific guidelines are given on the recognition, measurement and disclosure of environmental costs and liabilities.

Chapter II is a synthesis of the current national guidance on accounting for environmental costs and liabilities. It is based on a review of the work that has been, or is currently being, undertaken by ISAR, the European Advisory Forum, accounting organizations and standard-setting bodies in Canada, the United Kingdom and the United States, and on surveys conducted on Brazil, China, the Czech Republic, Germany, Mauritius, the Netherlands, Pakistan, Poland, the Republic of Korea, the Russian Federation and Switzerland.

Chapter III attempts to go beyond the conventional accounting model to identify key environmental performance indicators and examine their relation to financial performance. It reviews best practices used to measure and communicate environmental performance and how such environmental data are increasingly being used by the financial community to make investment decisions. It concludes by making recommendations to improve environmental performance indicators so that environmental performance can be reported in a coherent and useful manner.

The last chapter deals with information disclosure and transfer pricing. Governments have enacted legislation to determine transfer pricing and prevent abuses in this area. But these regulations are not uniform, particularly in their disclosure requirements. Further, the current reporting requirements may provide insufficient information for users of financial statements. This report makes recommendations for improved accounting and reporting measures which would make the transfer-pricing practices of transnational corporations more transparent for accounting purposes.

CONTENTS

CHAPTER I

POSITION PAPER: ACCOUNTING AND FINANCIAL REPORTING FOR ENVIRONMENTAL LIABILITIES AND COSTS

CHAPTER II

ACCOUNTING AND REPORTING FOR ENVIRONMENTAL LIABILITIES AND COSTS WITHIN THE EXISTING FINANCIAL REPORTING FRAMEWORK

CHAPTER III

LINKING ENVIRONMENTAL AND FINANCIAL PERFORMANCE: A SURVEY OF BEST PRACTICE TECHNIQUES

CHAPTER I

POSITION PAPER: ACCOUNTING AND FINANCIAL REPORTING FOR ENVIRONMENTAL LIABILITIES AND COSTS

SUMMARY AND CONCLUSIONS

After a brief introduction by the secretariat, the representative of the **Canadian Institute of Chartered Accountants (CICA)** introduced agenda item 3(a) "Examination of national standards and regulations for environmental financial accounting", based on document TD/B/COM.2ISAR/2. He provided evidence of the perceived need for guidance in this area:

- Users of financial reports need information on the enterprise's environmental performance with its consequences for the financial health of the enterprise; this information is currently absent from financial reports;

- Financial statements were designed to report on financial performance, and additional guidance is needed if environmental performance is to be reported;

- Interpretation of existing international and national standards in environmental accounting and financial reporting at the corporate level is needed to prevent fundamental differences in amounts being measured and disclosed; furthermore, companies are devising their own solutions.

Some of the problem areas discussed by the experts included the definition of "environmental costs"; when to expense or capitalise environmental costs; what constitutes an "obligation" in the environmental context; when to recognise an environmental liability; measurement of an environmental liability; and treatment of recoveries, all of which were contained in the original version of "Environmental financial accounting and reporting at the corporate level" (TD/B/COM.2/ISAR/2).

In the discussions, it was suggested that the title of the background paper be changed. The Group unanimously agreed that the present title, "Interim statement of best practice guidance for environmental financial accounting and reporting", was inappropriate, especially the use of the word "interim". Also, various delegates recommended avoiding the term "best practice", because practice in this area was still evolving and it would be premature to refer to "best practice". The terms "position paper" and "guidelines" were suggested as alternatives since ISAR was not a standard-setting body.

A number of experts made the point that reliable and transparent environmental disclosure was needed by a wide audience of users such as governments, investors, creditors, consumers and environmentalists. Similarly, the "guidelines" should apply to a larger group of preparers of financial statements, including banks and government enterprises. Environmental issues were increasingly relevant to public enterprises, not just the private sector, although it was originally developed in that context. Experts stressed the importance of the guideline as "value added" to developing countries and economies in transition, as well as to developed countries. UNCTAD/ISAR should therefore synthesise and publish the guideline for a wide circulation.

It was suggested that the paper could also give guidance concerning accounting for environmental benefits as opposed to just costs and liabilities. It was pointed out that benefits were even harder to measure and this would have to be the subject of subsequent work; furthermore, not everything could easily fit into the conventional accounting framework.

The first technical point addressed by the Group was the definition of environmental costs, which were all the internal costs resulting from steps taken to manage the environmental impacts of an enterprise's activity. A number of examples of environmental costs were given, including disposal and avoidance of waste, preserving or improving air quality, and cleaning up oil spills. Not included were fines and penalties, but these should be disclosed separately. Normally, environmental costs should be charged to income in the period in which they were identified, unless the criteria for recognition as an asset had been met, in which case they should be capitalized. Experts discussed the fact that what was included as an environment cost would require judgement. Some enterprises might choose to include only those costs that were wholly attributable to environmental measures. Others might choose to make an arbitrary allocation when a cost was only partly environmental. Therefore, <u>disclosure</u> of what had been included as an environmental cost was essential.

There was considerable debate on the description of and distinctions between various types of obligations. There was a clear understanding of a legal obligation, but in the opinion of many speakers it was necessary to go beyond them, particularly if one considered substance over form. The debate focused on the terms "constructive obligations" and "equitable obligations", and on whether they were distinct or overlapped. Constructive obligations arose out of a business-type obligation or a business policy. Some experts felt that equitable obligations could be omitted because they were difficult to determine and could constitute a subset of constructive obligations based on ethical or moral considerations. However, other experts insisted that not all equitable obligations were constructive. An example was given of TNCs which often accounted for and reported on their environmental liabilities arising from legal obligations in developed countries but were silent on such liabilities arising in developing countries where there was no legislation. In the view of some experts the term "equitable obligation" would close a loophole in that most companies now reported liabilities only when they had "no discretion" **not** to report them. The concept of obligations needed to be expanded beyond legal obligations, which were too narrow, particularly when viewed in an environmental context. It was pointed out that the current conceptual accounting frameworks mentioned equitable obligations. The Group agreed that the term "equitable obligation" should remain in the guideline as a footnote to the term "constructive obligation".

Views differed about which method should be used to recognise environmental liabilities relating to future site restorations, or closure and removal, decommissioning costs and other situations where expenditures were not expected to be incurred for a considerable period of time. The discussion centred on whether full provision should be made immediately for the entire future cost or whether it should be built up gradually over the life of the operation. It was agreed that in the case of long-term decommissioning costs an enterprise could choose to provide for such costs over the life of the related operations. The Group also agreed that when environmental damage related to the enterprise's own property for which there was no obligation to clean up, consideration should be given to disclosing this fact. The rationale was that this information was needed by the shareholders, especially when they were different from management.

In concluding its discussion of item agenda item 3(a) the Group agreed to entitle the paper "Position paper: Accounting and financial reporting for environmental costs and liabilities", and endorsed its contents for consideration by Governments, organisations and other interested parties. It was felt that this title better reflected the contents of the paper.

I.   PURPOSE AND FOCUS OF THE POSITION PAPER

Since the late 1980s, the Intergovernmental Working Group of Experts on International Standards of Accounting and Reporting (ISAR) has given extensive attention to issues relating to environmental accounting, and has undertaken a number of surveys at the national as well as at the enterprise level. In 1991, it reached agreement on a number of items that it felt could be considered by the board of directors for disclosure in its report or management discussion, in order to deal with relevant environmental issues. In 1995, its thirteenth session was devoted exclusively to the subject of environmental accounting. During that session, ISAR noted that, although considerable research was already under way, a significant effort was still required to study and evaluate the information being produced, so as to identify the most appropriate guidance that should be given to governments and other interested parties. It concluded that providing such guidance was important. Without its prompt development, ISAR felt that differences would arise, and member States would subsequently find themselves in the position of having to reconcile their independent standards and procedures with those of other member States.

The purpose of this *Position Paper on Accounting and Financial Reporting for Environmental Costs and Liabilities* is to provide assistance to enterprises, regulators and standard-setting bodies on what is considered best practice in accounting for environmental transactions and events in the financial statements and associated notes. The sections on measurement and presentation are based on a synthesis of positions developed, or being developed, by standard-setting and other organisations, and includes extracts taken from some of the related documents. The section on disclosure is more extensive than that included in the documents referred to, and includes some of the disclosures previously proposed by ISAR.

ISAR recognises that a number of these issues are under consideration by the International Accounting Standards Committee (IASC). This position paper attempts to bring together in one place most of the issues which have been raised in corporate accounting and reporting of environmental impacts. It is unlikely that the IASC will issue such a comprehensive statement in the near future. It is more likely that it will incorporate environmental issues in each of its individual standards, as appropriate. This approach could take a number of years.

The focus of this Position Paper *is on the accountability of the management of an enterprise for financial implications of managing the environmental resources entrusted to it and that are linked to the enterprise's activity*.

The stated objective of financial statements as contained in the *Objectives of Financial Statements* issued by ISAR (1989) is to provide information about the financial position of an enterprise, which is useful to a wide range of users in making decisions and is necessary for the accountability of management for resources entrusted to it. The environment is a resource that is significant to many enterprises, and it must be managed efficiently for the benefit of both the enterprise and society.

II.   NEED TO ACCOUNT FOR ENVIRONMENTAL COSTS AND LIABILITIES

Accounting for the environment has become increasingly relevant to enterprises (whether they be businesses, non-profit organisations or government enterprises, such as municipalities and crown corporations) because issues such as the pollution of the environment have become a more prominent economic, social and political problem throughout the world. Steps are being taken at the national and international level to protect the environment and to reduce, prevent and mitigate the effects of pollution. As a consequence, there is a trend for enterprises to disclose to the community at large information about their environmental policies, environmental objectives, and programmes undertaken, and the costs and benefits related to these policies, objectives and programmes, and to disclose and provide for environmental risks.

How an enterprise's environmental performance affects its financial health and how financial information relating to such performance can be used to assess environmental risk, and the management of such risk, are often matters of concern to investors and their advisers. Creditors have similar needs, but an added factor is the possibility of having to take on the responsibility for rectifying environmental damage should a debtor default on a loan for which it has pledged land as security; the amount involved may be significantly greater than that of the original loan. Owners and shareholders are particularly interested because of the potential impact environmental costs may have on the financial return on their investment in the enterprise. Other interested parties would include customers, suppliers, regulators, the general public, and those acting on their behalf. The information provided should be presented in such a manner so as not to jeopardise business confidentiality in sensitive areas or the competitive position of the enterprise.

III.   SCOPE

This *Position Paper* deals with accounting for and reporting of environmental costs and liabilities arising from transactions and events that affect, or will likely affect, the financial position and results of an enterprise and, as such, should be reported in an enterprise's financial statements. The recognition and measurement of costs or events that are not absorbed by the enterprise are not covered. Examples of such costs (often referred to as external costs) can include those relating to the negative impacts of air pollution and water pollution on the environment which are borne by society at large rather than the enterprise.

IV. DEFINITIONS

The following terms are used in this *Position Paper* with the meanings specified:

- The *environment* comprises our natural physical surroundings and includes air, water, land, flora, fauna and non-renewable resources, such as fossil fuels and minerals.
- An *asset* is a resource controlled by an enterprise as a result of past events and from which future economic benefits are expected to flow to the enterprise.
- A *liability* is a <u>present</u> obligation of the enterprise arising from past events, the settlement of which is expected to result in an outflow from the enterprise of resources embodying economic benefits.
- A *contingent liability* is a <u>potential</u> obligation arising from past events that exists at the balance sheet date, but whose outcome will be confirmed only on the occurrence or non-occurrence of one or more uncertain future events that are outside the control of the enterprise.
- *Environmental costs* comprise the costs of steps taken, or required to be taken, to manage the environmental impacts of an enterprise's activity in an environmentally responsible manner, as well as other costs driven by the environmental objectives and requirements of the enterprise[1].
- *Environmental assets* are environmental costs that are capitalised because they satisfy the criteria for recognition as an asset.
- *Environmental liabilities* are obligations relating to environmental costs that are incurred by an enterprise and that meet the criteria for recognition as a liability. When the amount or timing of the expenditure that will be incurred to settle the liability is uncertain, "environmental liabilities" are referred to in some countries as "provisions for environmental liabilities".
- To *capitalise* is to record an environmental cost as an integral part of a related asset, or as a separate asset, as appropriate.
- An *obligation* is a duty or responsibility to others that entails settlement, by future transfer or use of assets, provision of services or other yielding of economic benefits, at a specified or determinable date, on occurrence of a specified event, or on demand.
- A *legal obligation* is a statutory, regulatory or contractually based obligation. A *constructive obligation* is one that can be created, inferred or construed from the facts in a particular situation, rather than being legally based[2] or that arises from ethical or moral considerations[3] and that an enterprise has little or no discretion to avoid.

Accounting for environmental costs and liabilities is covered by various basic concepts of accounting that have evolved. Of particular relevance are the definitions of "liabilities" and "assets". Additional disclosures may, however, be necessary or desirable to fully reflect various environmental impacts arising from the activities of a particular enterprise or industry.

V. RECOGNITION OF ENVIRONMENTAL COSTS

Environmental costs should be recognised in the period in which they are first identified. If the criteria for recognition as an asset have been met, they should be capitalised and amortised to the income statement over the current and appropriate future periods; otherwise they should be charged to the income statement immediately.

Issues relating to environmental costs centre on the period or periods in which costs should be recognised, and whether they should be capitalised or charged to income.

In some cases, an environmental cost may relate to damage that has taken place in a prior period. Examples include environmental damage to property that occurred prior to acquisition, an accident or other activities in a prior period that now require clean up, clean up of property disposed of in a prior period, and costs of disposing or treating hazardous waste created in a prior period. Accounting standards, however, generally preclude environmental costs being treated as a prior period adjustment unless there is a change in accounting policy or unless there was a fundamental error. The examples referred to above would, therefore, generally not qualify as prior period adjustments.

Environmental costs should be capitalised if they relate, directly or indirectly, to future economic benefits that will flow to the enterprise through:
(a) increasing the capacity, or improving the safety or efficiency of
     other assets owned by the enterprise;
(b) reducing or preventing environmental contamination likely to occur
     as a result of future operations; or
(c) conserving the environment.

The definition of an asset indicates that where a cost incurred by an enterprise will result in future economic benefits, it would be capitalised and charged to income in the periods in which those benefits are expected to be realised. Environmental costs that comply with such a criterion would, therefore, be capitalised. Capitalisation is also considered appropriate when environmental costs are incurred for safety or environmental reasons, or where they reduce or prevent potential contamination, or conserve the environment for the future. While they may not directly increase economic benefits, incurring such costs may be necessary if the enterprise is to obtain, or continue to obtain, future economic benefits from its other assets.

Many environmental costs do not result in a future benefit, or are not sufficiently closely related to future benefits to enable them to be capitalised. Examples would include treatment of waste products, clean up costs relating to current operating activities, clean up of damage incurred by the reporting enterprise itself in a prior period, ongoing environmental administration, and environmental audits. Fines and penalties for non-compliance with environmental regulations, and compensation to third parties for environmental damage are regarded as environmentally related costs, and are also instances of costs incurred that do not result in future benefits. Such costs would therefore be charged to the income statement immediately.

When an environmental cost that is recognised as an asset is related to another asset, it should be included as an integral part of that asset, and not recognised separately.

In most instances, environmental costs that are capitalised are related to another capital asset. There is no specific or separate future benefit that results from incurring the environmental costs themselves. The future benefit of such costs lies in another productive asset that is used in the enterprise's operations. For example, the removal of asbestos from a building does not in itself result in a future economic or environmental benefit. It is the building that receives the benefit. It would therefore be inappropriate to recognise such asbestos removal as a separate asset. A piece of machinery that removes pollution from the water or atmosphere, on the other hand, could have a specific or separate future benefit and could, therefore, be recognised separately.

When an environmental cost is capitalised and included as an integral part of another asset, the combined asset should be tested for impairment and, where appropriate, written down to its recoverable amount.

The integration of capitalised environmental costs with the related asset could, in some instances, result in the combined asset being recorded above recoverable amount. Consequently, the combined asset should be tested for impairment. Similarly, capitalised environmental costs recognised as a separate asset should also be tested for impairment[4]. Whilst the recognition and measurement of environmental impairment involves the same principles as other forms of impairment, the uncertainties may be greater. In particular, the "stigma" effect of environmental pollution on the value of neighbouring properties has to be considered.

VI.   RECOGNITION OF ENVIRONMENTAL LIABILITIES

An environmental liability would normally be recognised when there is an obligation on the part of the enterprise to incur an environmental cost.

An obligation does not have to be legally enforceable for an environmental liability to be recognised. There may be cases where an enterprise has a constructive obligation, either in the absence of a legal obligation or that expands on the legal obligation. For example, it may be the enterprise's established policy to clean up contamination to a higher standard than that required by law, because its business reputation would be affected if it did not live up to this commitment, or because it is the right and proper thing to do. For an environmental liability to be recognised in such situations, however, there has be a commitment on the part of management of an enterprise to incur the related environmental costs (for example, a board decision recorded in minutes that are publicly available, or communicated by way of a public announcement). At the same time, an enterprise should not be precluded from recognising an environmental liability simply because its management, at a later date, is unable to meet the commitment. If this eventuality does occur, there should be disclosure of that fact in the notes to the financial statements, together with the reason why the enterprise's management is unable to meet the commitment.

In rare situations, it may not be possible to estimate, in whole or in part, the amount of an environmental liability. This does not exempt an enterprise from disclosing the fact that there is an environmental liability. In such a situation, the fact that no estimate can be made, together with the reason therefor, should be disclosed in the notes to the financial statements.

When environmental damage relates to the enterprise's own property, or is caused by the enterprise's operations and activities to other property for which there is no obligation on the enterprise's part to rectify, consideration should be given to disclosing the extent of the damage in the notes to the financial statements or in a section of the report outside the financial statements themselves. When there is a reasonable possibility that such damage may have to be rectified in some future period, a contingent liability may have to be disclosed.

Although there may not be an obligation at the balance sheet date for an enterprise to rectify environmental damage, the situation may change in future periods, for example, due to new legislation or due to a decision by the enterprise to dispose of its property, in which case there will then be an obligation. In any event, owners and shareholders are entitled to know the extent to which there is environmental damage to the enterprise's own property, as well as to the property of others.

Costs relating to site restoration or the closure or removal of long-lived assets which the enterprise is under an obligation to incur should be recognised as an environmental liability at the time of identifying the need to undertake the remedial action relating to such site restoration, closure or removal. In the case of long-term decommissioning costs, however, an enterprise may choose to provide for such costs over the life of the related operations.

Since the obligation relating to future site restoration or closure or removal of long-lived assets arises when the related damage to the environment originally takes place, an environmental liability would be recognised at that time, and not deferred until the activity is completed or the site is closed. Because of their nature, however, an enterprise may choose to recognise decommissioning costs over the life of the related operations (see paragraph 40).

Future site restoration costs that relate to damage incurred in prior periods to prepare an asset or activity for operation, and that are recognised as an environmental liability at the time the related damage is incurred, should be capitalised.

In many situations, environmental damage has to be incurred before an enterprise can commence a particular activity and also throughout the life of that activity. For example, mining operations could not be commenced without related excavation work being undertaken. Enterprises are frequently required to undertake site restoration once the activity has been completed. Such restoration costs would be accrued when the environmental damage to which they relate is incurred (see paragraphs 26 and 27). The amount would also be capitalised and amortised to the income statement over the life of the related operations.

VII.   RECOGNITION OF RECOVERIES

An expected recovery from a third party should not be netted against the environmental liability, but should be separately recorded as an asset, unless there is a legal right of set off. Where the amount is netted because there is a legal right of set off, the gross amounts of both the environmental liability and the recovery should be disclosed.

In most cases, an enterprise will remain primarily liable for the whole of the environmental liability in question such that, if the third party fails to pay for any reason, the entity would have to meet the full cost. If the enterprise is not responsible for the third party's portion should it default, only the enterprise's portion would be recorded as an environmental liability.

Expected proceeds from the sale of related property and salvage proceeds should not be netted against an environmental liability.

For an asset with limited life, salvage and residual values are normally taken into consideration in arriving at the amount to be amortised. It would be double counting to reduce an environmental liability by such amounts.

VIII. MEASUREMENT OF ENVIRONMENTAL LIABILITIES

When there is difficulty in estimating an environmental liability, the best possible estimate should be provided. Details on how the estimate was arrived at should be disclosed in the notes to the financial statements. In those rare situations where no estimate can be provided, this fact and the reasons therefor should be disclosed in the notes to the financial statements.

In some situations, an estimate of an environmental liability may be difficult to determine because of the uncertainty about a number of factors. Such factors include the extent and type of hazardous substances at a site, the range of technologies that can be used, and evolving standards as to what constitutes acceptable remediation. Even though it may not be practical to estimate the actual liability, it will often be possible to estimate a "range of loss". In such an instance, the best estimate within the range should be provided. Where it is not possible to arrive at a "best estimate", at least the minimum estimate should be recognised. It would be a rare situation when no estimate can be made. In such a case, note disclosure should be provided.

For environmental liabilities that will not be settled in the near term, ISAR expresses a preference for measuring the liability at the present value of the estimated future expenditures that will be needed, based on the current cost of performing the required activities and existing legal and other requirements. Measuring the liability at the full current cost amount is also considered acceptable. For long-term decommissioning costs, providing for the anticipated future expenditures over the life of the related operations is also considered acceptable. The approach used should be disclosed. Where the provisioning approach is used, the estimated amount of the full provision needed to cover the long-term decommissioning costs should also be disclosed.

A number of approaches have been proposed for measuring liabilities relating to future site restoration, or closure and removal, costs and for other situations where expenditures relating to the settlement of the liability are not expected to be incurred for a considerable period of time. They include the following:
   (a) the "current cost" approach;
   (b) the "present value" approach;
   (c) providing for the anticipated expenditures over the life of the
      related operations.
Both the present value approach and the current cost approach require the determination of the estimated cost to perform the site restoration, closure or removal activities in the current period based on existing conditions and legal requirements (the current cost estimate). Under the current cost approach, this amount would be reflected as the environmental liability. Under the present value approach, however, the measurement of the environmental liability would be based on the present value of the estimated future cash outflows required to satisfy the obligations. Providing for the anticipated expenditures over the life of the related operations would be based on an estimate of the cash outflows that would eventually be required, rather than the amount that would currently be required.

The present value approach requires additional information about the time value of money and the factors that may affect the timing and amount of the estimated cash flows required to satisfy the obligations. Those latter items attempt to estimate the outcome of future events and, consequently, increase the level of uncertainty about that approach. As a result, some believe that the reliability of the present value approach is not sufficient to require recognition of a liability in the financial statements. They believe that the current cost approach is inherently more reliable than the present value approach because of the absence of uncertainties about future events.

Others believe, however, that the decision usefulness of the current cost approach decreases with increases in the length of time between the initial recognition of the liability and its eventual settlement, and that the relevance of the present value approach outweighs the perceived reliability of the current cost approach.

In some industries, it is acceptable practice to provide for long-term decommissioning costs over the life of the related operations, for example, with respect to the decommissioning of drilling platforms or nuclear power plants. The reasons for applying this practice are often pragmatic, in that it may avoid what some see as excessive volatility in reported income and financial position brought about by changes in the estimates of such costs.

In measuring an environmental liability based on the present value approach, the discount rate used to measure present value would normally be a risk-free rate, such as that used for a government security that has a similar term. Advances in technologies that are expected to take place in the near term would be taken into consideration, but those of a longer-term nature would not be considered. Expected inflation that will affect the costs to be incurred would also be taken into consideration. Further, the amount of the environmental liability would be reviewed each year, and adjusted for any changes made in the assumptions used in arriving at the estimated future expenditures. Measurement of a new or additional obligation will be based on factors relevant to the period in which that obligation arises.

For environmental liabilities that will be settled in the near-term, the current cost approach would normally be used.

IX. DISCLOSURE[5]

Disclosure of information relating to environmental costs and liabilities is important for the purpose of clarifying or providing further explanation of the items included in the balance sheet or the income statement. Such disclosures can either be included in those financial statements, in the notes to the financial statements or, in certain cases, in a section of the report outside the financial statements themselves. In deciding on whether an item of information, or an aggregate of such items, should be disclosed, consideration should be given as to whether the item is material. In determining materiality, consideration would be given not only to the significance of the amount, but also to the significance of the nature of the item.

Environmental costs

The types of items that an enterprise has identified as environmental costs should be disclosed.

Environmental costs arise in a number of ways. Costs incurred by an enterprise may improve the operational efficiency of the enterprise, as well as its environmental efficiency. What is included as an environmental cost will require judgement. Some enterprises may choose to include only those costs that are "wholly and exclusively" attributable to environmental measures. Others may choose to make an arbitrary allocation when a cost is only partly environmental. Disclosure of what has been included as an environmental cost should, therefore, be provided.

The amount of environmental costs charged to income, distinguished between operating and non-operating costs and analysed in a manner appropriate to the nature and size of the business and/or the types of environmental issues relevant to the enterprise, and the amount of environmental costs capitalised during the period, should be disclosed in the notes to the financial statements.

The types of items identified could include, but would not necessarily be restricted to: liquid effluent treatment; waste, gas and air treatment; solid waste treatment; site restoration; remediation; recycling; and analysis, control and compliance.

Environmentally related costs incurred as a result of fines and penalties for non-compliance with environmental regulations and compensation to third parties as a result of loss or injury caused by past environmental pollution and damage should be separately disclosed.

Fines, penalties and compensation are different from other types of environmental costs in that they provide no benefit or return to the enterprise. Separate disclosure is therefore appropriate.

An environmental cost recorded as an extraordinary item should be separately disclosed.

Environmental Liabilities

Environmental liabilities should be separately disclosed either in the balance sheet or in the notes to the financial statements.

The basis used to measure environmental liabilities (the present value approach, or the current cost approach) should be disclosed.

For each material class of liabilities, the following should be disclosed:
(a) brief description of the nature of the liabilities;
(b) general indication of the timing and terms of their settlement.
When there is significant uncertainty over the amounts of the liabilities, or the timing of settlement, this fact should be disclosed.

Any significant measurement uncertainties relating to a recognised environmental liability and the range of possible outcomes should be disclosed.

Where the present value approach has been used as the basis of measurement, consideration would be given to disclosing all assumptions critical to estimating the future cash outflows and the environmental liability recognised in the financial statements, including:

(a) the current cost estimate of settling the environmental liability
(b) the estimated long-term rate of inflation used in computing the environmental liability
(c) the estimated future cost of settlement
(d) the discount rate(s)

The disclosure called for in this section will assist users of the information in their assessment of the nature, timing and an enterprise's commitment of its future financial resources.

Accounting policies

Any accounting policies that specifically relate to environmental liabilities and costs should be disclosed.

General

The nature of environmental liabilities and costs recognised in the financial statements should be disclosed, including, inter alia, *a brief description of any environmental damage, any laws or regulations that require its remediation, and any reasonably expected changes to these laws or to existing technology that are reflected in the amount provided for.*

The type of environmental issues that are pertinent to an entity and its industry should be disclosed, including
   i.   *the formal policy and programmes that have been adopted by the entity*
   ii. *in cases where no such policy and programmes exist, this fact should be stated*
   iii. *the improvements in key areas that have been made since the introduction of the policy, or over the past five years, whatever is shorter*
   iv. *the extent to which environmental protection measures have been undertaken due to governmental legislation, and the extent to which governmental requirements (for example, a timetable for the reduction of emissions) have been achieved*
   v.   *any material proceedings under environmental laws* [6]

It would be desirable to disclose any government incentives, such as grants and tax concessions, provided with respect to environmental protection measures.

The disclosure advocated in this section could be provided either in the notes to the financial statements or in a separate section outside the financial statements. It enables users of the information to assess an enterprise's current and future prospects regarding the impact of environmental performance on the financial position of the enterprise.

Notes

1.   Examples include costs of disposal and avoidance of waste, preserving or improving air quality, cleaning up oil spills, removing asbestos from buildings, researching for more environmentally friendly products, carrying out environmental audits and inspections, etc. What is included as an environmental cost will require judgement.

     Fines, penalties and compensation would be regarded as environmentally related costs, and would not be included in this definition of environmental costs, but would be disclosed separately.

2.   For example, there may not be any legal obligation for an enterprise to clean up an oil spill in a particular jurisdiction, but the enterprise's reputation, and its future ability to operate in that jurisdiction, may be significantly at risk if it fails to do so.

3.   Sometimes referred to as an equitable obligation

4.   Refer to the work being undertaken by the IASC on "Impairment of Assets" for further guidance on this subject.

5.   ISAR acknowledges that the disclosure proposed goes beyond that advocated by standard setting organisations. On the other hand, minimal disclosure is currently being provided by most enterprises.

6.   This is taken from ISAR's Conclusions on Accounting and Reporting by Transnational Corporations, (United Nations publication, Sales No.E.94:II.A.), New York, paragraph 209.

CHAPTER II

ACCOUNTING AND REPORTING FOR ENVIRONMENTAL LIABILITIES AND COSTS WITHIN THE EXISTING FINANCIAL REPORTING FRAMEWORK*

SUMMARY

The chapter is a synthesis of current guidance on environmental accounting issues provided by governmental and non-governmental organizations. It presents environmental costs within the context of the existing financial reporting framework. The scope of the existing financial reporting framework does not extend to "external costs". The chapter begins by defining basic concepts such as liabilities, assets and contingencies from the perspective of the existing framework and then these concepts are applied to environmental accounting. The chapter proceeds to the more technical issues of recognition and disclosure of environmental costs. Concepts such as contingencies and commitments for future environmental expenditures are also addressed. Appendix 1 presents specific references to current guidance that formed the basis for the chapter. Appendix 2 provides examples of the treatment of environmental costs relating to environmental damage.

I.   INTRODUCTION

A. Objective of Chapter

The objective of this chapter is to synthesize the current guidance provided by governmental and non-governmental organizations on environmental accounting issues, and identify best practices that may be considered by national standard setters in the development of their own accounting standards, rules or regulations.

B. Scope of Coverage

This Chapter covers only those environmental costs that can be dealt with under the existing financial reporting framework. These are often referred to as "internal costs" and

---

*   UNCTAD would like to express its gratitude to expert David Moore, Canadian Institute of Chartered Accountants, for his contribution to this chapter.

generally arise because of a transaction between the reporting entity and another party. The Chapter does not cover the recognition and measurement of costs that are external to the entity, such as the impact of air pollution and water pollution on the environment, and that are not currently absorbed by the entity (often referred to as "external costs"). It should be noted, however, that the boundaries of internal costs are not static. Legislation and other measures can impose an obligation on an entity to undertake specific action for which there was previously no such obligation, thereby converting an "external cost" into an "internal cost". It should also be noted that a number of entities and industry associations are exploring appropriate ways of reporting "external costs" relating to the environmental impacts of their operations.

C. Work Undertaken

This Chapter is primarily based on work that has been, or is currently being, undertaken by the Intergovernmental Working Group of Experts on International Standards of Accounting and Reporting (ISAR) (primarily in the area of disclosure), the European Accounting Advisory Forum, and accounting organizations and standard-setting bodies in Canada, the United Kingdom and the United States. A survey other countries was undertaken, and responses were received from Brazil, China, the Czech Republic, Germany, Korea, Mauritius, the Netherlands, Pakistan, Poland, Russia and Switzerland. Germany noted that there were accounting requirements on environmental matters in its country. Under Section 249 of its Commercial Code, provisions must be set up for uncertain liabilities and uncompleted transactions. A specific requirement is to set up a provision for land reclamation expense that will be incurred during the following year. Korea indicated that there is a disclosure requirement relating to environmental issues in its Financial Accounting Standards (see Appendix 1, Section VII). A number of countries indicated that they had Statements on the basic concepts on accounting similar to those that had been issued by ISAR and the International Accounting Standards Committee (IASC), which, as is noted in Section IV of this Chapter, provide the basic underpinning for accounting for environmental costs and liabilities.

Further, no general standards or guidance that are specific to particular industries have been identified.

II.   THE NEED FOR STANDARDS ON ENVIRONMENTAL FINANCIAL ACCOUNTING

The need for specific standards or guidance on accounting for environmental liabilities and costs has been questioned by some on the grounds that sufficient guidance is already provided in pronouncements issued by international organizations, such as the IASC (through its "Framework for the Preparation and Presentation of Financial Statements" and its International Accounting Standards) and ISAR (through its Conclusions on Accounting and Reporting by Transnational Corporations), and those issued by standards-setting organizations in a number of countries.

Several reasons have, however, been provided as to why there is a need for more specific guidance. For example, the document issued by the European Accounting Advisory Forum (EAAF) on "Environmental Issues in Financial Reporting" notes that "issues associated with the accounting for the environment, environmental audit and related issues have become increasingly relevant to businesses as the pollution of the environment has become a more prominent economic, social and political problem throughout the world. Steps are being taken at national and international level to protect the environment and to reduce, prevent and mitigate the effects of pollution. As a consequence, companies are now being expected or required to disclose information about their environmental policies and objectives, programmes undertaken and expenses incurred in pursuit of these objectives and to provide for and disclose environmental risks. In the area of accounting, initiatives are being taken to facilitate the collection of data and to increase companies' awareness of the financial implications of environmental issues."[1]

The CICA Task Force on Environmental Costs and Liabilities has noted other reasons why standards on Environmental Financial Accounting are needed:

- environmental liabilities fall under the definition of liabilities [set out in various Statements of Concepts and Objectives], but they are generally not being reported; even when reported, there are inconsistencies in measuring the liability and in the type and amount of information that is disclosed;
- the investment community may have concerns about how environmental performance affects the financial health of an organization, and uses environmental information to assess environmental risk and how it is being managed, and to determine the effects of environmental performance on financial results; when a 1992 focus group of institutional investors was asked to prioritize what types of environmental information were most important in making decisions, it stated that financially relevant data were considered the most important, in particular, environmental liabilities and expenditures;
- creditors' concerns are similar to those of the investment community, but an additional concern that can overwhelm the rest is that, if an asset pledged as security is environmentally damaged, the creditor may be required to take on the liability for rectifying such damage should the debtor default on the loan; if an environmental liability exists, the amount is often significantly greater than that of the original loan; creditors look for evidence that an organization is actively and effectively managing its environmental performance and liabilities;
- financial information comparability may be suffering from the absence of specific guidance dealing with the accounting for environmental liabilities and costs;
- a large number of entities that are required to set up the liability or provisions for site restoration costs avoid doing so on the basis that such costs cannot be reasonably determined;
- there is confusion about when an environmental cost meets the definition of an asset;
- environmental costs are often different from other costs because they may produce future benefits that are not strictly economic.[2]

III. DEFINITIONS

A. Environment

The EAAF document on "Environmental Issues in Financial Reporting" defines environment as "our natural physical surroundings [which] includes: air, water, land, flora, fauna and non-renewable resources, such as fossil fuels and minerals."[3] An almost identical definition is included in the Canadian Research Report.[4]

B. Environmental Costs

The EAAF document notes that "Environmental Expenditures include the costs of steps taken … to prevent, reduce or repair damage to the environment which results from its operating activities, or to deal with the conservation of renewable and non-renewable resources. These costs include, inter alia, the disposal and avoidance of waste, the protection of surface and ground water, preserving or improving air quality, noise reduction, the removal of contamination in buildings, researching for more environmentally friendly products, raw materials or production processes etc." It specifically excludes from the definition "costs incurred as a result of fines or penalties for non-compliance with environmental regulations, compensation to third parties as a result of loss or injury caused by past environmental pollution and similar environmentally related costs." [5]

The ICAEW October 1996 Paper has, however, noted that "this distinction may be difficult to sustain as costs of this nature need to be taken into account in any assessment of environmental performance."[6]

Unlike the EAAF document, however, the Canadian Research Report includes fines, penalties and compensation to third parties in its definition of environmental costs. It notes that "'Environmental costs' include: (a) the costs of environmental measures; and (b) environmental losses." The items included under "environmental measures" are similar to those included in the EAAF definition of "environmental expenditures." "Environmental losses" are those costs for which there is no return or benefit, and covers those items excluded by the EAAF, as well as assets of the entity that have to be written off because the costs cannot be recovered due to environmental concerns. The Canadian Research Report definition specifically excludes costs relating to product and workplace safety activities.[7]

In its Statement of Principles, the CICA Task Force on Environmental Liabilities and Costs has broadly defined "Environmental Costs" as those incurred:
- to prevent, remove, contain or rectify damage to the environment,
- to help in the preservation or conservation of the environment, or
- as a result of activities or inactions that damage the environment [8]

Like the Canadian Research Report, the CICA Task Force regards fines, penalties and compensation to third parties that are environmentally related as environmental costs, since they result from activities or inactions that damage the environment. Additional examples of environmental costs are restoring a mine site after completion of mining operations (rectifying damage to the environment), site investigations, and systems and controls for monitoring environmental compliance.[9]

The EAAF document has noted that "the main problem in defining environmental expenditures is to determine which costs should be included. Only the additional and identifiable costs to prevent, reduce or repair damage to the environment should be included. In a number of areas it will be difficult to make this distinction, for example, in the area of research and development, health and safety but also with respect to capital investments in, for example, a new plant or production process. There is a risk that environmental expenditures will be overstated, for instance for publicity reasons. In order to qualify as an environmental expenditure, the primary purpose of the expenditure should be to prevent, reduce or repair damage to the environment. On the other hand, for instance in a company which is engaged in the environmental business such as the treatment of waste, it could be argued that all expenditures incurred by this company should be included as environmental expenditures. This can clearly not be the intention, as it would be in contradiction with the definition of environmental expenditures. Similarly, in the case where a group of companies contains a separate legal entity which is involved in, say, the environmental protection business, the costs of goods or services provided by this entity to third parties outside the group would not qualify as environmental expenditures in the consolidated accounts of the group. The costs of goods or services provided by this entity to other companies included in the consolidation, on the other hand, may qualify as environmental expenditures in the consolidated accounts. Whatever definition of environmental expenditures is adopted, it is likely that there will always remain grey areas where judgement is needed to decide whether expenditures qualify as environmental expenditures."[10]

In its background paper, the CICA Task Force notes that "the cost of environmental activities that are directly undertaken by employees of the entity would only be included to the extent that they are an essential element of the environmental costs and are incurred in lieu of incurring similar costs with outside parties." It also notes that "some costs incurred may be only partly environmental in nature. For example, a piece of equipment may be acquired to both help rectify, stabilize or contain damage to the environment and improve the overall efficiency of the business. Trying to identify and segregate the environmental portion of such a cost may, however, be difficult and the benefit of doing so may be questionable. It should therefore be left to management's judgement whether the environmental portion should be separately identified. In any event, only the portion that specifically relates to the environmental matters [previously referred to] would be included."[11]

The ICAEW April 1995 Discussion Paper notes that "costs of environmental measures are sometimes difficult to distinguish. There is an argument that such costs should be confined to those which relate 'wholly and exclusively' to preventing, reducing or repairing damage to the environment and should exclude, for example, costs incurred so as to conserve energy, and closure costs, even if the closure takes place for environmental reasons. On the other hand, it is important that any information about future costs should be as complete as possible, subject to the technical constraints in quantifying such costs. On balance, the working party therefore takes the view that, provided disclosure is accompanied by adequate explanation, a 'wholly and exclusively' condition would be unduly restrictive."[12]

This idea is developed further in the ICAEW October 1996 Paper. It notes that "where an entity wishes to make a comprehensive allocation of costs, this should be regarded as an acceptable practice, provided that a rational approach is adopted and the basis of allocation is described. ...As a basis for comparison, [however], a 'wholly and exclusively' condition may offer the most satisfactory approach. However, to avoid misleading a user of accounts due to the possible overlap with other costs and benefits, it is important that there is adequate disclosure of what environmental costs include or, in some cases, exclude."[13]

Conclusion on Definition of Environmental Costs

The primary difference between those organizations that have issued documents on this subject is whether fines, penalties and compensation to third parties relating to environmental activities or inactions should be included in the definition of environmental costs/expenditures.

A compromise position may be to require that such items be classified in a separate category. It is also evident that what is included in environmental costs is, to some extent, judgmental and it will be up to the individual entity to decide what comprises environmental costs in its particular circumstances, using the guidance provided in the EAAF document, the ICAEW Discussion Paper, the CICA Task Force and the Canadian Research Report and any similar such guidance. It is suggested that the entity provide a brief description of what constitutes environmental costs.

C. Environmental liabilities

For the purpose of this chapter, environmental liabilities are obligations relating to environmental costs that are incurred by an entity and that meet the criteria for recognition as a liability (as set out in Section IVB). In certain countries, environmental liabilities are classified as "provisions." The IASC's November 1996 Draft Statement of Principles on "Provisions and Contingencies" notes that "provisions need to be distinguished from other liabilities such as trade creditors and accruals. The distinguishing feature is that, in the case of provisions, there is uncertainty over either the timing or amount of the future expenditure."[14] Such may be the case for certain (but not all) environmental liabilities. The term "environmental liabilities" as used in this Chapter covers both those that are certain and those for which there is some uncertainty.

IV.   BASIC CONCEPTS

A. Introduction

There seems to be general agreement that accounting for environmental costs and liabilities should be governed by the basic concepts of accounting. The ISAR group, the International Accounting Standards Committee and standard setting bodies in several countries have issued Statements of Objectives, Principles of Accounting and Reporting or Conceptual Framework statements. The positions issued or being developed on accounting for environmental costs and liabilities are considered to be in accordance with these statements. Of particular relevance are the definitions of "liabilities" and "assets." The various accounting standards on "contingencies" are also frequently referred to as a benchmark when considering measurement of and reporting environmental liabilities.

B. Liabilities

"Liabilities" has been defined by the US Financial Accounting Standards Board as "probable future sacrifices of economic benefits arising from present obligations of a particular entity to transfer assets or provide services to other entities in the future as a result of past transactions or events."[15] This can be considered representative of the definition adopted by other organizations.

It is generally acknowledged that there are three essential characteristics for a liability:
   (a) settlement by future transfer or use of assets, provision of services, or giving up other economic benefits, at a specified or determinable date, on occurrence of a specified event, or on demand;
   (b) an obligation that the entity has little or no discretion to avoid; and
   (c) a transaction or event that obligates the entity that has already occurred.[16]

It is also noted that the obligation referred to in (b) does not have to be legally enforceable: it can be constructive (inferred from the facts of a particular situation, rather than being contractually based) or equitable (based on ethical or moral considerations).

The IASC Framework for the Preparation and Presentation of Financial Statements notes that a liability would be recognized in the balance sheet "when it is probable that an outflow of resources embodying economic benefits will result from the settlement of a present obligation and the amount at which the settlement will take place can be measured reliably."[17]

C. Assets

"Assets" are defined in the Canadian conceptual framework as "economic resources controlled by an entity as a result of past transactions or events and from which future economic benefits may be obtained."[18] This can be considered representative of the definition adopted by other organizations.

It is also generally acknowledged that there are three essential characteristics for an asset:
    (a) it embodies a future benefit that involves a capacity to contribute to future net cash inflows;
    (b) the entity can obtain access to the benefit and control others' access to it;
    (c) the transaction or event giving rise to the entity's right to, or control of, the benefit has already occurred.[19]

The right to obtain and control access does not have to be legally enforceable as long as the entity can control its use by other means.

The IASC Framework notes that an asset will be recognized in the balance sheet "when it is probable that future economic benefits will flow to the enterprise and the asset has a cost or value that can be measured reliably."[20]

D. Contingencies

An accounting standard that is frequently referred to in the context of Environmental Liabilities is "Accounting for Contingencies," primarily because there is often uncertainty over the amount or timing of the event that will be required to settle the entity's obligations.

The AICPA, in its Statement of Position 96-1 on "Environmental Remediation Liabilities" refers to the FASB's Statement No. 5, "Accounting for Contingencies" and notes that it "requires accrual of a liability if (a) information available prior to issuance of the financial statements indicates that it is probable that an asset has been impaired or a liability has been incurred at the date of the financial statements and (b) the amount of the loss can be reasonably estimated."[21] The UK and CICA Accounting Standards Boards and the IASC have issued standards that are similar.

The issues of "probability of a loss" and "the amount of the loss can be reasonably estimated" have often been presented as reasons for not recognizing a contingent liability, and this logic has been extended to "environmental liabilities." Accounting standards organizations are, however, starting to counteract the nonrecognition of an environmental liability on these grounds. US-FASB Interpretation No. 14, "Reasonable Estimation of the Amount of a Loss" concluded that the criterion for recognition of a loss contingency that "the amount of the loss can be reasonably estimated" is met when a range of loss can be reasonably estimated.[22]

The US-FASB notes that its Exposure Draft on "Accounting for Certain Liabilities Related to Closure or Removal of Long-Lived Assets" "does not change existing requirements for recognition of liabilities, for example, the general principles in [FASB] Statement No. 5 ['Accounting for Contingencies']."[23]

The Canadian Research Report notes that CICA Section 3290, Contingencies, provides guidance with respect to recording accruals for contingent losses, and that "the conceptual literature of both the CICA and the FASB suggests that recognition of a liability is to take place only when a reasonable estimate can be made... ." It also notes that the CICA standard on future removal and site restoration costs also calls for a reasonable estimate (i.e., "when reasonably determinable"). It refers to a commentary (by R.M. Skinner) that not formally recording a liability relating to the probable amount of future costs, because it cannot be reasonably estimated, is unsatisfactory because the decision is subjective, and "there is a danger that judgement might be biased by a desire to omit liabilities in order to present a better picture of financial condition."[24]

E. Application of the Basic Concepts to Environmental Accounting

There seems to be general agreement among those who are developing standards on environmental accounting and disclosures, or certain aspects thereof, that the basic concepts presented in the various frameworks are equally applicable to environmental costs and liabilities. These frameworks have, however, been developed in the context of providing information on the financial position, performance and changes, aiding users in making economic decisions, and showing the results of the financial stewardship and accountability of management for the resources entrusted to it. In this context, a number of the financial reporting frameworks indicate the primary users are investors and creditors.

It may therefore be questioned whether standards developed in this context are necessarily fully appropriate when the objective is providing information on the environmental position, performance and changes, aiding users in making environmental decisions, and showing the results of the environmental stewardship and accountability of management. From the discussion that follows, it would seem apparent that the information produced by following the basic concepts that have been developed for financial accounting and reporting would indeed be appropriate, but additional disclosures may be desirable.

V. ENVIRONMENTAL LIABILITIES/PROVISIONS FOR ENVIRONMENTAL LIABILITIES

A. Recognition

As previously indicated in this Chapter, recognition of an environmental liability (or a provision for an environmental liability) is considered to be governed by the characteristics and criteria for a liability (as set out in Section IVB above). The EAAF document also notes that "in accordance with Article 20(1) of the 4th Directive, provisions for liabilities and charges are intended to cover losses or debts the nature of which is clearly defined and which at the date of the balance sheet are either likely to be incurred, or certain to be incurred but uncertain as to the amount or as to the date on which they will arise. These general conditions for the recognition of provisions, naturally, apply equally to provisions for environmental risks and liabilities."[25] Guidance is deemed necessary, however, because, as noted by the CICA Task Force, environmental liabilities are not generally being reported (see Section II above). The EAAF document notes that "given the number of uncertainties involved, with regard to environmental issues, it seems useful to give guidance to assist interpretation of the general recognition criteria for provisions in the 4th Directive as they relate to environmental risks and liabilities. Such uncertainties relate, among others, to changes in clean-up technologies, future legislation and the extent or nature of the clean-up required."[26]

The following summarizes the guidance set out the various documents that have been issued.

1. Likelihood of future settlement

In the documents issued by various organizations, no specific commentary with respect to the likelihood of future settlement was noted. It is nevertheless deemed to be an essential characteristic for recognition of an environmental liability.

2. Need for an obligation

As noted in Section IVB above, another essential characteristic of a liability is that there is an obligation that the entity has little or no discretion to avoid. Three types of obligation have been identified:

(a) Legal obligation

In all the documents that were reviewed, there is general agreement that a legal obligation would result in recognition of an environmental liability, provided the requirements for recognition set out in Section IVB above are met.

(b) Constructive obligation

There also seems to be a consensus that a constructive obligation would be recognized as an environmental liability, provided the requirements for recognition set out in Section IVB above are met. As noted in the UK-ASB Discussion Paper, "the notion of an obligation is wider than a legal obligation. There may be cases where an entity has a constructive obligation to clean up contamination in the absence of a legal liability or, alternatively, a constructive obligation that expands its legal liability. For example, a company may have identified contamination in land surrounding one of its production sites that it is legally obliged to clean up. Because of its concern for its long-term reputation, the company may effectively be obliged to clean up to a higher standard than that required by law, even if this is considerably more costly. Provided the entity can demonstrate ... that it has no realistic alternative to restoring to the higher standard, the incremental costs of remedying to that higher standard should be provided for."[27]

The US-FASB Exposure Draft sets out some conditions (stated to be not all-inclusive) that may provide evidence that "the actions or representations of the entity's management have left the entity with little or no discretion to avoid performing closure or removal activities.

a) the adverse economic consequences ... are so dire that they assure that those activities will be performed.
b) there is an established pattern of past practice for certain ... activities that would be extremely difficult to change.
c) the ... activities are the most reasonable course of action considering (1) other actions that are or would be required of the entity and (2) alternatives available to the entity should the ... activities not be completed."[28]

The IASC November 1996 draft SoP has a similar "no discretion" requirement and also notes that "a board decision, of itself, is not sufficient for the recognition of a provision."[29]

In its August 1997 Exposure Draft, the IASC states that "a provision should be recognised when, and only when: (a) an enterprise has a present legal or constructive obligation to transfer economic benefits as a result of past events. .... A present obligation exists when the enterprise has no realistic alternative but to make the transfer of economic benefits."[30] It stresses the fact that there has to be "no realistic alternative." One of the two examples of constructive obligations that the IASC Exposure Draft provides is "an enterprise that has identified contamination in land surrounding one of its production sites. The enterprise is not legally obliged to clean up, but because of concern for its long-term reputation and relationship with the local community, and because of its published policies or past actions, [it] is obliged to do so." In the minds of some, including the author of this chapter, this constitutes an equitable obligation. The point seems to be, however, that irrespective of whether the obligation is classified as constructive or equitable, there has to be no realistic alternative but to transfer economic benefits before such an obligation can be recognized. The IASC Exposure Draft specifically states that "in cases where the enterprise retains discretion to avoid making any expenditure, a liability does not exist and no provision is recognised. It follows that a board decision, of itself, is not sufficient for the recognition of a provision. Such a decision does not mark the inception of an obligation since, in the absence of something more, the enterprise retains the ability to reverse the decision and thereby avoid the expenditure."

The other consideration the IASC Exposure Draft mention is "that the legal or constructive obligation arises as a result of a past event. The mere intention or necessity to undertake expenditure related to the future is not sufficient to give rise to an obligation." Also, "provisions are not made for general business risks since they do not give rise to obligations that exist at the balance sheet date."

The June 1997 Financial Reporting Exposure Draft (FRED) of the UK Accounting Standards Board takes a similar stance to that of the IASC Exposure Draft. It states that "an obligation exists when an entity has no realistic alternative to making a transfer of economic benefits."[31] The Exposure Draft includes the same example regarding contamination in land that is provided in the IASC Exposure Draft[32] and is identical to the IASC Exposure Draft in the other items referred to.

The EAAF document notes that environmental liabilities or risks would qualify for recognition as a provision if "the company's management is committed to prevent, reduce or repair environmental damage. Such commitment would exist, for instance, where management has little discretion to avoid action on the basis of statements of policy or intention, industry practice or public expectations or where the company's management has decided to prevent, reduce or repair environmental damage and has communicated this decision internally to another company organ or externally."[33]

The ICAEW April 1995 Discussion Paper noted the fact that "a liability may crystallise if ... as the result of a public statement or declared policy, management is otherwise *irrevocably* committed to take such measures."[34]

(c) Equitable obligation

The IASC August 1997 Exposure Draft, the US-FASB Exposure Draft, the UK-ASB Discussion Paper and its June 1997 Exposure Draft, and the EAAF document only refer specifically to legal and constructive obligations, and do not mention, or cover, equitable obligations. For example, the US-FASB Exposure Draft states that "In addition to legal obligations, the obligations addressed by ... this Statement include certain constructive obligations ... that are incurred when the actions or representations of the entity's management have directly influenced the reasonable expectations or actions of those outside the entity and, consequently, leave the entity with little or no discretion to avoid the future sacrifice of the entity's resources to perform the closure or removal activities."[35] The UK-ASB Discussion Paper states that "expenditure that management can avoid by its own actions does not fall within the definition of a liability and should not result in recognition of a provision."[36] The EAAF document refers to "the company's management [being] committed to prevent, reduce or repair environmental damage."[37]

The Canadian Research Report, however, notes that "the definition of a liability includes not only legally enforceable obligations but also equitable obligations." It notes that these are defined by the US-FASB as "[stemming] from ethical or moral constraints rather than ... from a duty ... to do that which an ordinary conscience and sense of justice would deem fair, just, and right - to do what one ought to do rather than what one is legally required to do." The Canadian Report notes that this means that, "even if there is no legally enforceable obligation to clean up a site, there may be a moral obligation to do so ..."[38]

By not acknowledging equitable obligations, the IASC, US-FASB, and the UK-ASB seem to be narrowing the definition of liabilities contained in their conceptual frameworks or related statements. There also seems to be some reluctance, particularly, to permit the recognition of an environmental liability based solely on management's intent. As already noted in subsection 2(b) above, however, it may be argued that "ethical or moral obligations" need to have some of the features of a constructive obligation before they should be recognized. This seems to be the approach that has been taken in the EAAF document and the IASC August 1997 and UK-ASB June 1997 Exposure Drafts (see the quote/positions set out in subsection 2(b) above). It is suggested, however, that where there is the intent on management's part to prevent, reduce or repair environmental damage, the entity should not be prohibited from recognizing an environmental liability simply because management may, at a later date, be unable to meet the commitment. If that eventuality does in fact occur, there should be disclosure of that fact, and the reason, in the notes to the financial statements.

Some respondents to the ICAEW April 1995 Discussion Paper felt that an even broader approach should be taken. According to the ICAEW October 1996 Paper, they felt that "provision for cleaning up past contamination should be made as soon as the entity becomes aware of the problem rather than when it has an obligation to rectify the damage." The ICAEW working group indicated that "this widely held view emphasises the need for adequate disclosure when there is no obligation."[39]

3. Transaction or event has already occurred

In most of the documents reviewed, there is general agreement that the transaction or event obligating the enterprise must have already occurred in order for a liability to be recognized. Again, this is identified as a key characteristic of a liability in the various Concepts Statements that have been issued.

The Canadian Research Report indicates that there have been some problems in the interpretation of this characteristic, for example, does the signing of a contract create a transaction or event that has already occurred? If environmental damage that the entity is obligated to clean up has occurred, it can be argued that one part of the contract has been performed and a liability exists. Environmental damage that has occurred would therefore have one of the three characteristics of a liability - whether it would be recognized as such would depend on whether the two remaining characteristics exist.[40]

If an entity knows, or it is highly likely, that its future operations will cause environmental damage, a liability would not be recorded until such damage does in fact take place. Disclosure of this eventuality may be desirable, however, unless it is already evident from the nature of the entity's operation (for example, the fact that, in the oil transportation business, tanker spills are occasionally going to occur).

4. Extent to which amount is known or estimable

Again, concepts statements and other standards issued by a number of organizations indicate that liabilities should only be recognized in financial statements if they are probable and can be reasonably estimated. The various "Contingencies" standards have been used as a basis for establishing what is probable. The Canadian standard states that if the chance of the occurrence (or non occurrence) of the future event(s) is high, the future loss is to be recognized if it can be reasonably estimated.[41] The FASB standard calls for the occurrence of the future event to be probable ("the future event or events are likely to occur").[42]

The failure of enterprises to record liabilities of this nature on the grounds that the amounts are not reasonably determinable has caused a number of organizations to consider this matter. For example, the Canadian Institute of Chartered Accountants has issued a standard on "Measurement Uncertainties." More specific to the subject of Environmental Costs and Liabilities is the work that has been undertaken by the American Institute of Certified Public Accountants in its Statement of Position on "Environmental Remediation Liabilities." The AICPA has taken as its benchmark the FASB's Statement of Accounting Standards No. 5, Accounting for Contingencies. It goes on to note that "an entity's environmental remediation obligation that results in a liability generally does not become determinable as a distinct event, nor is the amount of the liability generally fixed and determinable at a specific point in time. Rather, the existence of a liability for environmental remediation costs becomes determinable and the amount of the liability becomes estimable over a continuum of events and activities that help to frame, define and verify the liability."[43]

With respect to the ability to reasonably estimate the liability, the AICPA notes that "in the early stages of the process, cost estimates can be difficult to derive because of uncertainties about a variety of factors." Such factors include the extent and types of hazardous substances at a site, the range of technologies that can be used for remediation, evolving standards of what constitutes acceptable remediation, and the financial responsibility and status of other parties.[44]

The AICPA notes that the requirement on reasonably estimating the amount of a loss is met when the "Range of loss" can be reasonably estimated. It notes that "an estimate of the range of an environmental remediation liability typically is derived by combining estimates of various components of the liability. ... For some of those component ranges, there may be amounts that appear to be better estimates than any other amount within the range; for other component ranges, there may be no such best estimates. ... At the early stages of the remediation process, particular components of the overall liability may not be reasonably estimable. This fact should not preclude recognition of a liability. Rather, the components of the liability that can be reasonably estimated should be viewed as a surrogate for the minimum in the range of the overall liability." The amount recognized should be the best estimate of the liability. If no "best" estimate can be made, an entity should recognize the "minimum estimate" of its share of the liability.[45]

While the focus of the AICPA draft Position Paper is relatively narrow, in that it has been developed in the context of the US Superfund and other US environmental remediation liability laws, the approach advocated with respect to estimation and recognition of an environmental remediation liability seems to be capable of general adaptation to other types of environmental liabilities when the amount is not easily quantifiable.

Recognition of the best estimate is now becoming the generally required practice for environmental liabilities. The UK-ASB Discussion Paper on Provisions states that where there is uncertainty over the amount, the best estimate, which should be unbiased and based on informed judgements, should be used. When it is not possible to arrive at a single figure, a range may be possible. At least the minimum amount in the range should be used as the best estimate, or a higher amount if that is a better estimate.[46]

The EAAF document also notes that "the best estimate should be based on the existing situation taking into account known future developments both technical and in legislation. ... If there is a possibility of loss in excess of the amount provided, such additional exposure to loss should be disclosed as a contingent liability in the notes." [underlining added for emphasis].[47]

The IASC November 1996 draft SoP notes that "it would often be the case that there would be no market in obligations of the kind being provided for. ...Assuming that it is possible to specify all the possible outcomes and their associated probabilities, the amount to be provided for could variously be estimated as: [a] the most likely outcome (that is, the outcome with the highest probability); [b] the maximum amount (that is, the highest possible outcome); [c] at least the minimum amount in the range (that is, any amount from the lowest possible outcome to the highest possible outcome); or [d] the expected value (that is, the amount that takes account of all possible outcomes using probabilities to weight the outcomes)." Under the expected value approach, if there is a 40% probability of a loss of $1,000,000 and a 60% probability of a loss of $500,000, an amount of $700,000 (40% of $1,000,000 + 60% of $500,000) would be recognized. The IASC Steering Committee that produced this draft SoP expressed the view that "the expected value is still the most relevant measure because it reflects all possible outcomes and their probabilities." [48]

The August 1997 IASC Exposure Draft, however, notes that "where the obligation measured does not involve a large population of items, there may be insufficient evidence of the various possible outcomes and their probabilities to permit an explicit calculation of expected values. In these situations other methods of estimation are used." [49] An similar position is set out in the UK-ASB June 1997 Financial Reporting Exposure Draft. [50]

In any event, there seems to be general agreement that it cannot be argued that the minimum in the range is zero, and therefore nothing needs to be accrued - if a future expenditure is probable, the amount cannot be zero.

5. Limitations of information produced

As has been noted above, before an environmental liability can be recognized, it must fall within the definition of a liability, in particular, there must be an obligation that the entity has little or no discretion to avoid. Consequently, the environmental damage that has taken place on the entity's own property would not be recognized, since there is no obligation for the entity to rectify such damage. Similarly, any damage to other property for which there is no legal or constructive obligation for the entity to rectify would not be recognized. While this may be completely justifiable when looking at the financial responsibilities of an entity, it may be somewhat more questionable when considering an entity's environmental responsibilities. Indeed, it is suggested that even the primary users of financial statements, investors and creditors, would be interested in information on the extent to which the entity's own property has been damaged, and the extent to which its operations have caused environmental damage to other property which it is under no obligation to rectify. It is, therefore, suggested that an entity be required to disclose the extent to which its own property has been damaged environmentally, and the extent to which its operations have caused environmental damage to other property which it is under no obligation to rectify.

B. Obligations relating to Long-Lived assets

A number of organizations have issued, or are in the process of issuing, standards that specifically pertain to obligations relating to long-lived assets. (For example, the US-FASB Exposure Draft on "Accounting for Certain Liabilities Related to Closure or Removal of Long-Lived Assets"; the UK-ASB Discussion Paper on "Provisions;" the section in the EAAF document on "Provisions for long-term decommissioning costs," and the CICA's accounting standard on "Capital Assets - Future Removal and Site Restoration Costs.") In its Exposure Draft, the US-FASB has set out some of the types of such closure and removal activities; they include decommissioning of nuclear facilities, certain closure, reclamation and removal costs of mining facilities, and closure and post closure costs of landfills and certain hazardous wastage storage facilities, all of which may constitute, in whole or in part, obligations that may be categorized as environmental obligations.[51] The question arises as to whether the total amount of the obligation should be recorded or whether the amount should be built up by annual charges to income over the period to settlement.

1. Total amount

Both the US-FASB Exposure Draft and the UK-ASB Discussion Paper call for the obligation to be recognized in full. The US-FASB Exposure Draft states that "the amount of the liability shall be based on the specific closure or removal activities that the entity currently would be obligated to perform based on an assessment of existing conditions, facts and circumstances."[52] The UK-ASB Discussion Paper states that "the amount provided for should be the best estimate that can be made of the expenditure that will be required to settle the obligation."[53]

2. Build up provision over period to settlement

The EAAF document, however, takes a somewhat different approach. It notes that "in some industries it is common practice that provisions for long-term de-commissioning costs, for instance with respect to drilling platforms or nuclear power plants, are not created for the full amount at inception, but rather are gradually built up over the useful life of the asset. The reasons for applying this practice are often pragmatic, in that it may avoid what some may see as excessive volatility in annual results and financial position caused by changes in the estimate of the amount of such costs and in that a gradual built-up does better correspond to an appropriate matching of income and expenditure. Provisions for long-term decommissioning costs can be distinguished from provisions for expected future environmental expenditures. It is therefore recommended that, as an exception [to the general requirement to recognize the full amount of the liability], gradually building up provisions for long term de-commissioning costs should be allowed. However, in this case, the enterprise should disclose in the notes on the accounts an accounting policy note which explains this practice as well as the amount of the full provision needed to cover all long term de-commissioning costs under the heading of contingent liabilities."[54]

The Canadian Standard on "Capital Assets" also states that "when reasonably determinable, provisions should be made for future removal and site restoration costs, net of expected recoveries, in a rational and systematic manner by charges to income."[55] It should be noted that this standard was issued in December 1990 when few companies were recognizing any portion of such obligations. The Canadian Research Report has, however, noted that this approach is deficient, in that the amount accrued, at any point in time, may not correspond closely to the entity's obligation for remediation of damage that has already taken place, and has recommended to the CICA Accounting Standards Board that the standard set out in CICA Handbook Section 3060, "Capital Assets" be changed to require that the full amount of the obligation be recognized.[56] The CICA Task Force, in its Statement of Principles, has supported the position taken in the Research Report.

C. What approach should be adopted to arrive at amount to be recognized?

Three approaches have been noted for measuring a liability

1. Current cost

This approach would measure the liability based on the estimated cost to perform the remediation, closure or removal activities in the current period.

2. Present value based on estimated future cash outflows

This approach would measure the liability based on the present value of the estimated future expenditures that will be required to settle the remediation, closure or removal obligations, based on conditions, legal and other requirements that are expected to exist in the period of settlement.

3. Present value based on current cost estimate

This approach would measure the liability based on the present value of the estimated future expenditures that will be required to settle the remediation, closure or removal obligations, based on conditions, legal and other requirements that currently exist.

The Canadian Research Report generally favoured the Current Cost approach. It noted that, "pending further study, and based on alternatives that are generally in use, ... it is preferable in most cases to recognize a liability for future environmental expenditures at its estimated current cost." It was acknowledged, however, that "if the amount of the expenditure is very significant and the date of the expenditure is some distance into the future, ... the estimate based on current cost should be discounted using a presumed 'real' rate of interest."[57]

An EITF Issue on Accounting for Environmental Liabilities, issued by the FASB's Emerging Issues Task Force in 1993, indicated that "discounting environmental liabilities for a specific clean-up site to reflect the time value of money is allowed, but not required, only if the aggregate amount of the obligation and the amount and timing of the cash payments for that site are fixed or reliably determinable. To be considered 'reliably determinable', the estimate of the expected costs to be incurred should be based on a site-specific plan for the clean up or remediation of the contamination and the amount and timing of the cash payments should be based on objective and verifiable information. The undiscounted estimated cash flows should be the estimated amounts expected to be paid at the dates of settlement (including estimates of inflation) and should be computed using explicit assumptions and methods derived from the remediation plan, such that a knowledgeable third party could review the computation and concur with the estimated cash flows ... If the effect of discounting is material, the financial statements should disclose the undiscounted amounts of the liability ... and the discount rate used."

The US-FASB Exposure Draft looked at both the "current cost" and the "present value based on current cost estimate" approaches. While noting that attempting to estimate the outcome of future events increases the level of uncertainty, and may be considered by some not to be reliable enough in arriving at an amount to be presented in the financial statements as the liability, the present value approach was deemed to be inherently more relevant than the current cost approach in respect of the obligation for closure and removal activities, in that the decision usefulness of the current cost approach decreases with increases in the length of the period of time. The Board noted that estimates and approximations are commonplace in financial statements, and felt that estimated future costs of closure and removal can be measured with sufficient reliability at justifiable cost, and that such reliability of measurement will be enhanced with experience. Nevertheless, it did feel that the estimate of future cash outflows should be based on the current cost estimate. Changes in existing legal or other requirements should not be reflected in estimated future cash flows until those new or revised requirements become effective. A change in existing legal or other requirements is an event that has economic consequences for an economic entity in the year that the change occurs.[58]

The UK-ASB Discussion Paper advocates a similar approach - forecast future cash flows in terms of today's prices, and discount them at a rate that excludes any allowance for inflation.[59] It should be noted that, "under this approach, the amount of the provision [liability] will need to be increased each year to reflect both amortization of the discount and price increases."[60]

None of the organizations referred to above is advocating the present value based on estimated cash outflows approach. The US-FASB Exposure Draft notes that, "conceptually, an entity should consider the effect that changes in existing legal or other requirements would have on the estimated future cash outflows," but "those changes are difficult to estimate or predict because they are not necessarily related to current or past events." Recognition of those changes "in the year of change permits a more reliable measurement of the economic effects of those new or revised requirements."[61] Similarly, the UK-ASB Discussion Paper notes that, "in concept, discounting is best achieved by forecasting the actual amount of future cash flows that will ultimately be paid and discounting them at a rate that includes an allowance for inflation: ... such an approach takes into account the different rates of inflation that apply to different expenditures." It notes, however, that "forecasting future price changes will be extremely difficult."[62]

The IASC November 1996 draft SoP is somewhat more general on its coverage of this aspect. It states that "where an obligation is discharged over a period of time the amount of a provision should be the present value of the expenditures required to settle the obligation.... If the amount of the obligation is unable to be estimated from market value, the amount should be estimated by discounting the estimated future cash flows. However, discounting should be applied only if the result is material. If discounting is applied, the cash flows and discount rate should be consistent as regards the effects of matters such as uncertainty and inflation."[63]

The IASC August 1997 Exposure Draft, however, explicitly states that "where the effect of discounting is material, the amount of a provision should be the present value of the expenditures expected to be required to settle the obligation." It notes that "provisions related to cash outflows that arise soon after the balance sheet date are more onerous than those where the same cash flows arise later, because of the time value of money. If the cash flows were not discounted, two provisions giving rise to the same amount with different timings would be recorded at the same value, although rational economic appraisal would regard them as different."[64] The UK-ASB June 1997 Exposure Draft also states that "the amount recognised should be discounted where this has a material effect."[65]

The EAAF document specifically states that it does not address this issue.[66]

4. Components of the current cost estimate

The US-FASB Exposure Draft states that "direct internal costs of the entity should be included in the current cost estimate to the extent that those costs are essential to closure or removal activities," since they "are incurred in lieu of incurring similar costs with outside parties. ... Recurring indirect internal costs such as administrative and occupancy costs should be charged to expense as incurred. ... The current cost estimate should [also] include consideration of unforeseeable circumstances associated with projects of similar scope and complexity," and it should also "be adjusted for inflation and for advances in technology that are expected to be available for use in the near term."[67]

Inflation rate

Only the US-FASB Exposure Draft specifically mentions the inflation rate. It states that the inflation rate that is appropriate will depend on the nature of costs that will be incurred or services that will be needed.[68]

Discount rate

The Canadian Research Report suggests that, if discounting is used, "the estimate based on current cost should be discounted using a presumed 'real' rate of interest (i.e., the actual rate of interest adjusted for inflation)."[69]

The UK-ASB Discussion Paper states that "where the liability is funded by assets that match the liability in terms of timing, amount and risk, the discount rate used should be the effective rate of the assets placed in the fund. In other cases, the discount rate used should be the effective rate of a government bond of a similar remaining term and in a similar currency to that in which the liability has been measured."[70]

The UK-ASB June 1997 Exposure Draft states that "because the amount being discounted has been determined on a prudent basis (i.e., having regard to the risks associated with the cash flows), the rate used to discount should be a risk-free rate, i.e., a rate determined from the effective rate of a government bond of a similar remaining term and in a similar currency to that in which the liability has been measured. Where the provision is discounted: a) the amount recognised should be calculated either by discounting cash flows measured at current prices using a real discount rate or by discounting cash flows measured at estimated future prices using a nominal discount rate. b) the cash flows should be estimated post-tax and discounted using a post-tax discount rate. c) the post-tax amount should be adjusted by the amount of tax that would be recognised separately under SSAP 15 "Accounting for deferred tax" and any tax amount recognised separately. The amortisation of the discount should be included in interest, but separately disclosed from other interest on the face of the profit and loss account."[71]

The US-FASB Exposure Draft states that the "discount rate used ... shall be the interest rate in effect when the obligations are incurred on monetary assets that are essentially risk-free and for which the cash flows match as nearly as possible the timing and amount of expenditures required to satisfy the closure or removal obligations." It also notes that "the discount rate applied when the liability is recognized shall not be subsequently adjusted."[72]

The IASC August 1997 Exposure Draft states that "If discounting is applied, an enterprise ensures that the cash flows and discount rate are consistent. Thus if cash flows are projected in nominal terms, a nominal rate of discount is used and conversely if cash flows are projected in real terms the discount rate is a real discount rate The provision is measured on a pre-tax basis..."[73]

5. Advances in Technology

Another issue is whether the amount estimated should take into consideration improvements in technology. The general view is that "reasonably expected" changes can be taken into consideration. The US-FASB Exposure draft indicates, as noted above, that adjustments should be made for advances in technology that are expected to be available for use in the near term. The IASC November 1996 draft SoP and the IASC August 1997 Exposure Draft both point out, however, that "the development of a completely new technology for cleaning up is not anticipated."[74]

D. Offsetting/Treatment of Recoveries

1. Recoveries from third parties

Under established accounting principles, offsetting is generally only permitted when there is a legal right of set off. This is generally in the context of an account receivable being offset against an account payable, with the entity only being responsible for the net amount. A question arises as to whether, when setting up an environmental liability, an estimated recovery from another party can be offset, with only the net amount being recognized.

One approach is that, when recovery from a third party is probable, it should be taken into consideration since it is simply a factor in the determination of the amount that should be recognized as a liability. When determining the net recoverable amount of an asset, both the gross recoveries and the related outflows are taken into consideration. Similarly, a possible recovery from others could be included in determining the amount to be recognized as a liability. In addition, standards on Contingencies, such as CICA Handbook 3290 and US-FASB Statement No. 5, indicate that the amount of a likely/probable recovery should be taken into account in determining the amount to be accrued. (If the loss is less than likely/probable, however, it would not be taken into account, but disclosure might be desirable.)

Both the CICA Handbook and the Canadian Research Report permit recovery from third parties to be taken into consideration in computing the environmental liability provided the recovery is at least probable. The CICA Handbook makes reference to "provisions for future removal and site restoration costs being net of expected recoveries."[75] The Canadian Research Report, however, indicates that "it is desirable that the gross amount of the liability and the amount of the expected recovery that has been deducted from it be disclosed."[76]

The UK-ASB Discussion Paper, the EAAF document, the US-FASB Exposure Draft, and the IASC November 1996 draft SoP, however, take a somewhat different position. The UK-ASB Discussion Paper notes that "in most cases the reporting entity will remain primarily liable for the whole of the costs in question such that if the third party failed to pay for any reason, the entity would have to meet the full cost. Consistently with FRS 5 [the Statement on Reporting the Substance of Transactions] and companies legislation, this should be reflected in the accounts by recognising a provision for the full liability and a separate asset for the anticipated recovery."[77] The EAAF document notes that "Article 7 of the Fourth Directive prohibits the offsetting of assets and liabilities, except where a legal right of set-off exists. ... Even if the undertaking ... has a related legal right for a claim for recovery, it is recommended that the gross liability and the expected recoveries are shown separately in the balance sheet." (It should be noted, however, that the EAAF document states that "when estimating [an environmental] loss, any contingent recovery-payments should be taken into account.")[78]

The IASC August 1997 Exposure Draft states that "where some or all of the expenditure required to settle a provision is expected to be recovered from a third party, the asset in respect of the anticipated recovery should be offset against the liability and the net amount reported in the balance sheet where, and only where, the enterprise has no obligation for the part of the expenditure that is to be met by the third party. In other cases, the anticipated recovery and provision should be presented as a separate asset and a separate liability. The anticipated recovery should be measured using assumptions that are comparable to those used to measure the obligation. In the income statement, the expenditure may be presented net of the recovery."[79]

The position in the UK-ASB June 1997 Exposure Draft is similar, although there are some differences in wording and there is no reference to income statement presentation[80]. The AICPA Statement of Position 96-1 seems to infer that recoveries should be taken into consideration in arriving at environmental remediation liabilities, unless a third party is not likely to be able to pay its share. It states that "once an entity has determined that it is probable that an environmental remediation liability has been incurred, the entity should estimate that liability based on available information.... The estimate of the liability includes the entity's:

    (a) Allocable share of the liability for a specific site;

    (b) Share of amounts related to the site that will not be paid by other potentially responsible parties (PRPs) or the government."[81]

It should be noted that the focus of this document is on allocating the costs among the PRPs, with each party recognizing its share, rather than on one party being primarily responsible with the other parties providing offsetting amounts, even though at the outset only a limited number of PRPs may be identified by the Environmental Protection Agency; it is up to those parties to perform an investigation to find others who may be liable.

The EITF on "Accounting for Environmental Liabilities," issued by the US-FASB's Emerging Issues Task Force in 1993, noted that "any asset that is recognized relating to the recovery of a portion or all of the liability that is measured on a discounted basis also should be discounted" and that "the undiscounted amount of any related recovery should be disclosed."

2. Recoveries from sale of property

The Canadian Research Report covers recoveries from sale of property in the context of site restoration and removal costs. It notes that the CICA Handbook is not specific on this particular issue, since it merely refers to "net of expected recoveries." If including recoveries from sale of property "means....that no provision for future site restoration costs is necessary if expected recoveries from the sale of the property exceed such expected costs, the future removal and site restoration costs would effectively be matched against expected future benefits from the sale of the site." This means that a possible net gain on a sale of property is being offset against a known liability. The Research Report states that this does not appear to be in accordance with the basic principles of the existing accounting model, and indicates that "the CICA Handbook ... should be changed with respect to environmental remediation costs to clarify the reference to 'net of expected recoveries' and to indicate that it does not include recoveries from sale of the related asset."[82]

None of the other pronouncements examined covered this particular issue

3. Expected recoveries from salvage and residual values

The Canadian Research Report notes that, for an asset with a limited life, salvage and residual values are taken into consideration in arriving at the amount to be amortized (i.e., cost less salvage/residual value). The Canadian Petroleum Association Removal and Site Restoration Task Force in its "Guide for Estimating Future Site Restoration Costs" interpreted the CICA recommendation on removal and site restoration costs to mean that salvage values could be deducted in determining future site restoration costs. The Research Report suggested that the CICA Handbook be changed to clearly reflect that the amount to be recognized as an environmental liability should not be net of the residual or salvage values.[83]

Again, none of the other pronouncements examined covered this particular issue.

4. Providing for additional depreciation in lieu of recognition of a liability

The US-FASB Exposure Draft notes that "an obligation that meets the requirement for liability recognition shall be recognized when the obligation is incurred.... Providing for additional depreciation ... is not an acceptable substitute for recognition of a liability. Accumulated depreciation shall not exceed, and depreciation expense shall not be computed using a depreciation base that exceeds, the historical cost of an asset."[84]

E. Contingent Environmental Liabilities

The UK Standard on "Accounting for Contingencies" (SSAP 18) defines contingency as "a condition which exists at the balance sheet date, where the outcome will be confirmed only on the occurrence or non-occurrence of one or more uncertain future events."[85] In the US, SFAS 5 defines it as "an existing condition, situation or set of circumstances involving uncertainty as to possible gain... or loss... to an enterprise that will ultimately be resolved when one or more future events occur or fail to occur."[86]

For an accrual to be recognized in respect of a loss contingency, two conditions have to be met: it must be probable that an asset has been impaired or a liability incurred at the balance sheet date; and the amount of the loss can be reasonably estimated.

The dividing line between "environmental liabilities" and "contingencies" is often not too clear, usually because it is clearly apparent that a loss has occurred; it is only the amount of the loss that lacks precision.

The ICAEW October 1996 Paper notes that the UK-ASB Discussion Paper on Provisions, proposes "restricting the recognition of provisions to those circumstances where an entity has an obligation to transfer economic benefits as a result of past events and is not free to avoid an outflow of resources. The discussion paper on provisions does not cover contingent liabilities leaving them to be dealt with by SSAP 18."[87]

The ICAEW Paper also expresses the view that "there would be advantages in reviewing the requirements of SSAP 18 so as to address the issues raised by contingent environmental liabilities. For example, unless there is a demonstrable commitment, a chemical company reporting under the going concern concept does not recognise the costs that would be associated with cleaning up contaminated land within its own premises, as these costs would only arise in the event of closure and sale. In such a case, the going concern concept does not assume indefinite occupation but it should be clarified whether an eventual disposal of the site constitutes an 'uncertain future event.' "[88]

It is questionable, however, whether the situation indicated in this example would be regarded as a contingent liability unless there is some evidence indicating that closure or sale is a possibility.

The CICA Research Report on Environmental Costs and Liabilities concluded that Disclosure of Contingent Environmental Liabilities should include:
  (a) "reasonably possible" future environmental expenditure related to past events or transactions; and
  (b) "reasonably possible" asset impairment losses that could have a significant effect on future cash flows.

In addition, if the possibility of environmental loss is remote, but there could be significant impact on the financial position of the entity, the CICA Research Report Study Group felt that it is desirable to disclose this possibility.[89]

The ICAEW October 1996 Paper noted that this went beyond the current UK requirement for contingencies, and the view was expressed that there would be a risk that users may draw unreliable conclusions from this information. Also, it was questionable whether a distinction can be made between "probable" loss and "reasonably possible" loss and the focus should therefore be on "probable loss."[90]

F. Conclusions on Environmental Liabilities

Based on the review of material that is being developed by standard setting bodies and other organizations, it is suggested that the following positions be adopted with respect to environmental liabilities:
1. An environmental liability should be recognized in respect of environmental damage when:
  (a) there is an obligation on the part of an entity to prevent, reduce or rectify such damage, and the entity has little or no discretion to avoid such an obligation (that is, (i) there is a legal or contractual obligation in respect of such action, or (ii) statements of management policy or intention, industry practice, or public expectations give management little discretion to avoid such action, or (iii) management has communicated its decision to undertake such action either externally or internally to another branch of the entity), and
  (b) a reasonable estimate can be made of the amount required to settle the liability.

2. Where the environmental damage relates to the entity's own property, or to environmental

damage to other property caused by the entity's operations or activities for which there is no obligation on the entity's part to rectify, the extent of the damage should be disclosed.

3. When there is difficulty in estimating the amount of an environmental liability, a reasonable estimate should be provided. The estimate may be based on information that provides a range of amounts of loss, and the best estimate within the range should be provided. Where practical, experts should be used in arriving at the estimate. Known developments, both technical and in legislation, should be taken into consideration, but any anticipated technological developments that have not been proven should not be taken into consideration.

4. The amount recorded as an entity's liability for expected future environmental expenditures should be an estimate of the total amount of the liability arising from past transactions or events (or the entity's best estimate where the actual amount is not known).

   - The liability should be measured based on either the present value of the estimated future expenditures that will be needed to settle the liability at the estimated future settlement date, but based on <u>existing</u> (not future) conditions, legal and other requirements (the "present value approach") or the estimated expenditures that would be required to settle the liability in the current period (the "current cost approach"). The method used should be disclosed.

   - If the liability is measured based on the present value of estimated future expenditures, in arriving at the amount to be recognized, the following should be taken into consideration:
     (a) the estimate of the future settlement expenditures should be based on the estimated current cost of performing the required action;

     (b) this amount should then be adjusted for:
         (i) expected inflation;
         (ii) advances in technology that will be available for use in the near term;

     (c) the adjusted amount should then be discounted using a risk free rate; the such rate could be based on that used for a government bond for a similar term;

     (d) when further obligations are incurred in a future period, the incremental liability relating to those further obligations will be measured using a risk free rate in effect for that period. A corresponding weighted average discount rate should be used to measure the entire liability;

     (e) changes in the present value of the liability due to the passage of time should be recognized as period costs;

     (f) changes in the estimates of the future cash flows required for settlement of the liability that are caused by changes in assumptions and by new legal requirements should be accounted for as changes in the estimate of the liability; they should not affect the discount rate used.

5. An expected recovery from a third party should <u>not</u> be netted against an environmental liability, but should be separately recorded as an asset, unless there is a legal right of set off.

When there is a legal right of set off, the gross amounts of both the liability and the recovery should be disclosed

6. .Expected proceeds from the sale of the related property and salvage proceeds should <u>not</u> be netted against an environmental liability.

7. The setting up of provisions on a systematic basis over the life of the related asset or activity or providing additional depreciation are <u>not</u> acceptable alternatives to recognizing the full amount of an environmental liability

VI.   ENVIRONMENTAL COSTS

Issues relating to accounting for environmental costs centre on the period or periods in which such costs should be written off, and include

- the circumstances, if any, in which they can be treated as a prior period adjustment;
- the circumstances in which they can be capitalized, or recorded as an asset, rather than expensed

A. Prior Period Adjustment

In some cases, an environmental cost may relate to damage that has taken place in a prior period. A question arises whether such cost should be charged to the prior period and matched against the benefits arising from the operating activities in that prior period.

Only the Canadian Research Report and the ICAEW Discussion Paper discuss this issue. The Canadian Research Report notes that treatment as a "prior period adjustment is ... severely restricted by current accounting standards." Examples of environmental costs that might be considered for prior period adjustment treatment are the following:

(i)   environmental damage to property that occurred prior to acquisition

(ii)   an accident or other activities in a prior period that caused damage that now requires cleanup

(iii)   cleanup of damage to property disposed of in a prior period, due to a law that existed in that prior period

(iv)   costs of disposing of, or otherwise dealing with, hazardous waste created in the prior period

(v)   an environmental cost that involves a correction of an error in prior period financial statements

With the exception of item (v), the situations referred to in the examples listed above would generally not qualify for treatment as a prior period adjustment, and would be charged to income of the current period, unless they comply with the criteria set out in a particular accounting standard for "prior period adjustments."[91]

The ICAEW April 1995 Discussion Paper notes that "prior period adjustments are defined as "material adjustments applicable to prior periods arising from changes in accounting policies or from the correction of fundamental errors. They do not include normal recurring adjustments or corrections of accounting estimates made in prior periods." It notes that this definition "would generally prevent environmental costs being treated as a prior period adjustment." It also notes that the definition in the IASC's standard on "Net Profit or Loss for the Period, Fundamental

Errors and Changes in Accounting Policies" (IAS 8) is similar to that indicated above.[92]

B. Capitalization of Environmental Costs

Whether or not an environmental cost can be capitalized depends on whether it is deemed to comply with the definition of an "asset" as set out in section IVC.

EITF Issue #90-8 on "Capitalization of Costs to Treat Environmental Contamination," issued by the FASB's Emerging Issues Task Force in 1990, states that these costs may be capitalized if recoverable, but only if any one of the following conditions exist.

1. The costs extend the life, increase the capacity, or improve the safety or efficiency of property owned by the company. For purposes of this criterion, the condition of that property after the costs are incurred must be improved as compared with the condition of that property when originally constructed or acquired, if later.

2. The costs mitigate or prevent environmental contamination that has yet to occur and that otherwise may result from future operations or activities. In addition, the costs improve the property compared with its condition when constructed or acquired, if later.

3. The costs are incurred in preparing for sale that property currently held for sale.

An earlier EITF Issue #89-13, "Accounting for the Cost of Removal of Asbestos," issued by the FASB's Emerging Issues Task Force in 1989, had considered whether the costs incurred to remove or treat asbestos (a) when a property with a *known* asbestos problem is acquired, or (b) in an existing property, should be capitalized or charged to expense. In both cases, capitalization is permitted, in (a) as part of the property acquired, and in (b) as a betterment. Both situations were subject to an impairment test for that property. No supporting argumentation was provided for the positions taken in EITF Issue #89-13. EITF Issue #90-8, however, did confirm that such capitalization is appropriate, based on condition 1 set out above.

The Canadian Research Report, however, questions whether capitalization should be permitted in such circumstances. One condition for capitalization is that the service potential for a capital asset is enhanced. This concept of increased service potential is incorporated in one of the characteristics of an asset - that it embodies a future benefit that involves a capacity to contribute to future net cash inflows (i.e., there is an increase in future economic benefits). The Canadian Research Report notes that while environmental costs may result in future benefits to the entity, they are not necessarily future economic benefits. For such costs to be capitalized, they have to increase expected future economic benefits of an asset – if the environmental cost simply maintains the service potential of the asset, it should be charged to income currently.

The Research Report recognized that this approach differed from that in EITF #90-8, but felt that its interpretation complied more closely to the definition an "asset." It also identified two basic approaches that can be taken with respect to "capitalization"; the "increased future benefits" approach, and the "additional cost of future benefits approach."

(a) *Increased future benefits approach*
Under the "increased future benefits approach," environmental costs must result in an

increase in expected future benefits if such costs are to be capitalized. The purchase of new equipment must result in the generation of future net cash inflows, or an expenditure relating to the improvement of an asset must result in increased future net cash inflows if they are to be capitalized. Consequently, the removal of asbestos or the installation of a scrubber to reduce air pollution would only be capitalized if it could be demonstrated that such activity results in an increase in future net cash inflows. If such activity in fact reduces such future net cash inflows, because of an additional obligation to amortize the new or improved "asset" over its estimated life, it cannot be capitalized – it does not result in a future economic benefit; such costs, even though undertaken for a good and valid reason, are excessive. It can be argued that management is <u>only</u> undertaking those costs because there is an obligation to do so, and that the obligation is not profit motivated. Those who support this approach would argue that it would be rare for environmental costs to be capitalized. Basically, the only situation where they would be capitalized is where the incurrence of environmental costs actually improves the operating capability of an enterprise, and therefore does result in the generation of future net cash inflows.

(b) *Additional cost of future benefits approach*

Under the "additional cost of future benefits approach," environmental costs must result in future economic benefits, but not necessarily an <u>increase</u> in future economic benefits, if they are to be capitalized. The impact of adopting this approach for the purchase of a piece of new equipment is the same as that under the "increased future benefits approach" – future net cash inflows must be generated if the environmental cost is to be capitalized. But for an expenditure relating to the improvement of an existing asset, the philosophy is different – it is not necessary that the future net cash inflows be increased as a result of incurring the cost; all that is necessary is that future cash inflows from the improved asset continue to be generated. In effect, a new assessment is made – is that improved asset going to generate economic benefits? Those who support this approach consider it logical. If the expenditure relating to environment cost is being (or is to be) incurred because of a regulatory requirement, failure to do so could result in a cessation of business or reduced future net cash inflows through the imposition of fines and penalties. If an enterprise chooses to improve its operations environmentally, that decision is going to result in future benefits, and the cost of those future benefits should be spread over future periods, irrespective of whether they are, or are not, future economic benefits.

The Research Report goes on to apply the two approaches to specific solutions, as follows:

(a) Those involving discretionary expenditures. Since such expenditures would normally be undertaken with the expectation of increased future economic benefits, they would normally be capitalized under both approaches. If taken simply to clean up damage that existed at the time an asset was acquired, but was not discovered until later, such expenditures would be expensed under the "increased future benefits approach," but might be capitalized under the "additional cost of future benefits approach." If the expenditures are undertaken solely for public relations reasons, they would be expensed under both approaches.

(b) Those involving expenditures undertaken as a result of an existing law or regulation. Under the "increased future benefits approach," the expenditures would only be capitalized if there is an expected increase in future net cash inflows. The Research Report also states that knowledge of the damage is a factor – if the damage is known at the time the original asset was purchased or constructed, it would have been taken into account in arriving at the purchase price, and the anticipated expenditures relating to the environmental cost should therefore be capitalized in the purchase price; any future expenditure should not be capitalized. This may, however, be a somewhat esoteric from a practical standpoint. Under the "additional costs of future benefits approach," such cost would be capitalized. If the damage occurred during past operating activities, contrary to a law that existed at the time, the cost of rectifying the damage should be expensed under both approaches.

(c) Those expenditures undertaken as a result of a new law or regulation.

   (i)   Relating to modification of existing assets. Under the "increased benefits approach," these expenditures would normally be expensed, since they could not be viewed as increasing future economic benefits beyond those that existed at the acquisition or construction date of the original asset. Some argue, however, that even under this approach, such costs should be capitalized, since the passing of the new law or regulation results in a new "assessment point" for deciding whether expenditure relating to the asset increase future economic benefits. Under the "additional cost of future benefits approach," such costs would be capitalized.

   (ii)   Relating to damage caused by past activities. Under both approaches, arguments can be made for both capitalizing and expensing such expenditures (the "new assessment point" argument under the "increased future benefits approach" is advocated by some as permitting capitalization; the fact that such expenditures relate to a previous period in which operating activities took place is advocated by some, who support the "additional cost of future benefits approach," that they should be expensed).

It should be noted that the Study Group that prepared the Research Report was divided over which of the two approaches should be required.[93]

The EAAF document states that, "where environmental expenditures are incurred to prevent or reduce future environmental damage or conserve resources, they may qualify for recognition as an asset if, in accordance with Article 15(2) of the 4th. Directive, they are intended for use on a continuing basis for the purpose of the undertaking's activities <u>and</u> if in addition one of the following two criteria is met:

(a) the costs relate to anticipated environmental benefits and extend the life, increase the capacity, or improve the safety or efficiency of assets owned by the company; or

(b) the costs reduce or prevent environmental contamination that is likely to occur as a result of future operations."[94]

The EAAF goes on to note that "fixed assets may be acquired for safety or environmental reasons. The acquisition of such fixed assets, while not directly increasing the future economic benefits of any particular existing items of fixed assets may be necessary in order for the undertaking to obtain the future economic benefits from its other assets. Where this is the case, such acquisitions of fixed assets qualify for recognition as assets, in that they enable future economic benefits from related assets to be derived by the undertaking in excess of those it could derive if they had not been acquired. For example, a chemical manufacturer may have to install certain new chemical handling processes in order to comply with environmental requirements on the production and storage of dangerous chemicals; related plant enhancements are recognised as an asset to the extent they are recoverable because without them, the enterprise is unable to manufacture and sell chemicals.

"It is further recommended that environmental expenditures incurred after an asset is acquired, constructed or developed are capitalised, provided they are recoverable, whether or not the expected future economic benefits from the asset increase as a result of the expenditure. For example, following this approach, environmental expenditures that relate to an existing fixed asset and are required as a result of new law or regulation are viewed as additional cost of the anticipated future benefits from the asset and can therefore be capitalised, subject to the application of a recoverability test."[95]

The ICAEW April 1995 Discussion Paper took the view that the "increased future benefits approach" with a reasonably wide interpretation of the term "economic benefits" should be the principle adopted.[96] The ICAEW October 1996 Paper notes that "the [UK] ASB has adopted the criterion of access to future economic benefits rather, than *increased* future economic benefits. This approach dispenses with the need to demonstrate an increase in economic benefits; for example, expenditure that is necessary to maintain an operating licence so as to continue operations, or to avoid closure, could qualify for capitalisation."[97]

C. Costs relating to Closure or Removal of Long-lived assets

A liability for closure and removal obligations is also required to be capitalized under certain proposed pronouncements that have been issued for comment. The US-FASB Exposure Draft on Accounting for Certain Liabilities Related to Closure or Removal of Long-lived Assets states that "initial recognition of a liability for closure or removal obligations shall be capitalized as part of the cost of the related long-lived asset because incurrence of those obligations is integral to or a prerequisite for operating the asset. Subsequent changes in the estimated future cash outflows required to satisfy the closure or removal obligations ... also shall be capitalized as part of the cost of the long-lived asset. Depreciation of the asset, including capitalized closure or removal costs, shall be revised prospectively over its remaining estimated useful life."[98] The UK-ASB Discussion Paper takes the same approach. It notes that "an entity normally assumes an obligation for abandonment costs only because it is required to do so in order to obtain the economic benefits of the facility. Hence, the costs meet the test ... of providing access to economic benefits and may be properly capitalised as part of the cost of the facility."[99]

The IASC August 1997 Exposure Draft, by reference in an example relating to site restoration costs (replacement of the overburden, which has been necessarily removed before mining operations could commence) requires capitalisation of such costs. It states that "as removal of the overburden provides access to future benefits from the mine, the amount provided is capitalised as part of the cost of the mine and recognised as an expense over the life of the mine."[100] The UK-ASB June 1997 Exposure Draft states that "provisions should be capitalised as assets when, and only when, the expenditure provides access to future economic benefits; otherwise the provision should be charged immediately to the profit and loss account."[101]

The CICA Handbook, however, does not permit such costs to be capitalized with respect to site restoration. It states that "when reasonably determinable, provisions should be made for future removal and site restoration costs, net of expected recoveries, in a rational and systematic manner by charges to income."[102] The accumulated amount would, presumably, be recorded as a deferred charge on the balance sheet. As noted previously, the CICA standard on future...site restoration costs (which is reputed to be the first accounting standard released on an environmental issue) was issued in December 1990, and may be subject to some review in view of what has taken place in accounting thinking on this subject over the past 6 years. In fact, the Canadian Research Report Study Group noted that "if an obligation for site restoration of a capital asset were recognized as a liability [as is recommended in the Research Report], ... the cost would be either capitalized, if considered to be a cost of the capital asset in question, or reflected as a deferred charge. This deferred charge would be amortized to income as appropriate."[103] The CICA Task Force is also recommending to the CICA Accounting Standards Board that costs relating to closure and removal of long-lived assets be capitalized.[104]

The US-FASB Exposure Draft also considers whether closure and removal costs should be capitalized as part of the cost of the long-lived asset, or capitalized as the cost of a separately identified intangible asset. It decided on the former, arguing that "current accounting practice includes all costs that are necessary to get an asset ready for its intended use ... Capitalized closure or removal costs are not a separate asset, just as other costs that may be capitalized in the historical cost of a long-lived asset are not separate assets. That is, there is no specific and separate future economic benefit that results from those costs. The future economic benefit of those costs lies in the productive asset that is used in the entity's operations."[105] This position is also supported by the CICA Task Force in its Statement of Principles. It also notes that it "does not regard the deferred charge treatment or offsetting against the related liability as acceptable accounting treatments of these types of environmental costs."[106]

As noted previously in Section VB2, the EAAF document suggests that expected future expenditures for long-term decommissioning costs be built up gradually, and not recognized in full at inception. The document is silent on how the corresponding "asset" would be accounted for (it is presumed that it would be accounted for as a deferred charge).

D. Recoverability and Impairment

(a) Recoverability

It is generally acknowledged, either explicitly or implicitly, that the capitalization of environmental costs is subject to the test of recoverability. US-FASB-EITF 90-8 indicates that "those costs may be capitalized if recoverable"; the UK-ASB Discussion Paper states that "it would, however, be necessary to ensure that [capitalization of abandonment costs] did not result in the facility being stated at above its recoverable amount."[107] The Canadian Research Report notes that "a further condition for capitalization is that the particular costs must be recoverable from the related expected future benefits."[108]

(b) Impairment

Certain of the pronouncements issued also refer to impairment. The EAAF document that "a value adjustment should be made if the amount recoverable from the use of the site has declined below its carrying amount and it is expected that this reduction in value will be permanent. The carrying amount of the site should however not be written down below its fair value."[109] The UK-ASB Discussion Paper on Provisions, in talking about the facility not being stated above its recoverable amount, indicates that "this is particularly likely if the estimate of abandonment costs increases beyond that originally made; such an eventuality would indicate that a review for impairment was required."[110] The US-FASB Exposure Draft states that "FASB Statement No. 121, *Accounting for the Impairment of Long-lived Assets and for Long-lived Assets to Be Disposed Of*, shall be applied for the recognition and measurement of impairment of those long-lived assets."[111]

The ICAEW October 1996 Paper indicates that, although the ICAEW April 1995 Discussion Paper noted that the issue of impairment is not unique to assets affected by environmental factors, "this type of impairment carries particular uncertainties regarding timescale and amount." The Paper also notes that "some respondents to [that] discussion paper suggested that there is a risk of double counting of environmental losses if the impairment of assets is recognised as well as making provision for environmental costs" but the working group felt that "provided the process is properly applied, double counting should not arise."[112]

The Canadian Research Report notes that "environmental developments or concerns may result in the impairment of the net carrying value of an existing capital asset." It states that "the focus in determining 'net recoverable amount' is [not just] on estimated future net cash flow from use, but it also includes 'residual value,' which is the estimated net realizable value at the end of the asset's useful life." Capital assets that have been impaired because of environmental considerations should be written down.

The Canadian Research Report also notes that where management does not intend to undertake cleanup or modifications relating to environmental damage, net carrying amount would be reduced if it exceeds net realizable value. Where management does intend to undertake such modification or cleanup, however, the Research Report suggests that "the estimated costs of these modifications should be deducted from the 'net recoverable amount' of the modified/cleaned up asset and then compared to the net carrying value of the existing asset to determine if a write-down is necessary." It also notes that Canadian accounting standards would not permit the reversal of any such write down.[113]

The IASC issued an Exposure Draft on "Impairment of Assets" in May 1997. It does not specifically cover environmental assets, although the general principles would equally apply to such assets. There is a view, however, that additional guidance is needed because the uncertainties may be greater, for example, the "stigma" effect of environmental pollution on the value of neighbouring property.

E. Assets Held for Sale

A number of pronouncements permit capitalization of environmental costs if they pertain to assets held for sale. US-FASB-EITF Issue #90-8 states that "in general, environmental contamination treatment costs should be charged to expense. Those costs may be capitalized if recoverable but only if one of the following criteria is met, [the third of which is that] the costs are incurred in preparing for sale that property currently held for sale."

The Study Group that prepared the Canadian Research Report, however, did not support the position that all environmental costs relating to an asset held for sale should be capitalized. It felt that the "capitalize vs. expense" decision should depend on the particular circumstances of the situation. Where the environmental expenditure is discretionary and it results in higher proceeds, the costs may be capitalized; if it is not discretionary, the "increased future benefits approach" would call for the environmental expenditure to be charged to expense; under the "additional costs of future benefits approach," it would either be viewed as relating to expected benefits from the asset, and therefore capitalized; for other types of expected benefits, such as being a good corporate citizen, it would be charged to expense.[114]

F. Expensed to Current Period

When an environmental cost does not satisfy the criteria for capitalization, it is expensed.

Because of the situations being covered, the UK-ASB Discussion Paper, the US-FASB Exposure Draft and the AICPA Statement of Position do not cover environmental costs that are expensed. As noted in Appendix 2, US-FASB-EITF Issue #90-8 has provided a number of examples of situations where environmental costs would have to be expensed rather than capitalized.

The Canadian Research Report covers in some depth the issue of where such costs would be expensed (this is in addition to the "difference of opinion" whether, except in rare situations, environmental costs can be capitalized under any circumstances). The Canadian Research Report notes that the environmental costs related directly or indirectly to benefits of the current period would be expensed, as would costs viewed as "period costs" or losses. Examples provided are:

(a) Costs related directly to current period benefits
   • Treatment of waste products
   • Costs of hazardous waste disposal
   • Clean up costs relating to current operating activities.

(b) Costs related indirectly to current period benefits
   • Ongoing environmental administration, compliance, assessment and audit activities
   • Employees attendance at study groups and seminars re environmental issues.

(c) Costs viewed as "period" costs or losses
   1. those that do not have sufficient ties to future benefits and therefore cannot be capitalized or deferred
      • Research costs to redesign products and processes to
         (i)   prevent and abate damage to the environment
         (ii)   conserve renewable and non renewable resources
      • Donations to programs relate to the environment
      • Recycling programs

   2. those related to activities of and benefits received in prior periods
      • clean up of polluted site that has been abandoned
      • clean up costs related to prior period activities in excess of the estimated recorded in prior periods (benefits received in those prior periods)
      • clean up of non-owned site previously used, the clean up being required as a result of new laws or regulations

   3. costs that do not yield any benefit (i.e., losses)

- fines or penalties for non compliance related to operating activities.[115]

G. Conclusions with respect to environmental costs

Based on the review of material that is being developed by standard setting bodies and other organizations, it is suggested that the following positions be developed with respect to environmental costs:

1. Costs relating to environmental damage incurred in prior period would generally be recognized when it first becomes evident that they have been incurred (that is, as soon as they are identified). They would not be treated as a prior period adjustment unless they meet the restrictive criteria set out in accounting standards relating to the treatment of prior period adjustments.

2. Environmental costs should be capitalized if they relate, directly or indirectly, to future economic benefits that will flow to the enterprise through:
   (a) increasing the capacity, or improving the safety or efficiency of other assets owned by the enterprise;
   (b) reducing or preventing environmental contamination likely to occur as a result of future operations; or
   (c) conserving the environment.

   They should also be capitalized if they are incurred to prepare an asset or activity for operation and, in doing so, damage is done to the environment that cannot be avoided and that has to be rectified at some future point in time.

3. When an environmental cost that merits recognition as a capital asset is related to another capital asset, it should be included as an integral part of that asset, and not recorded separately.

4. All capital assets, including environmental costs that are recognized as a capital asset, should be tested for impairment to ensure that they are not recorded above recoverable amount. Where an environmental cost is included as an integral part of another capital asset, that capital asset should be tested for impairment.

5. Where an environmental cost does not qualify for recognition as an asset, it would be expensed.

6. Where an environmental cost is recognized as a capital asset, it would be amortized to income over its remaining life, or the remaining life of the asset to which it relates, as appropriate.

VII. COMMITMENTS

The Canadian Research Report states that if a commitment to undertake future environmental expenditures relating to future transactions and events that are not expected to yield any benefits, a provision should be made currently for the future loss. If such future expenditures are expected to yield future benefits, however, they would not be recognized prior to their occurrence. The Research Report also suggests a number of disclosure requirements.[116] These are set out in Appendix I, Section VI.

VIII. DISCLOSURE

Generally, the various documents that have been issued call for varying degrees of disclosure relating to environmental liabilities, environmental costs and the accounting policies relating thereto that have been followed. The disclosures called for in the US-FASB Exposure Draft, the UK-ASB Discussion Paper on Provisions and the AICPA draft Statement of Position are related to the specific area that such Statements cover. Extensive disclosure is advocated by the Canadian Research Report. The EITF Issues published by the US-FASB Emerging Issues Task Force deal with accounting treatment and tend not to get into disclosure issues. The disclosures called for by the EAAF document and the CICA Task Force are more general in nature.

A. Disclosures relating to Environmental Liabilities

There seems to be support among those that have issued documents on Environmental Financial Accounting that there should be disclosure of the amount of environmental liabilities and the valuation methods used. The EAAF document states that "environmental provisions should be shown in the balance sheet under the caption 'other provisions' and, if material, separately disclosed in the notes to the accounts, in accordance with Article 42 of the 4th Directive and Article 29(1) of the 7th Directive." It also calls for disclosure in the notes on the accounts of "the valuation methods applied on environmental issues, as part of the disclosure required by Article 43(1)(1) of the 4th Directive and Article 34(1) of the 7th Directive."[117]

The US-FASB Exposure Draft advocates disclosure of the liability either on the face of the statement of financial position or in the notes to the financial statements. As noted in Section VC, this Exposure Draft also advocates that the liability for closure and removal obligations be reflected at the present value of the estimated cash flows that will be required to satisfy those obligations. With respect to the related disclosure, it calls for disclosure of all assumptions that are critical to estimating the future cash flows and the liability recognized in the financial statements. They would include the current cost estimate of closure or removal obligations; the estimated long-term rate of inflation used in computing the liability; the estimated total future cost of closure or removal obligations; the discount rate(s); and the general estimated timing of closure or removal activities.[118] Other disclosures are set out in Appendix 1, Section III.

The UK-ASB Discussion Paper on Provisions indicates that its general disclosures on provisions should be applied to provisions for environmental liabilities. They include a brief description of the nature of the obligation, including an indication of the timing of payment; the amount provided for and, if estimated, the basis on which the estimate is made; and, where the amount provided for is discounted, this should be stated. The type of rate used, though not its amount, should be disclosed and, where relevant, the fact that no allowance has been made for risk should be stated.[119] (See also Appendix I, Section IV).

The Canadian Research Report goes somewhat further in the amount of the disclosure it advocates for environmental liabilities. In addition to separate disclosure of environmental liabilities in financial statements, it advocates that any liability that is individually material should be disclosed separately; and that the nature of any significant measurement uncertainties relating to a separately-disclosed recognized liability, and the range of reasonably possible outcomes, should be disclosed. It also calls for disclosure of the aggregate of payments to be made in each of the next five years for future environmental expenditures that have been recognized as a liability. If such disclosure cannot be made because there is considerable uncertainty about the timing of the future expenditures, this fact should be disclosed. A number of disclosures are advocated relating to environmental liabilities that have not been recognized in financial statements because no estimate can be made of them.[120] (See Appendix I Section VI).

Noting that "the measurement of liabilities may be difficult and is particularly vulnerable to the effect of changes in the current state of the environmental technology," the ICAEW April 1995 Discussion Paper notes that "to be useful, disclosure needs to strike a balance between a broad unquantified statement and a very detailed description of specific valuation methods that may tend to confuse the reader."[121] This idea is repeated in the ICAEW October 1996 Paper.[122]

B. Disclosure of Environmental Costs

An argument commonly raised against separate disclosure of environmental costs charged to income in the current period is that it is very difficult to determine the amount involved. In particular, it is difficult to distinguish environmental costs from other costs, such as operating costs, and to assemble the information. A Report issued by UN-ISAR in 1992 on "Accounting for Environmental Measures" refuted this argument against separate disclosure. It noted that "the difficulties of definition and allocation of expenses to different accounts, raised in the 1989 survey [which was based on seven German and Swiss enterprises that disclose considerable information regarding expenditures relating to environmental costs], have not posed insurmountable obstacles, provided use is made of non-accounting personnel with appropriate expertise." That Report did also note, however, that "while environmental expenditures are capable of definition, that definition is likely to be arbitrary. Ultimately, a judgement must be made as to the items which constitute environmental expenses." The companies surveyed also "claimed the publication of this information was valuable. They received fewer questions on their environmental performance in shareholders' meetings and local governments were more likely to grant approvals for their projects based on their reputation for being 'open' about information disclosure."[123]

In its Statement of Principles, however, the CICA Task Force has decided not to advocate disclosure, in the notes to the financial statements, of the amount charged to income in the current period. In the background paper to this Statement of Principles, the Task Force states that it "concluded that determining the amount of environmental costs charged to income might be difficult, and it is questionable whether a sufficient degree of detail could be included in the notes in order to provide useful information. Unless the descriptive information is provided in sufficient detail, the quantitative information could in certain situations be misinterpreted. Discussion in management's discussion and analysis, or in a separate section of the report, would normally be a more appropriate means of providing users with meaningful information on environmental performance."[124]

The EAAF document, however, recommends (but, presumably, does not require) disclosure in the notes of "the amount of environmental expenditure charged to the profit and loss account, analysed in a manner appropriate to the nature and size of the business and/or the types of environmental issues relevant to the enterprise, as well as the amount of environmental expenditures capitalised ... ." It also recommends disclosure of "the amount of environmentally related costs including costs incurred as a result of fines and penalties for non-compliance with environmental regulations and compensation to third parties as a result of loss or injury caused by past environmental pollution, which are excluded from the [EAAF] definition of environmental expenditures ... ."[125]

The EAAF document also calls for disclosure of "extraordinary environmental items, in accordance with Article 29 of the 4th Directive and Article 17 of the 7th Directive."[126]

C. Disclosure of Accounting Policies relating to Environmental Costs and Liabilities

There would appear to be general agreement regarding the disclosure of accounting policies relating to environmental costs and liabilities. In fact ISAR, IASC, and the standard-setting organizations of most countries have issued general positions or Statements of Accounting Policies[127] and these can be applied to the disclosure of accounting policies relating to environmental liabilities and costs. The ISAR Group notes that "as accounting policies are normally described in the notes to the financial statements, the following environment-related accounting policy notes could be included therein: (a) recording liabilities and provisions; (b) setting up catastrophe reserves (through appropriation of retained earnings); disclosure of contingent liabilities."[128] The EAAF document requires disclosure in the notes of "the valuation methods applied on environmental issues, as part of the disclosure required by Article 43 (1)(1) of the 4th Directive and Article 34(1) of the 7th Directive."[129] The US-FASB Exposure Draft calls for disclosure of "the funding policy for closure or removal obligations."[130] The ICAEW April 1995 Discussion Paper notes that "under SSAP 2 'Disclosure of accounting policies,' the accounting policies followed for dealing with items which are judged material or critical in determining profit or loss for the year and in stating the financial position should be disclosed by way of note to the accounts." It suggests that "a specific accounting policy for recognition and measurement of environmental costs and liabilities should be provided when such items are material to the financial statements."[131] The ICAEW October 1996 Paper states that "where environmental costs and liabilities are significant, the accounting policies should explain whether the amounts concerned are those which relate 'wholly and exclusively' to preventing, reducing or repairing damage to the environment or whether they are based on a comprehensive allocation of cost."[132]

The Canadian Research Report also notes that "it has become accepted practice to provide information in the financial statements about the accounting policies of the entity....the Study Group believes that the following disclosures should be made about an entity's accounting policies with respect to environmental costs:

- what is included in the definition of 'environmental costs';
- the basis on which environmental costs are expensed or capitalized;
- how environmental costs are amortized to income;
- the basis on which environmental liabilities are recognized."[133]

The CICA Task Force Background Paper states that "as a minimum, [the entity] should disclose what is included in the definition of 'environmental costs' and a description of the method of amortizing environmental costs to income."[134]

D. Commitments

The Canadian Research Report sets out a number of suggested disclosure requirements relating to environmental commitments. These are set out in Appendix I, Section VI.

E. Other

The EAAF Document states that "an indication of government incentives related to environmental protection measures, such as grants and tax concessions," could usefully be given in the annual report, as could "the extent to which environmental protection measures, resulting from changes in future legal requirements that have already been enacted - or substantially enacted - into law, are in process of implementation."[135]

F. General

A number of organizations require, or have suggested that various general disclosures be made with respect to environmental costs. Some of these relate to "external costs" which are not covered by this Report (see Section IB, Scope of Coverage). Others, however, are relevant to environmental costs that can be accounted for under the existing accounting and reporting framework.

The ISAR Group calls for disclosure of "the type of environmental issues that are pertinent to the enterprise and its industry, including (i) the formal policy and programmes that have been adopted by the enterprise; (ii) in cases where no such policy and programmes exist, this fact could be stated; (iii) the improvements in key areas that have been made since the introduction of the policy, or over the past five years, whatever is shorter, (iv) the extent to which environmental protection measures have been undertaken due to governmental legislation, and the extent to which governmental requirements (for example, a timetable for the reduction of emissions) are being achieved; (vi) any material proceedings under environmental laws. ..."[136] Other items are set out in Appendix 1.

The US-FASB Exposure Draft states that there should be disclosure of "a description of the closure or removal obligations and of the related long-lived assets."[137] The UK-ASB Discussion Paper also calls for disclosure of "a brief description of the nature of the obligation...." and notes that, for environmental liabilities and costs "appropriate disclosures would include, *inter alia*, a brief description of the environmental damage, any laws or regulations that requires its remediation, any reasonably expected changes to these laws or to existing technology that are reflected in the amount provided for...."[138]

In view of the different types of disclosure called for, and the importance of disclosures in respect of environmental costs and liabilities, the various requirements or disclosures advocated by various organizations are set out in Appendix 1.

G. Disclosure Outside the Financial Statements

A number of countries, such as the United Kingdom, Canada and the United States, call for certain disclosures outside the financial statements, such as the Management's Discussion & Analysis (MD&A) (Canada and US), other filings with the Securities & Exchange Commission (US) or the Operating and Financial Review (OFR) (UK). The MD&A or OFR, and associated documents, often call for, both directly and indirectly, the disclosure of environmental information.

(a) *United Kingdom*

The Accounting Standards Board in the UK has issued a statement of "best practice" on the Operating and Financial Review. The statement is intended to have persuasive rather than mandatory force; its use is commended by the Financial Reporting Council, the Hundred Group of Finance Directors and the London Stock Exchange. It notes that "an OFR would include a discussion and interpretation of the business, the main factors, features as well as uncertainties that underlie it and the structure of its financing. Although it is a report on the year under review, not a forecast of future results, it should nevertheless draw out those aspects of the year under review that are relevant to an assessment of future prospects."[139] It specifically advocates a "discussion identifying the principal risks and uncertainties in the main lines of business, together with a commentary on the approach to managing these risks and, in qualitative terms, the nature of the potential impact on results." One of the examples considered relevant, depending on the nature of the business is "environmental protection costs and potential environmental liabilities."[140]

Although not specifically referring to environmental costs and expenditures, they would be covered by other items that would be discussed in the OFR, such as capital expenditures both the current level of expenditure and planned (committed and authorized, but not committed) future expenditures. Discussion of other activities and expenditures which can be regarded as a form of "investing in the future" is also advocated.

The ICAEW October 1996 Paper has noted that "it is necessary to strike a balance between making a general statement about the treatment of environmental issues and providing a detailed description of specific valuation methods."[141]

The Advisory Committee on Business and the Environment in its Report on "Environmental Reporting and the Financial Sector - An approach to good practice" considers that "the OFR should also state whether a formal environmental management system is in operation, and the extent to which management action has led to changes in the business's environmental performance. It should for example, include a statement of the business's record as regards its compliance with environmental requirements, with an indication of significant infringements of them, The policy for managing environmental risks should be stated: this will help to demonstrate and ensure appropriate Board responsibility towards environmental issues and their integration throughout the business."[142]

(b) *Canada*

In Canada, the Ontario, Quebec and Saskatchewan Provincial Securities Acts, or pronouncements associated therewith, require the filing of an Annual Information Form (AIF) by companies registered with the Securities Commissions of those Provinces. One of the requirements for the AIF is a discussion of "the financial or operational effect of environmental protection requirements on the capital expenditures, earnings and competitive position of the issuer for the fiscal current year and any expected impact on future years."[143]

It should be noted that the ISAR conclusions also include this requirement.[144]

Again there are general requirements in the MD&A itself that could have relevance to the disclosure of environmental information, such as the requirement to describe any unusual or infrequent events or transactions or any significant economic changes which materially offset income from continuing operations and the extent to which such income was affected, and "description and amounts of matters that have had an impact on reported expenditures and are not expected to have an impact on future operations."

(c) *United States*

The country that has the most extensive non-financial statement requirements relating to the disclosure of environmental information is the United States, through requirements specified by its Securities and Exchange Commission. The SEC requirements are, however, often quite specific to environmental legislation enacted in the US. Regulation S-K calls for a number of disclosure requirements relating to non financial items. Item 101, "Description of Business," item 103 "Legal Proceedings" and item 303 "Management's Discussion and Analysis" refer to required disclosures of environmental matters. In addition, the SEC has issued interpretive releases and letters that contain further disclosure requirements.

Item 101, "Description of Business" includes a paragraph that states that:
"...Appropriate disclosure also shall be made as to the material effects that compliance with Federal, State and local provisions which have been enacted or adopted regulating the discharge of materials into the environment, or otherwise relating to the protection of the environment, may have upon the capital expenditures, earnings and competitive position of the registrant and its subsidiaries. The registrant shall disclose any material estimated capital expenditures for environmental control facilities for the remainder of its current fiscal year and its succeeding fiscal year and for such further periods as the registrant may deem material." (paragraph (c) 1 (xii))

An interpretive release makes it clear that if compliance costs are expected to be materially higher in the period(s) beyond the mandatory disclosure period, this fact must be disclosed.

Item 103, "Legal Proceedings" requires the disclosure of any material pending legal requirements. It exempts, however, ordinary routine litigation immaterial to the business. Instruction 5 to item 103 addresses proceedings relating to environmental matters and indicates that administrative or judicial proceedings concerning discharge of materials into the environment or primarily for the purpose of the protecting the environment shall not be deemed "ordinary routine litigation incidental to the business." Such an administrative or judicial proceeding must be described if:

    (i)   it is material to the business or financial condition of the registrant;

    (ii)   it involves primarily a claim for damages or involves potential monetary sanctions, capital expenditures, deferred charges or charges to income and the amount involved, exclusive of interest and costs, exceeds 10% of the current assets of the registrant and its subsidiaries on a consolidated basis; or

    (iii)   a governmental authority is a party to such proceeding and such proceeding involves potential monetary sanctions, unless the registrant reasonably believes that such proceeding will result in no monetary sanctions, or in monetary sanctions exclusive of interest and costs, of less than $100,000. Proceedings which are similar in nature may be grouped and described generically.

Various interpretative releases have been issued on this matter.

Item 303, Management's Discussion and Analysis of Financial Condition and Results of Operations may also call for disclosure of certain environmental information of a softer nature, where it has an impact on liquidity, capital resources and results of operations, including those that would have an impact on future operations. For example, the registrant may have to allocate financial resources to upgrading equipment so as to comply with environmental legislation. New and proposed environmental rules and regulations may affect future operations.

H. Conclusions with respect to Disclosures

Based on the review of material that is being developed by standard setting bodies and other organizations, it is suggested that the following positions be developed with respect to disclosures:

Definition

1. The definition of environmental costs should be disclosed.

Environmental Liabilities

2. Environmental Liabilities should be disclosed as a separate caption in the balance sheet.

3. The basis, or bases, used to measure environmental liabilities (for example, the "current cost" approach or the "present value" approach) should be disclosed.

4. For each material class of liabilities, the following should be disclosed
   (a) a brief description of the nature of the liabilities,
   (b) a general indication of the timing and terms of their settlement,
   (c) when there is significant uncertainty over the amounts of the liabilities, or the timing of settlement, this fact should be disclosed.

5. Where the "present value" approach has been used as the basis of measurement, consideration should be given to disclosing all assumptions critical to estimating the future cash outflows and the liability recognized in the financial statements, including:
   (a) the current cost estimate of settling the liability;
   (b) the estimated long-term rate of inflation used in computing the liability;
   (c) the estimated future cost of settlement;
   (d) the discount rate(s).

Environmental Costs

6. The amount of environmental expenditure charged to income, distinguished between operating and non operating costs and analyzed in a manner appropriate to the nature and size of the business and/or the types of environmental issues relevant to the enterprise, should be disclosed. The amount of environmental expenditures capitalized in the current period should be separately disclosed.

7. Costs incurred as a result of fines and penalties for non compliance with environmental regulations and compensation to third parties as a result of loss or injury caused by past environmental pollution should be disclosed

8. Any environmental costs recorded as extraordinary items should be separately disclosed.

Accounting policies

9. Any accounting policies that specifically relate to environmental liabilities and costs should be disclosed.

General

10. The nature of environmental liabilities and costs recognized in the financial statements should be disclosed, including, *inter alia*, a brief description of any environmental damage, any laws or regulations that requires its remediation, and any reasonably expected changes to these laws or to existing technology that are reflected in the amount provided for.

11. The type of environmental issues that are pertinent to an entity and its industry should be disclosed, including
    (a) the formal policy and programmes that have been adopted by the entity;
    (b) in cases where no such policy and programmes exist, this fact should be stated;
    (c) the improvements in key areas that have been made since the introduction of the policy, or over the past five years, whatever is shorter,
    (d) the extent to which environmental protection measures have been undertaken due to governmental legislation, and the extent to which governmental requirements (for example, a timetable for the reduction of emissions) have been achieved;
    (e) any material proceedings under environmental laws.

12. It would be desirable to disclose any government incentives, such as grants and tax concessions, provided with respect to environmental protection measures.

Management's Discussion and Analysis or Operating and Financial Review

13. Consideration should be given to including a discussion of issues relating to environmental costs and liabilities in the MD&A or OFR. Such a discussion could include the matters referred to in items 10 to 12 above.

IX.   POLLUTION ALLOWANCES AND SIMILAR ECONOMIC INSTRUMENTS

As a means of achieving national pollution emission targets, some countries have introduced, or are considering introducing, "pollution allowances." Such allowances are a limited authorization to emit specified gases into the atmosphere. For example, under an allowance allocation system, the US Environmental Protection Agency grants each regulated sulphur dioxide source annual allowances equaling the number of tons of sulphur dioxide targeted for that entity per year. If the entity releases emissions below its targeted level, allowances left over after compensating for the released emissions may be held for future use or sold. If emissions exceed targeted levels, allowances must be purchased to cover the difference. Substantial fines are assessed if allowances held are inadequate to cover the emissions, and an entity may also lose its expected allowances for the following year.

A question arises as to how these "allowances" should be accounted for. Presumably, purchased allowances would be expensed, if used up during the year, or recorded as an asset at their cost, if not so used up. How does one value those allowances received by way of grant? Are they treated as a donated asset and valued at their market value? Is a gain recorded on those assets that are sold? What other ways are there of accounting for such "allowances"? This seems to be an issue on which guidance is needed.

Notes

1. Document for the [European] Accounting Advisory Forum "Environmental Issues in Financial Reporting, " December 1995 (referred to as the EAAF Document) paragraph 1.

2. CICA Task Force on "Environmental Liabilities and Cost" Background Paper, September 11-12, 1996, unpublished (referred to as the CICA Task Force Background Paper), paragraph 2.

3. EAAF Document, paragraph 9.

4. "Environmental Costs and Liabilities: Accounting and Financial Reporting Issues," published by the Canadian Institute of Chartered Accountants, 1993, (referred to as the Canadian Research Report), page 9

5. EAAF Document, paragraph 9.

6. "Environmental Issues in Financial Reporting," The Institute of Chartered Accountants in England and Wales, October 1996 (referred to as the ICAEW October 1996 Paper), page 8, paragraph 1.15.

7. Canadian Research Report, pages v, 9 and 11.

8. CICA Task Force Background Paper, paragraph 8.

9. CICA Task Force Background Paper, paragraph 9.

10. EAAF Document, paragraphs 10 and 11.

11. CICA Task Force Background Paper, paragraphs 9 and 10

12. "Financial Reporting of Environmental Liabilities - A Discussion Paper," The Institute of Chartered Accountants in England and Wales, April 1995 (referred to as the ICAEW April 1995 Discussion Paper), page 7, paragraph 1.5.

13. ICAEW October 1996 Paper, page 7, paragraphs 1.7 and 1.8

14. "Provisions and Contingencies," Draft Statement of Principles, International Accounting

Standards Committee, November 1996 (referred to as the IASC November 1996 draft SoP), page 13, paragraph 18.

15.   Statement of Financial Accounting Concepts No. 3, "Elements of Financial Statements of Business Enterprises," (SFAC 3) US Financial Accounting Standards Board, 1980, page 12, paragraph 28.

16.   See, for example, SFAC 3, page 13, paragraph 29.

17.   "Framework for the Preparation and Presentation of Financial Statements." International Accounting Standards Committee, July 1989, paragraph 91.

18.   CICA Handbook Section 1000, "Financial Statement Concepts," Canadian Institute of Chartered Accountants, paragraph 29.

19.   See, for example, SFAC 3, page 9, paragraph 20

20.   "Framework for the Preparation and Presentation of Financial Statements." International Accounting Standards Committee, July 1989, paragraph 89.

21.   Statement of Position, 96-1 "Environmental Remediation Liabilities," American Institute of Certified Public Accountants, October 10, 1996 (referred to as AICPA Statement of Position 96-1), page 35, paragraph 5.2.

22.   FASB Interpretation No. 14, "Reasonable Estimation of the Amount of a Loss." US Financial Accounting Standards Board, paragraph 2.

23.   Exposure Draft, Proposed Statement of Financial Accounting Standards, "Accounting for Certain Liabilities Related to Closure or Removal of Long-Lived Assets," US Financial Accounting Standards Board, February 7, 1996 (referred to as the FASB Exposure Draft), paragraph 36.

24.   Canadian Research Report, pages 47 and 48.

25.   EAAF Document, paragraph 12.

26.   EAAF Document, paragraph 12.

27.   "Provisions," Discussion Paper, UK Accounting Standards Board, 1995 (referred to as the UK-ASB Discussion Paper), page 56, paragraph 4.2.2.

28.   FASB Exposure Draft, paragraph 8

29.   IASC November 1996 draft SoP, page 18, paragraph 29.

30.   Proposed International Accounting Standard "Provisions, Contingent Liabilities and Contingent Assets," Exposure Draft 59, International Accounting Standards Committee, August 1997 (referred to as the IASC August 1997 Exposure Draft), paragraph 14. Also the discussion set out in paragraphs 15 to 21.

31. Financial Reporting Exposure Draft (FRED) 14, "Provisions and Contingencies", UK Accounting Standards Boar, June 1997 (referred to as UK-ASB June 1997 Exposure Draft), paragraph 5.

32. UK-ASB June 1997 Exposure Draft, paragraph 38.

33. EAAF Document, paragraph 14.

34. ICAEW April 1995 Discussion Paper, page 11, paragraph 4.3.

35. FASB Exposure Draft, paragraph 7

36. UK-ASB Discussion Paper, page 21, paragraph 1.2.2

37. EAAF Document, paragraph 14.

38. Canadian Research Report, page 45.

39. ICAEW October 1996 Paper, page 12, paragraph 3.7.

40. Canadian Research Report, page 44.

41. CICA Handbook, Section 3290.

42. Statement of Financial Accounting Standards No. 5, "Accounting for Contingencies" (US-SFAS 5), US Financial Accounting Standards Board, March 1975, paragraph 3.

43. AICPA Statement of Position 96-1, page 35, paragraph 5.3

44. AICPA Statement of Position 96-1, pages 36 and 37, paragraph 5.7

45. AICPA Statement of Position 96-1, pages 37 and 38, paragraphs 5.10. 5.11 and 5.13.

46. UK-ASB Discussion Paper, page 27, paragraphs 1.3.2 and 1.3.3.

47. EAAF Document, paragraph 15.

48. IASC November 1996 draft SoP, page 20 to 22, paragraphs 36 to 42.

49. IASC August 1997 Exposure Draft, paragraph 26.

50. UK-ASB June 1997 Exposure Draft, paragraph 52.

51. FASB Exposure Draft, paragraph 6.

52. FASB Exposure Draft, paragraph 9.

53. UK-ASB Discussion Paper, page 26, paragraph 1.3.2.

54.   EAAF Document, paragraph 18.

55.   CICA Handbook, Section 3060, "Capital Assets," paragraph 39.

56.   Canadian Research Report, page 51.

57.   Canadian Research Report, pages 57 and 58.

58.   FASB Exposure Draft, paragraph 51-54 and 56.

59.   UK-ASB Discussion Paper, page 30, paragraph 1.3.17.

60.   UK-ASB Discussion Paper, page 30, paragraph 1.3.17.

61.   FASB Exposure Draft, paragraph 56

62.   UK-ASB Discussion Paper, page 30, paragraph 1.3.17.

63.   IASC November 1996 draft SoP, page 23, paragraphs 43 and 45.

64.   IASC August 1997 Exposure Draft, paragraphs 33 and 34.

65.   UK-ASB June 1997 Exposure Draft, paragraph 9.

66.   EAAF Document, paragraph 8.

67.   FASB Exposure Draft, paragraphs 57-60

68.   FASB Exposure Draft, paragraph 59

69.   Canadian Research Report, pages 57-58.

70.   UK-ASB Discussion Paper, page 31, paragraph 1.3.20.

71.   UK-ASB June 1997 Exposure Draft, paragraphs 10 and 11.

72.   FASB Exposure Draft, paragraphs 11 and 14.

73.   IASC August 1997 Exposure Draft, paragraph 35.

74.   IASC November 1996 draft SoP, page 24, paragraph 49 and IASC August 1997 Exposure Draft, paragraph 37.

75.   CICA Handbook, Section 3060, "Capital Assets," paragraph 39.

76.   Canadian Research Report, page 55.

77.   UK-ASB Discussion Paper, page 32, paragraph 1.4.2.

78.   EAAF Document, paragraphs 22 and 15.

79.   IASC August 1997 Exposure Draft, paragraph 39.

80.   UK-ASB June 1997 Exposure Draft, paragraph 16.

81.   AICPA Statement of Position 96-1, page 43, paragraph 6.2

82.   Canadian Research Report, pages 52 and 53.

83.   Canadian Research Report, pages 55 and 56.

84.   FASB Exposure Draft, paragraph 10.

85.   Statement of Standard Accounting Practice No. 18, "Accounting for Contingencies" (UK-SSAP 18), UK-Accounting Standards Board, August 1980, paragraph 14.

86.   US-SFAS 5, paragraph 1.

87.   ICAEW October 1996 Paper, page 15, paragraph 4.2.

88.   ICAEW October 1996 Paper, page 13, paragraph 4.3

89.   Canadian Research Report, pages 91 and 92.

90.   ICAEW October 1996 Paper, page 15, paragraph 4.5.

91.   Canadian Research Report, pages 17 and 18.

92.   ICAEW April 1995 Discussion Paper, pages 7 and 8, paragraphs 2.3 to 2.5, and October 1996 Paper, page 9, paragraph 2.3.

93.   Canadian Research Report, pages 22 to 36.

94.   EAAF Document, paragraph 19.

95.   EAAF Document, paragraphs 20 and 21.

96.   ICAEW April 1995 Discussion Paper, page 9, paragraphs 3.3 and 3.4

97.   ICAEW October 1996 Paper, page 10, paragraph 2.9.

98.   FASB Exposure Draft, paragraph 17.

99.   UK-ASB Discussion Paper, page 63, paragraph 4.4.11.

100.   IASC August 1997 Exposure Draft, Appendix 1, Illustrative Examples, paragraph 4.

101. UK-ASB June 1997 Exposure Draft, paragraph 13.

102. CICA Handbook, Section 3060, "Capital Assets," paragraph 39.

103. Canadian Research Report, page 39.

104. CICA Task Force Background Paper, Principle 6(d).

105. FASB Exposure Draft, paragraph 75.

106. CICA Task Force Background Paper, Principle 7 and paragraph 57.

107. UK-ASB Discussion Paper, page 63, paragraph 4.4.11.

108. Canadian Research Report, page 23.

109. EAAF Document, paragraph 23.

110. UK-ASB Discussion Paper, page 63, paragraph 4.4.11.

111. FASB Exposure Draft, paragraph 18.

112. ICAEW October 1996 Paper, page 17, paragraphs 5.1 and 5.5.

113. Canadian Research Report, pages 65 and 66.

114. Canadian Research Report, pages 36-38.

115. Canadian Research Report, page 20.

116. Canadian Research Report, page 62.

117. EAAF Document, paragraphs 26 and 27(a)

118. FASB Exposure Draft, paragraph 25.

119. UK-ASB Discussion Paper, page 66, paragraph 4.5.1 and page 33, paragraph 1.5.2.

120. Canadian Research Report, page x.

121. ICAEW April 1995 Discussion Paper, page 19, paragraph 8.7

122. ICAEW October 1996 Paper, page 19, paragraph 6.3

123. Intergovernmental Working Group of Experts on International Standards of Accounting and Reporting, "Accounting for Environmental Protection Measures,"*International Accounting and Reporting Issues, 1991 Review* (New York, United Nations, 1992), pp. 101 and 105-107.

124. CICA Task Force Background Paper, Paragraph 70.

125. EAAF Document, paragraph 28(a) and (b)

126. EAAF Document, paragraph 27(b).

127. For example, see ISAR Group, Conclusions on Accounting and Reporting by Transnational Corporations, pages 15 and 16, paragraphs 98-101 and IASC IAS 1, Disclosure of Accounting Policies.

128. ISAR Group, Conclusions, page 32, paragraph 210.

129. EAAF Document, paragraph 27(a).

130. FASB Exposure Draft, paragraph 25(c).

131. ICAEW April 1995 Discussion Paper, page 18, paragraphs 8.1 and 8.4.

132. ICAEW October 1996 Paper, page 21, paragraph 6.13

133. Canadian Research Report, page 88.

134. CICA Task Force Background Paper, paragraph 62.

135. EAAF Document, paragraph 29(d) and (e)

136. ISAR Group, Conclusions, pages 31 and 32, paragraphs 209 to 211.

137. FASB Exposure Draft, paragraph 25(a) and (b).

138. UK-ASB Discussion Paper, page 33, paragraph 1.5.2 and page 66, paragraph 4.5.1.

139. Accounting Standards Board Statement, "Operating and Financial Review" (UK-ASB - OFR), UK-Accounting Standards Board, July 1993, Introduction, paragraph 2.

140. UK-ASB-OFR, paragraph 12

141. ICAEW October 1996 Paper, page 19, paragraph 6.3

142. "Environmental Reporting and the Financial Sector - An approach to Good Practice," Advisory Committee on Business and the Environment (UK), February ,1997, pages 6-7, paragraph 13.

143. For example, Ontario Securities Commission Policy Statement No. 5.10 Part II, item 3(2)c; Quebec Securities Act Regulations Schedule IX, Part II, item 3.2(3).

144. ISAR Group, Conclusions, page 32, paragraph 209 (a) (vii).

APPENDIX 1

DISCLOSURE REQUIREMENTS

I.   ISAR CONCLUSIONS ON ACCOUNTING AND REPORTING BY TRANSNATIONAL CORPORATIONS

209.   The following are items that could be considered by the board of directors for inclusion in their report/management discussion in order to deal with relevant environmental issues:

(a) The type of environmental issues that are pertinent to the enterprise and its industry;

(i)   The formal policy and programmes that have been adopted by the enterprise with respect to environmental protection measures;

(ii)   In cases where no such policy and programmes exist, this fact could be stated;

(iii)   The improvements in key areas that have been made since the introduction of the policy, or over the past five years, whichever is shorter;

(iv)   The environmental emission targets that the enterprise has set for itself, and how the enterprise is performing relative to those targets;

(v)   The extent to which environmental protection measures have been undertaken due to governmental legislation, and the extent to which governmental requirements (for example, a timetable for the reduction of emissions) are being achieved;

(vi)   Any material proceedings under environmental laws; management should disclose a known and potentially significant environmental problem unless it can objectively conclude that the problem is not likely to occur or, if it does, that the effect is not likely to be material;

(vii)   The financial or operational effect of environmental protection measures on the capital expenditures and earnings of the enterprise for the current period and any specific impact on future periods;

(viii) When material, the actual amount charged to operations in the current period, together with a description of the environmental measures to which they relate. This amount might be subdivided into the following general ledger accounts:

(1)   Liquid effluent treatment;
(2)   Waste gas and air treatment;
(3)   Solid waste treatment;
(4)   Analysis, control and compliance;
(5)   Remediation;
(6)   Recycling;
(7)   Other (for example, accidents, safety, etc.);

(ix)   In cases where it is not possible to segregate the amount that relates to environmental protection measures, this fact could be stated;

(x)   When material, the actual amount capitalized during the current period, the accumulated amount capitalized to date, and the period for amortizing, or writing off, such amounts, together with a description of the environmental measures to which they relate. This amount might be subdivided into categories. In cases where it is not possible to segregate the amount that relates to environmental measures, this fact could be stated.

210. As accounting policies are normally described in the notes to the financial statements, the following environment-related accounting policy notes could be included therein:

(a) Recording liabilities and provisions;
(b) Setting up catastrophe reserves (through appropriations of retained earnings);
(c) Disclosure of contingent liabilities.

211. As contingent liabilities are normally disclosed, if material, in the notes to financial statements,the following environment-related items could be included therein:

(a) Liabilities, provisions and reserves that have been set for the current period, and amounts accumulated to date;
(b) Contingent liabilities, with an estimate of the amount involved, unless the event is not likely to occur. The possible loss could be quantified to the extent reasonably practicable. If the possible loss cannot be reasonably calculated, a description of the contingent liability could continue to be furnished and the reason could be given why an estimate of the amount of the loss cannot be made. Completion of a feasibility study of remediation costs may be normally considered as the earliest date at which a reasonable estimate of the liability is possible.

II. EAAF DOCUMENT ON ENVIRONMENTAL ISSUES IN FINANCIAL REPORTING

General

24. Environmental issues related to financial reporting should only be disclosed in the accounts and annual report to the extent that they are material to the financial performance or financial position of the undertaking.

25. If Member States have introduced accounting exemptions for small and medium-sized companies, as defined in Article 11 and 27 of the 4th Directive, on the basis of this Directive, these exemptions would also be relevant for disclosures in relation with environmental issues.

Disclosure in the balance sheet

26. Environmental provisions should be shown in the balance sheet under the caption "other provisions" and, if material, separately disclosed in the notes on the accounts, in accordance with Article 42 of the 4th Directive and Article 29(1) of the 7th Directive.

Disclosure in the notes on the accounts

27. In conformity with the provisions of the 4th and 7th Directives, the following information should be given in the notes:

(a) The valuation methods applied on environmental issues, as part of the disclosure required by Article 43(1)(1) of the 4th Directive and Article 34(1) of the 7th Directive;
(b) Extraordinary environmental items, in accordance with Article 29 of the 4th Directive and Article 17 of the 7th Directive;
(c) Disclosure and details of "other provisions," in line with paragraph 26;
(d) Contingent liabilities, in conformity with Article 43(1)(7) of the 4th Directive and Article 34(7) of the 7th Directive, including narrative information in sufficient detail, so that the nature of the contingency can be understood.

28.   In addition to the requirements of 4th and 7th Directives, the following disclosures in the notes are recommended:

(a) As indicated in paragraph 11, the amount of environmental expenditure charged to the profit and loss account, analyzed in a manner appropriate to the nature and size of business and/or the types of environmental issues relevant to the enterprise, as well as the amount of environmental expenditures capitalized in accordance with paragraphs 19 to 21.

(b) As indicated in paragraph 11, the amount of environmentally related costs including costs incurred as a result of fines and penalties for non-compliance with environmental regulations and compensation to third parties as a result of loss or injury caused by past environmental pollution, which are excluded from the definition of environmental expenditures in paragraph 9, if not already separately disclosed as extraordinary items under 27 b);

(c) If other quantitative or qualitative environmental information is provided in a separate environmental report, in accordance with paragraph 7, a reference to this report (or under 29 f).

Disclosure in the annual report

29.   The following information could usefully be given in the annual report:

(a) Where environmental issues are relevant to the financial position of the undertaking, a description of the respective issues and the undertaking's response thereto;

(b) The policy that has been adopted by the enterprise in respect of environmental protection measures;

(c) The improvements that have been made in key areas of environmental protection;

(d) An indication of government incentives related to environmental protection measures, such as grants and tax concessions;

(e) The extent to which environmental protection measures, resulting from changes in future legal requirements that have already been enacted - or substantially enacted - into law, are in the process of implementation;

(f) If other quantitative or qualitative environmental information is provided in a separate environmental report, in accordance with paragraph 7, a reference to this report (or under 28 c).

III.   US-FASB EXPOSURE DRAFT ON ACCOUNTING FOR CERTAIN LIABILITIES RELATING TO CLOSURE OR REMOVAL OF LONG-LIVED ASSETS

25.   An entity that reports a liability for its closure or removal obligations shall disclose the following information:

(a) A description of the closure or removal obligations and of the related long-lived assets

(b) The liability for closure or removal obligations recognized in the financial statements (on the face of the statement of financial position or in the notes to financial statements)

(c) All assumptions that are critical to estimating the future cash outflows and the liability recognized in the financial statements, including:

      (1)   The current cost estimate of closure or removal obligations

      (2)   The estimated long-term rate of inflation used in computing the liability

      (3)   The estimated total future cost of closure or removal obligations

      (4)   The discount rate(s)

      (5)   The general estimated timing of closure or removal activities

(d) The funding policy for closure or removal obligations

(e) The fair value of assets, if any, dedicated to satisfy the closure or removal obligations

(f) The effects on the reported liability and capitalized costs of closure or removal activities resulting from changes in the current reporting period in the estimated future costs of closure or removal activities

(g) The individual components of the costs of closure or removal activities recognized in the statement of operations (depreciation, changes in the present value of the liability due to the passage of time, and investment earnings on any dedicated assets) and the total of those costs

(h) The caption or captions in the statement of operations in which the costs in (g) are aggregated if those costs have not been presented as a separate caption or reported parenthetically on the face of the statement.

IV.   UK-ASB DISCUSSION PAPER ON PROVISIONS

4.5.1. In view of the wide range of items that provisions for environmental liabilities may contain it is proposed that no disclosures should be specified other than the general disclosure applicable to provisions. These disclosures should be applied to the particular items provided for, with the amount of detail disclosed reflecting the relative significance of the item. For example, an entity may have recognised a substantial provision for the cost of cleaning up past contamination.

1.5.2. The following general principle for disclosure is proposed:

For each material class of obligation whether recognised or not, the following should be disclosed:

(a) a brief description of the nature of the obligation including an indication of the timing of payment and, where there is significant uncertainty over the amount or timing of the expenditure that will be made, the factors that are relevant to determining them (with respect to provisions for environmental liabilities, this would include, *inter alia*, a brief description of the environmental damage, any laws or regulations that require its remediation, any reasonably expected changes to those laws or to existing technology that are reflected in the amount provided for, and the likely timing of the expenditures (4.5.1)).

(b) The amount provided for and, if estimated, the basis on which the estimate has been made; and

(c) where the amount provided for is discounted, this should be stated. The type of rate used, though not its amount, should be disclosed and, where relevant, the fact that no allowance has been made for risk should be stated.

1.5.3. In addition to information on the amount provided at the year-end, the user needs to know by how much, and for what reasons, any recognised provision has changed in the year. It is therefore proposed that:

The movements in the year on each material class of recognized provision should be disclosed, showing separately:

(a) additional provisions made in the year;
(b) amounts used (ie paid and charged against the provision);
(c) amounts released unused;
(d) where the provision is discounted, interest; and
(e) exchange differences.

1.5.7. A provision should be used only for expenditures that relate to the matter for which the provision was originally recognised. Any release of an excess provision that was originally recognised in a previous period should be disclosed separately from a new provision recognised in connection with a different matter.

V. AICPA STATEMENT OF PRINCIPLES 96-1 ON ENVIRONMENTAL REMEDIATION LIABILITIES

Accounting Policies (7.10 to 7.13)

- whether the accrual for environmental remediation liabilities is measured on a discounted basis.
- the event, situation or set of circumstances that generally triggers recognition of the obligation (e.g., completion of a feasibility study (encouraged by not required)).
- the policy concerning timing of recognition of recoveries (encouraged).

Environmental Remediation Loss Contingencies (7.14 to 7.18)

- nature of the accrual and, in some circumstances, the amount accrued (SFAS 5).
- where no accrual is made, due to fact that loss is not deemed probable and/or a reasonable estimate cannot be made, the nature of the contingency and an estimate on the possible loss or range of loss, or a statement that such an estimate cannot be made.

Recognized Losses and Recoveries of Losses and Reasonable Possible Losses (7.19 to 7.23)

With respect to recorded accruals for environmental remediation loss contingencies and assets for third-party recoveries related to environmental remediation obligations:

(a) The nature of the accruals, if such disclosure is necessary for the financial statements not to be misleading, and, in situations where disclosure of the nature of the accruals is necessary, the total amount accrued for the remediation obligation, if such disclosure is also necessary for the financial statements not to be misleading.
(b) If any portion of the accrued obligation is discounted, the undiscounted amount of the obligation and the discount rate used in the present-valuing determinations.
(c) If an asset for third-party recoveries related to the environmental remediation obligation has been recognized, the amount of recovery recorded.

(d) An indication that it is at least reasonably possible that a change in the estimate of the obligation or of the asset will occur in the near term, if applicable.

With respect to reasonably possible loss contingencies, including reasonably possible loss exposures in excess of the amount accrued:

(a) The nature of the reasonably possible loss contingency, that is, a description, an estimate of the possible loss exposure or the fact that such an estimate cannot be made.
(b) An indication that it is at least reasonably possible that a change in the estimate will occur in the near term, if applicable.

Entities also are encouraged, but not required, to disclose the following:

(a) The estimated time frame of disbursements for recorded amounts if expenditures are expected to continue over the long-term.
(b) The estimated time frame for realization of recognized probable recoveries, if realization is not expected in the near term.
(c) The factors that cause the estimate to be sensitive to change, if applicable.
(d) If an estimate of the probable or reasonably possible loss or range of loss cannot be made, the reasons why it cannot be made.
(e) If information about the reasonably possible loss or the recognized and additional reasonably possible loss for an environmental remediation obligation related to an individual site is relevant to an understanding of the financial position, cash flows, or results of operations of the entity, the following with respect to the site.
   • The total amount accrued for the site
   • The nature of any reasonably possible loss contingency or additional loss, and an estimate of the possible loss or the fact that an estimate cannot be made and the reasons why it cannot be made.
   • Whether other PRPs are involved and the entity's estimated share of the obligation.
   • The status of regulatory proceedings
   • The estimated time frame for resolution of the contingency.

Probable but not Reasonably Estimable Losses (7.24 to 7.26)

• The nature of the probable contingency, that is, a description of the remediation obligation, and the fact that a reasonable estimate cannot currently be made.
• The estimated time frame for resolution of the uncertainty as to the amount of the loss (encouraged, but not required).

Unasserted Claims (7.27 and 7.28)

• If there is no current legal obligation to remediate a situation of probable or possible environmental impact, no disclosure is required.

• If an entity is required by existing laws and regulations to report the release of hazardous substances and to begin a remediation study or if assertion of a claim is deemed probable, the disclosures called for by the Statement on Accounting for Contingencies should be made.

Environmental Remediation Costs recognized Currently (7.29)

Encouraged, but not required, disclosures are:
- The amount recognized for environmental remediation loss contingencies in each period.
- The amount of any recovery from third parties that is credited to environmental remediation costs in each period.
- The income statement caption in which environmental remediation costs and credits are included.

VI.   CANADIAN RESEARCH REPORT

Environmental expenses
- Total environmental expenses, excluding the amortization of capital assets related to environmental concerns, should be disclosed in financial statements.
- It is desirable to disclose in financial statements the dollar amount and nature of each category making up the total environmental expense shown, particularly if one category is a significant component of the total. It is also desirable to indicate where each category (or part thereof) is reflected in the income statement, if not obvious.
- There should be separate disclosure in financial statements of a particular environmental expense if it is likely to differ in the future.
- Known trends with respect to environmental matters that have had a favourable or unfavourable impact on net sales, revenues or income from continuing operations should be disclosed in financial reports, but outside financial statements. Further, it is desirable to similarly disclose information that explains any significant change from year to year in any disclosed environmental expense figures.

Capital assets related to environmental concerns
- If current environmental expenditures on capital assets represent a significant component of current expenditures on capital assets or if they are likely to differ significantly in the future, their nature and amount should be disclosed in the financial statements.
- It is not necessary to segregate or disclose in financial statements the cost of capital assets related to environmental concerns.

Other assets related to environmental concerns
- If current expenditures on other assets related to environmental concerns are significant in relation to total current expenditures on capital and other assets, or if they are likely to differ significantly in the future, their nature and amount should be disclosed in the financial statements.
- The major categories of others assets related to environmental concerns should be separately disclosed, together with the basis of amortization, if any.

Impairment of assets as a result of environmental concerns
- If the impairment of assets as the result of environmental concerns is recognized through a loss accrual under *Handbook* Section 3290, the accrued loss should be shown as a liability and should be distinguished from other liabilities.

Environmental liabilities
- There should be separate disclosure in financial statements of environmental liabilities.

- Environmental liabilities that are individually material should be disclosed separately. If a counter-claim or claim against a third party has been deducted in determining the amount recognized, it is desirable that the gross amount of the liability and the amount deducted be disclosed separately .
- Any deferred charge that has resulted from the recognition of a liability for expected future environmental expenditures may be presented in the financial statements as a deduction from that related liability, provided there is note disclosure of the full amount of the liability and the disposition of the deferred charge.
- The nature of any significant measurement uncertainties relating to a recognized liability that is disclosed separately, and the range of reasonably possible outcomes, should be disclosed.
- Changes in the amount of the recorded environmental liability would not normally be disclosed.
- As a minimum, the aggregate of payments to be made in each of the next five years for future environmental expenditures that have been recognized as a liability should be disclosed. If such disclosure cannot be made because there is considerable uncertainty about the timing of the future expenditures, this fact should be disclosed.
- For environmental liabilities that have not been recognized in financial statements because no estimate can be made of them, the following should be disclosed:
    - the nature of the expected future expenditure or loss, including an indication of the likelihood of the expenditure being made or the loss being suffered;
    - a statement that an estimate of the expected future expenditures or loss cannot be made;
    - the timing of the expected future expenditure or loss, including an indication of any uncertainties related to timing.

Any unrecognized liabilities that are individually material should be disclosed separately.

Commitments
- Significant future environmental capital expenditures that involve "contractual obligations" or commitments, and that are abnormal in relation to financial position or usual business operations, should be disclosed in accordance with *CICA Handbook* Section 3280, "Contractual Obligations."
- Significant future environmental expenditures required because of environmental legislation or regulations and that are abnormal in relation to financial position or usual business operations should be disclosed. Such expenditures should also be disclosed if required by proposed legislation or regulation that it is virtually certain will come into force.
- If an entity has made a commitment with respect to significant future environmental operating expenditures that will govern the level of expenditures for a considerable period into the future, the particulars of the commitment should be disclosed (as required by Section 3280). Similarly, if existing environmental legislation or regulations will require significant future environmental operating expenditures for a considerable period into the future, the particulars of the regulations and related expenditures should be disclosed.
- It is desirable that there be disclosure in the financial report, but not necessarily in the financial statements, of environmental capital expenditures that are planned or are expected to be required under new legislation or regulations, for at least the following year.
- It is desirable that there be disclosure in the financial report, but not necessarily in the financial statements, of the environmental operating expenditures that are planned or are expected to be required under new legislation or regulations, for at least the following year.

Accounting policies
- An entity's accounting policies with respect to the following should be disclosed:
  - what is included in the definition of "environmental costs";
  - the basis on which environmental costs are expensed or capitalized;
  - how environmental costs are amortized to income;
  - the basis on which environmental liabilities are recognized.

Possible future environmental expenditures and impairment losses
- "Reasonably possible" future environmental expenditures related to past events or transactions or "reasonably possible" asset impairment losses that could have a significant impact on future cash flows should be disclosed in financial statements.
- If the probability of an environmental loss related to past events or transactions is remote, but the impact could have a significant adverse effect on the financial position of the entity, it is desirable to disclose this possibility.
- With respect to possible future environmental expenditures or losses that are disclosed in financial statements, the following details should be provided:
  - the nature of the expected future expenditure or loss, including an indication of the likelihood of the expenditure being made or the loss being suffered;
  - the size of the expected future expenditure or loss: an estimate of the expenditure or loss; or an estimate of the range of possible outcomes or a statement that an estimate cannot be made;
  - the timing of the expected future expenditure or loss, including an indication of any uncertainties related to timing.
- Possible future environmental expenditures, or losses due to asset impairment, that are individually material should be disclosed separately. Others with similar characteristics may be grouped.

Possible future environmental losses relating to future events or transactions
- There is normally no need to disclose normal business risks with respect to environmental concerns, unless the possibility of loss is imminent or could be very significant.
- An entity should disclose, in its financial statements, the industry in which it operates, the basic nature of its operations within that industry, and the particular circumstances of the entity, such as location of operations.
- If possible future environmental losses relating to future events or transactions and resulting from the public's concerns about the environment, as expressed either through legislation, regulation or public pressure, could have a significant adverse effect on the future cash flows of the entity, the nature and possible effect of these concerns should be disclosed in the financial report.
- If there is little or no risk related to environmental concerns, it may be desirable to disclose this fact in the financial report, along with an appropriate explanation.
- If the possibility of a future environmental loss exists because of a specific action by the entity or because of a specific action by others, the nature of the action and the possible effect should be disclosed in the financial report.
- If the possibility of a future environmental loss exists, but the probability of its occurrence has been reduced by actions taken by the entity, such actions should be disclosed in the financial report.

VII.   KOREAN INSTITUTE OF CERTIFIED PUBLIC ACCOUNTANTS

In its Financial Accounting Standards, which have been approved by the Ministry of Finance and Economy as of March 30, 1996, item 21 of Article 90, Additional Footnote Disclosures, calls for the following to be disclosed in the footnotes accompanying the financial statements:

> The company's environmental standards and policies, safety and accident related matters, environment related investments, consumption of resources and energy, and matters related to occurrence and treatment of by-products and scraps.

APPENDIX 2

EXAMPLES OF TREATMENT OF ENVIRONMENTAL COSTS RELATING TO ENVIRONMENTAL DAMAGE

As noted in Section VB, the extent to which environmental costs would be capitalised depends on the particular approach adopted. Under certain approaches, capitalisation would be rare; under others, capitalisation would be permitted providing certain criteria were met.

The FASB's Emerging Issues Task Force, in its EITF Issue 90-8, has provided a number of examples of where capitalisation would, or would not be appropriate. As noted in Section VB, it states that these costs may be capitalised if recoverable, but only if any one of the following conditions exist.

1. The costs extend the life, increase the capacity, or improve the safety or efficiency of property owned by the company. For purposes of this criterion, the condition of that property after the costs are incurred must be improved as compared with the condition of that property when originally constructed or acquired, if later.
2. The costs mitigate of prevent environmental contamination that has yet to occur and that otherwise may result from future operations or activities. In addition, the costs improve the property compared with its condition when constructed or acquired, if later.
3. The costs are incurred in preparing for sale that property currently held for sale.

Evaluation of Criteria	*Conditions*		
Example	*Decision*	*Apply*	*Do not apply*
1. Tanker oil spill (a) Clean up waterways and beach front (b) Re-enforce tankers hull to reduce risk of future spill	Expense Capitalise	 1,2	1,2,3
2. Rusty chemical storage tank (a) Remove rust that developed during ownership (b) Apply rust prevention chemical	Expense* Capitalise	2 (in part) 1, 2	1, 2 (in part)
3. Air pollution caused by manufacturing activities (a) Acquire & install pollution control equipment (b) Pay fines for violation of the Clean Air Act	Capitalise Expense**	1, 2	 1, 2

Evaluation of Criteria	*Conditions*		
Example	*Decision*	*Apply*	*Do not apply*
4. Lead pipes in office building contaminate drinking water (a) Remove lead pipes & replace with copper pipes	Capitalise Expense book Value of lead pipes	1, 2	
5. Soil contamination caused by operating a garbage dump (a) Refine soil on dump property (b) Install liner	Expense* Capitalise	2 (in part) 1 (in part)	1, 2 (in part) 1 (in part) 2
6. Water well contamination caused by chemical leak into wells that will be used for future beer production (a) Neutralise water in wells (b) Install water filters	Expense* Capitalise	1, 2	1, 2
7. Underground gasoline storage tanks leak and contaminate company's property (a) Refine soil (b) Encase tanks to prevent future leaks from contamination surrounding soil	Expense* Capitalise	1, 2	1, 2
8. Air in office building contaminated with asbestos fibre (a) Remove asbestos	Capitalise	1, 2 (in part)	2 (in part)

* Unless held for sale.
** Even if held for sale.

CHAPTER III

LINKING ENVIRONMENTAL AND FINANCIAL PERFORMANCE: A SURVEY OF BEST PRACTICE TECHNIQUES*

SUMMARY AND CONCLUSIONS

The Group also considered agenda item 3(b), the linkage between environmental performance and financial performance. The representative of the **Association of Chartered Certified Accountants (ACCA)**, presented document TD/B/COM.2/ISAR/2, which went beyond the traditional financial statements and identified key environmental performance indicators currently in use by leading-edge enterprises to measure and communicate environmental performance. He highlighted the apparent conflict between society's need to reduce the environmental impacts of enterprises and the ability of statutory or non-statutory mechanisms to make transparent the financial/economic consequences for the enterprise and its stakeholders of being a good environmental neighbour. As of late 1997 there had been no international consensus on how corporate environmental activity and impact should be reported.

Financial performance indicators were calculated on the basis of national accounting standards. Therefore, when financial analysts calculated these ratios for various enterprises they had reliable measures for comparing performance. This was not the case with regard to environmental performance.

The survey of environmental reports contained in document UNCTAD/ITE/EDS/Misc.9 revealed that there was no consensus on the use of standardized environmental performance indicators. Each company within an industry reported its performance using different environmental indicators, not necessarily using the same indicators from year to year. As a result, it was more difficult to compare the environmental performance of different companies, and to determine whether the company was improving over time, and the effect on financial performance as seen in terms of eco-efficient indicators. Eco-efficient indicators relate the change in environmental impacts to the change in financial results (i.e. sales, value added). The speaker explained that there was an increased level of business risk flowing from increasing levels of environmental legislation and growing public interest in corporate compliance.

---

* UNCTAD would like to express its gratitude to expert Roger Adams, Association of Chartered Certified Accountants for his contribution to this paper.

He indicated that pressure for improved reporting of environmental performance was coming from Governments, regulators, investors, customers, bankers, insurers and environmental lobby groups. There was a need to communicate environmental performance in a standardized and coherent way if it was to be useful to a potential user in understanding how corporate environmental strategy and performance impact on financial performance and shareholder value.

The representative of **Ellipson**, informed the Group that environmental variables such as environmental performance indicators (EPIs) had an economic value; users wanted to see them in the annual report, and therefore they had to be harmonized. They also had to be aggregated on the same basis as the financial data if they were to be combined with financial data when producing eco-efficient indicators. Some of these indicators, if appropriately constructed, could be part of the audited statements. The banking community was pressing for better EPIs because its concerns focused not only on asset quality but also on the quality of management, and for this it wanted reliable core indicators to be developed.

There was broad acceptance by the experts of the work undertaken so far. It was suggested that, in order to give users the full value and reflect the full richness of the inputs and discussion that had gone into document TD/B/COM.2/ISAR/2, it be published and distributed together with the background papers. Experts further suggested that these papers be translated into as many languages as possible, published and disseminated as widely as possible, including through regional workshops. The material would have to be adapted to produce the necessary training materials for the workshops. A number of experts expressed interest in holding the workshops in their countries.

A number of experts referred to complementary work being carried out by a number of international bodies such as International Accounting Standards Committee (IASC), International Federation of Accountants (IFAC) and International Organization for Standardization (ISO). It was agreed that these bodies should be brought into the research process and that ongoing collaboration should be established with them.

EXECUTIVE SUMMARY

A.   Objectives of the study

Public reporting of environmental data by enterprises is a phenomenon of the 1990s. With environmental legislation drawing tighter almost everywhere, financial sector stakeholders are beginning to demand improved levels of environmental data. They use such data for various purposes: to reduce their own exposure to lending or credit risk; to judge the entity's own exposure to risk; to interpret corporate managements' ability to manage environmental issues and integrate environmental issues into general long-term strategic issues; and to compare progress between companies and over time.

The specific objectives of the background paper from which this chapter is drawn are:
- to explore the limitations of the conventional financial reporting model as a vehicle for reporting environmental data;

- to identify and record the methods being used by leading edge companies to measure and communicate environmental performance;
- to identify and record the techniques used by financial sector stakeholders to integrate environmental performance data into their investment decisions;
- to review evidence concerning the relationship (if any) between environmental and shareholder value auditioned
- to make recommendations concerning the way(s) in which environmental performance is communicated in external corporate reporting and to suggest ways in which the use of environmental performance indicators can be improved

Underlying these objectives are the assumptions that:

(i)   there is a need to communicate environmental performance in a standardized and coherent way if it is to be useful or relevant to a potential user; and

(ii)   for financial market users in particular, there is a need to understand how corporate environmental strategy and performance impacts on financial performance and shareholder value.

B.   Limits of the conventional financial reporting model

Because neither national company legislation nor national generally accepted accounting principals (GAAP) frameworks have made broad environmental disclosures mandatory, disclosures in annual reports are usually confined to the largest enterprises, limited in extent and rarely comparable from enterprise to enterprise. As a result, such disclosures are seldom seen as being useful to external decision makers.

The conventional model of financial accounting and reporting is one which emphasizes the importance of financial performance. The annual report deriving from the conventional model highlights financial assets and liabilities, shareholder worth, operating income and taxes, and changes in the financial position of the enterprise over the reporting period. The conventional model contains relatively little by way of predictive or forward looking information.

The conventional model routinely ignores environmental issues unless they have a financial impact of sufficient materiality to trigger the recognition and measurement criteria contained in most established GAAP frameworks. Thus only a limited range of environmental disclosures are required by the conventional accounting framework: these few instances tend to centre on environmental liabilities and provisions, contingent liabilities and where appropriate, exceptional items, impaired assets and long term de-commissioning costs. Even these are underreported or unreported in the face of uncertainty on timing or estimation.

The conventional model of financial reporting minimizes the role given to non-financial data. Although the environment has played a larger role in corporate strategy over the last decade, it is nevertheless apparent that annual reports at present fail to convey either the significance of environmental issues to the reporting entity or any adequate description of how corporate management is attempting to integrate environmental strategy into overall corporate strategy. Reporting takes a minimalist approach and focuses largely on meeting legal obligations and targets.

C. Best practice in measuring and communicating environmental performance

A good summary of the current extent of disclosure of environmental data in company annual reports and stand alone environmental reports is the Klynveld Peat Marwick Goedeler (KPMG) "International Survey of Environmental Reporting 1996". This covers the 100 leading companies in each of the following 12 (developed) countries: Australia, Belgium, Canada, Denmark, Finland, the Netherlands, New Zealand, Norway, Sweden, Switzerland, the United Kingdom and the United States of America. Overall, 556 (69%) of companies surveyed mentioned the environment in their annual reports - an increase from 37% in 1993. With regard to stand-alone environmental reports, KPMG finds that 23% of companies surveyed (13% in 1993) produce corporate environmental reports, in addition to their annual report to shareholders. Interest in environmental disclosure and accounting for the environment is not confined, however, to the countries covered by the KPMG survey. Interest has been shown in countries as diverse as China, India, Japan, the Russian Federation, South Africa and Thailand.

Some problems arising with current environmental disclosures are set out in table 1. below.

<table>
<tr><td colspan="3">Table 1. Expected usefulness of environmental disclosures
Via the annual report to shareholders</td></tr>
<tr><td>Category of disclosure</td><td>Example of disclosure</td><td>Expected usefulness rating to financial community</td></tr>
<tr><td>Category 1: financially Quantified data relating to environmental liabilities and provisions; exceptional environmental costs; green levies and taxes</td><td>Balance sheet provisions in respect of future clean-up costs</td><td>High - accounting standards and statutory requirements only require separate disclosure of material (significant) items. Disclosure is covered by audit opinion.</td></tr>
<tr><td>Category 2: qualitative data relating to (inter alia) environmental policies, procedures and progress; other environmental costs</td><td>Statement of corporate environmental policies; description of environmental audit procedures and coverage</td><td>Moderate - discretionary disclosure(s) are susceptible to PR hype and are not covered by any audit opinion, but they are evidence of corporate commitment. Cost identification and allocation may be problematic.</td></tr>
<tr><td>Category 3: non-financial but quantified/verifiable data regarding environmental performance</td><td>Environmental performance data re emissions, resource use, efficiency measures</td><td>Moderate/low - unlikely to be externally verified or (currently) comparable with other companies in same sector</td></tr>
</table>

At present there appears to be a mismatch between corporate environmental disclosures and the needs of financial sector stakeholders. Based upon an analysis of (I) various stakeholder information needs studies and (ii) existing guidance/recommendations on environmental disclosures, this report makes recommendations which expand upon the earlier (1991) ISAR recommendations for environmental disclosure (UNCTAD Conclusions, 1994). Table 2 set out in D (below) presents a recommended framework for environmental disclosures within the annual report to shareholders.

D.   Methods used by leading-edge enterprises in measuring and communicating environmental performance

Possibly because of the relative novelty of environmental performance measurement, it appears that there is no one single accepted way of defining or measuring environmental performance. Various approaches are identified:

- reporting on compliance with statutory permits or toxic release inventory (TRI)-type requirements
- reporting reductions in absolute discharges
- reporting success in achieving emissions reduction targets
- relating emissions to significant environmental impacts ("environmental footprint")
- developing single (or multiple) index models to give an aggregate environmental performance
- developing an array of relevant environmental performance indicators (EPIs) which have general industry significance and which are computed on a consistent basis over time

The generic categories of environmental performance indicators identified by James and Bennett (1994) provide perhaps a useful synthesis of the current approach to monitoring, measuring and reporting environmental performance. It should be noted that there is a strong relationship between the categories of EPI identified below and those being developed for internal environmental management purposes by the International Standards Organisation (ISO - ISO 14031: Environmental Performance Evaluation).

Table 2.	
Categories of EPIs	Examples of EPIs
1. measures of ultimate environmental impact	• species diversity around plant • noise levels at specified points • ratio of actual to sustainable discharges
2. risk measures of potential impact	• usage of high risk chemicals/materials • risk of fatalities to exposed populations • risk of damage to ecosystems
3. emissions/waste measures (of mass and volume of emissions and wastes)	• emissions to air: TRI toxics, sulphur dioxides, nitrogen oxides, CO^2 etc. • waste to landfill: hazardous, non-hazardous • waste water discharges
4. input measures (of the effectiveness of business process)	• measures covering people, equipment, materials, physical setting, internal support
5. measures of resource consumption	• measures of energy, materials, water, etc. • electricity, gas, oil consumption • natural resource (paper/minerals/water) consumption)

6. efficiency measures (of energy and materials utilization)	• energy: ratio energy used/wasted • ratio actual/theoretical energy use • materials: percentage utilization • equipment: percentage utilization
7. customer measures (of satisfaction and behaviour)	• level of approval • number of complaints • product related environmental awareness • % adopting desired behaviour
8. financial measures	• cost of environment related capital expenditure • direct environment related operating costs • regulatory compliance, fines and penalties • costs of energy/materials • avoided costs plus measurable benefits

The significant amount of interest being demonstrated by the financial community in the relative environmental performance of enterprises has resulted in increasing attention being paid to the development of so-called "eco-financial" (or "eco-efficiency") indicators. Bodies such as the European Federation of Financial Analysts Societies and the Swiss Bankers Association have led the way in calling for the publication of standardized eco-efficiency/eco-financial indicators. Table 3. is illustrative of the range of such indicators which have been developed to date:

Table 3. Financially relevant ("eco-financial") environmental performance indicators	
1.	Cost of environment related capital expenditure
2.	Direct environment related operating or management costs as % of sales, value added, net earnings, divisional earnings or other unit of output costs, e.g. production cost or site cost of sales
3.	Total costs of regulatory compliance
4.	Fines and penalties, damages and remediation costs
5.	Cost of waste and waste-disposal charges to costs of materials
6.	Avoided costs/benefits of pollution prevention measures/reduced costs of purchased materials resulting from recycling or reuse
7.	Marginal cost of environmental protection measures
8.	Insurance premiums as measures of the effectiveness of risk-management activities
9.	Emission reduction/expenditure
10.	Average environmental expenditure per....
11.	Environmental investments/total investments
12.	Cost of energy or fuel consumption or packaging costs
13.	Donations and other voluntary environmental costs
14.	TRI emission per $m turnover

The above table reveals the diversity in environmental performance indicators. Enterprises within the same industry often report their performance using different indicators, and not necessarily using the same indicators from year to year. As a result, it is more difficult to compare the environmental performance of different enterprises; to determine if the enterprise is improving over time; and if so what strategy it adopted to achieve any improvements and whether it was the most cost-efficient strategy. The work currently under way on EPIs at the industry level or in conjunction with ISO 14031 aims at developing industry-specific indicators for internal management purposes and not for external reporting purposes. The identification and standardization of both generic and industry-specific EPIs could guide preparers in providing essential qualitative and quantitative environmental information for inclusion in the annual report. The use of standardized indicators could also stimulate enterprises to improve their environmental and financial performance by comparing them with competitors, that is benchmarking.

The widespread usage of such EPIs is dependent on there being:
- an accepted definition of environmental operating and capital expenditures;
- further development in the area of industry-specific EPIs;
- development of generic environmental impact EPIs, e.g., global-warming indicators

Regarding the first constraint, many enterprises appear able to disclose such data, but the analyst or would-be user needs to pay careful attention to the precise details of the accounting policy adopted by the reporting entity vis-à-vis the definition and disclosure of environmental operating and capital costs. With regard to the second constraint there is considerable experimentation going on at the industry/trade association level to derive appropriate generally accepted benchmark EPIs. With respect to the third constraint more work needs to be done in this area - a new ISAR project is reviewing generic EPIs in the context of such issues as Agenda 21 and various sustainability indicators.

Once measured, environmental performance is being communicated via a number of different media - and some companies use two, three or four different avenues to convey their environmental performance record to interested stakeholder groups. For example via:
- the annual report to shareholders
- a corporate stand-alone environmental performance report
- a local (site) report
- an Internet web site
- the official environmental register maintained by the regulator

As noted in para. 69 above, the number of enterprises disclosing non-financial and financially quantified environmental data is increasing at a steady rate.

But, as also noted in previous paragraphs, environmental reporting currently lacks credibility in the eyes of certain external stakeholder groups because certain "qualitative characteristics", which exist in the financial reporting domain, are absent. These include, inter alia:
- a guarantee of completeness
- comparability (through standardization of industry-relevant and generic EPIs)
- consistency of measurement
- absence of credible external verification

E. Conclusions and recommendations

In general the weight of available evidence indicates a strong (and growing) interest in corporate environmental performance - not just from the relevant national or regional environmental regulator, but from a variety of other stakeholders, most noticeably those from the financial sector (bankers, insurers, fund managers, etc.). At present these stakeholders find it difficult to interpret corporate environmental disclosures on a systematic basis because (a) of the voluntary nature of such reporting, and (b) because the general lack of standardization regarding the computation and disclosure of environmental performance indicators inhibits intercompany comparison.

The need for improved standards of environmental performance data is not restricted to enterprises based in developed countries, nor is it peculiar to the private sector. In many developing countries and transitional economies, access to external funding will depend in part upon improved environmental transparency and accountability.

1. Recommendations for annual report disclosures

Accepting that all material environmental liabilities and contingent liabilities are recognized, are appropriately measured and are properly disclosed by the conventional accounting system, what sort of additional information could be delivered in the annual report to shareholders on a cost-effective basis? Deliverable possibilities include those listed in the following table. It should be noted that the majority of these disclosures fall outside the audited financial statements themselves.

Table 4. An environmental reporting framework for the annual report	
Annual report element	Recommended environmental disclosure(s)
Chairman/CEOs report	• corporate commitment to continuous environmental improvement • significant improvements since last report
Business segment review	• segmented environmental performance data (if not provided in the environmental review (see below) • improvements in key areas since previous report
Environmental review	• scope of the review • corporate environmental policy statement • extent of worldwide compliance • key environmental issues facing the company • organizational responsibilities • description of environmental management systems and international standards (e.g., ICC/ISO/EMAS) • segmental performance data based around: energy use, materials use, emissions (CO_2, NOx, SO_2, CFCs, etc.) and waste disposal routes • sector-specific data including industry-agreed EPIs (including eco-efficiency-based EPIs) • financial data on environmental costs (energy, waste, remediation, staffing, exceptional charges and write downs, fines and penalties, green taxes paid, capital investment) • financial estimates of savings and benefits flowing from pro-environment efforts

	• cross-reference to other environmental reports • independent verification statement
Operating & financial Review/MD&A	• key environmental issues facing the company in the short-to medium-term and plans for addressing these • progress in addressing changes required by future legal requirements • actual and projected levels of environmental expenditure • legal matters pending
Report of the Directors	• environmental policy statement (if not provided elsewhere)
Accounting policy disclosure	• estimation of provisions and contingencies • capitalization policies • impairment policies • de-commissioning and land remediation policies • depreciation polices
Profit & loss account	• exceptional environmental charges (e.g. for remediation, de-commissioning or impairment charges) • other environmental costs and benefits (if not disclosed in separate environmental review - see above)
Balance sheet	• environmental provisions • de-commissioning provisions • environmental costs capitalized • expected recoveries
Notes to the accounts	• contingent environmental liabilities plus explanations
Other	Environmental data can also be put in the summary financial statements

2.   Recommendations for improving stand-alone environmental reports

Some general suggestions might be appropriate regarding the form and content of stand-alone environmental reports as they appear at present:

- clearer statements regarding the key environmental issues facing the reporting entity;
- more use could be made of the sort of segmental reporting techniques used for consolidated financial reporting purposes;
- a clear statement regarding the completeness of the environmental reporting should be made;
- a statement of the number of contaminated sites, the current state of remediation at each site and the likely timing and cost of future remediation procedures;
- the provision of industry relevant and industry accepted benchmarked environmental performance indicators (including experimentation with eco-efficiency indicators; and
- the provision of externally verified third party opinions based upon accepted and tested verification procedures (though these may still be developing).

3.   Recommendations for future work

The major issues to be resolved relating to the disclosure of environmental data would seem to be:

- agreeing <u>financial accounting definitions</u> in respect of environmental costs and revenues;
- developing a widely accepted range of <u>standardized environmental performance indicators</u> suitable for external reporting purposes;
- gaining acceptance for a <u>standardized format for external environmental reporting</u>: whether through the annual report to shareholders or through a stand-alone performance report; and
- improving the credibility of corporate environmental reporting activities by <u>formalizing the external attestation process</u>.

REPORT OVERVIEW

Part I provides a comprehensive overview of the financial and environmental accounting and reporting issues involved in trying to establish a link between environmental and financial performance. A brief overview of each section is provided immediately below:

Section I   examines the ability of the conventional accounting - financial reporting - model to deal effectively with issues relating to overall environmental performance. It also reviews the results of research aimed at elucidating the environmental information needs of stakeholder groups - especially the equity investor group.

Section II   reviews methods currently being used by companies to communicate corporate environmental performance - whether through the annual report to shareholders or in some separate stand alone environmental performance report. The section also discusses the problems which arise when trying to arrive at financial quantification of environmental costs and benefits.

Section III   the focus of this section is on the emergence of various generic and specific frameworks for reporting environmental performance indicators. The issue is eco-efficiency is considered and the section includes a detailed review of 6 industry sectors.

Section IV   describes methods used by equity investors to identify environmentally superior investment opportunities - and reviews the results of research directed at determining whether or not such investments also perform on a par with the market portfolio

Section V   summarises extant guidance on environmental reporting in the annual report to shareholders and makes a number of recommendations regarding (a) a standardised disclosure package and (b) future developmental work which needs to be undertaken.

Part II is (in effect) a "resources" section.

In Section VI, under a number of technical headings, various aspects of current best practice are illustrated (e.g. aspects of environmental financial accounting, environmental indices and EPI disclosure).

PART I

LINKING ENVIRONMENTAL AND FINANCIAL PERFORMANCE - A SURVEY OF CURRENT THEORIES AND PRACTICES

SECTION I: ENVIRONMENTAL PERFORMANCE COMMUNICATIONS AND THE CONVENTIONAL ACCOUNTING MODEL

A.   Introduction

This section examines the ability of the conventional accounting - financial reporting - model to deal effectively with issues relating to overall environmental performance. It also reviews the results of research aimed at elucidating the environmental information needs of stakeholder groups - especially the equity investor group.

The issue that is addressed in this paper primarily concerns the conflict that appears to exist between the universally supported need to reduce the environmental impact of enterprise (be it private or public sector) and the ability of statutory or non-statutory mechanisms (specifically financial reporting regimes) to make transparent the financial/economic consequences to the enterprise - and its stakeholders - of being a "good environmental neighbour".

It is apparent that (as of late-1997) there is still no international consensus as to how corporateenvironmental activity and impact should be reported, nor as to the extent towhich environmentally beneficial activity favourably influences overall financial out-turn and hence shareholder value.

If there is no obvious consensus on these issues, it is still clear, however, that environmental issues are viewed with an increasing degree of concern by the financial community. How else to explain the publication in the London *Financial Times* on November 14 1996 of an "Index of Corporate Environmental Engagement"? The index is based upon the answers to a self-assessment questionnaire sent to the 100 largest UK listed companies (the "FT 100" or "footsie 100"). This compilation of this index is intended to be an annual event - the underlying intention being to promote awareness at boardroom level of the growing importance attached by the financial community to environmental achievements and the integration of environmental strategies into broader corporate strategies.

It seems to be a useful exercise to replicate the index results at the start of this paper (see Figure 1 below) because, if nothing else, it demonstrates the importance which is now being attached to environmental performance by the financial community. And in the United Kingdom at least, there is no more central pillar of the Financial Establishment than the *Financial Times*.

Figure 1. The FT/ BiE - Index of Corporate Environmental Engagement				
1st quintile	**2nd quintile**	**3rd quintile**	**4th quintile**	**5th quintile**
British Airways	Allied Domecq	Argos	Abbey National	Bass
BT	Asda Group	Bank of Scotland	Barclays	Burmah Castrol
Enterprise Oil	***BAA***	Blue Circle	British Aerospace	Burton
ICI	BAT Industries	***Boots***	Cable & Wireless	Commercial Union
Marks & Spencer	***BP***	***British Gas***	C'bury Schweppes	Gen Accident
National Power	British Steel	Courtaulds	Carlton Comms.	Granada
NatWest Bank	GEC	Glaxo Wellcome	Dixons	GUS
RTZ Corporation	Grand Met	Guinness	***Kingfisher***	Land Securities
Safeway Stores	Hanson	***National Grid***	Ladbroke	Rank Org.
Scottish Power	***J Sainsbury***	P&O	Legal & general	Reuters
Shell	Lasmo	Pilkington	Reckitt & Colman	Royal B. Scotland
S/kline Beecham	***Powergen***	Redland	RMC	Royal Sun Alliance
Thames Water	***Severn Trent***	Southern Electric	Rolls Royce	Scottish & N'castle
Unilever	Smith & Nephew	Tate & Lyle	United Utilities	Tesco
	Thorn EMI		3i Group	TI Group
Ranks favourably >> Ranks poorly				

By way of footnote to Table 1 it might be useful to know that

(a)   those FT 100 companies ***highlighted thus*** are known to have issued an environmental report - those ***highlighted thus*** are also past winners or commendations in the annual Environmental Reporting Award Scheme run by the Association of Chartered Certified Accountants (ACCA), one of the UKs major accounting bodies.

(b)   those responsible for the Index have every intention of making it an annual benchmark of corporate environmental engagement - the exercise will even be independently reviewed (verified) in its second year.

B.   Why should environmental performance be expected to influence financial performance?

A company which recognises its environmental responsibilities, as defined by law, and which institutes appropriate and effective systems of environmental management to ensure *inter alia* both competitiveness and compliance will minimise its exposure to future financial risk/loss arising from environmental incidents. At the same time -

* such a company should be able to secure lower insurance premiums, reflecting the reduced risk
* a favourable environmental risk rating may secure the company better borrowing terms - either when issuing corporate debt or borrowing or when issuing new equity
* pure compliance costs should not result in a market penalty unless, $ for $, a company can be demonstrated to be incurring higher compliance costs than its sector peers (however, in the absence of any requirement to disclose such compliance costs, the market may be forced to rely on proxy measures - e.g. in the USA, the Toxic Release Inventory (TRI) disclosures have been argued to serve as an indicator for environmental performance)

A company which, in addition to recognising and responding to its statutory environmental responsibilities, also determines to be at the leading edge in terms of utilising environmentally friendly technologies or moving towards a more sustainable mode of operations should reap additional benefits:

- increased staff/employee commitment
- lower / eliminated "green" taxes, levies and fines
- lower operating costs and waste disposal costs
- improved corporate profile
- increased market opportunities (including public sector public procurement opportunities)

Research [such as that reported in the book *"Green Ledgers"* (WRI 1995)] identifies numerous cases where cost savings can be achieved through the exploitation of opportunities to reduce environmental impacts and costs, to recycle what was formerly considered waste, or to access new markets without sacrificing the original base position.

Whilst the impact of general compliance costs will have a negative effect on cash flows and the bottom line, it is axiomatic, in accounting terms, that reducing a cost (through reduced waste or more eco-efficient production) or accessing new sales revenues without sacrificing the old, will have a positive influence on "the bottom line".

There are many case study examples of how such savings and benefits can be achieved -see for example:

- *"Benefiting Business & the Environment"* - Institute of Business Ethics 1994: which features 21 UK company case studies
- *"Case Studies in Environmental Management in Small and Medium Sized Enterprises"* International Network for Environmental Management 1995: which surveys 13 case studies in countries including Columbia, Brazil, India, Tunisia, Hungary, The Czech Republic, Germany, Ireland and France
- *"Cleaner production World-Wide"* UNEP 1995: this features case studies from (amongst others) Chile, Egypt, Japan, the Philippines, Poland and the Republic of Tanzania,.

It is, however, quite a different thing to suggest that environmentally derived financial benefits will automatically flow through into superior share price performance. Many different factors affect "the bottom line", and the level of environmental costs is only one factor among many.

Similarly, many different factors can influence an analyst's view of a company. For example, analysts and fund managers may rate a company positively in terms of its environmental exposure but may be dissatisfied if an excessive proportion of sales is earned overseas. For such a company, adverse currency movements may impact negatively on share price despite superior environmental performance and increased revenues and profits generally.

Some in-depth market based accounting research is required to track the share price performance of portfolios of those companies commonly acknowledged to be environmentally sound or superior against either matched samples of not-so environmentally sound companies or against the market portfolio as a whole. Some examples of the findings of such market based research is described in below.

It is perhaps also worth recording at the start of this paper that the concept of shareholder wealth maximisation (as supported by the conventional accounting model) and the concept of sustainable development (as favoured by the environmental lobby) may not be easily reconcilable. The types of initiatives described in the case studies cited in a previous paragraph show costs and savings as conventionally measured - they are not concerned with cost internalisation or related issues which are at the heart of the notion of sustainability.

Financial accounting cannot solve these issues on its own. A broader concept of corporate performance may need to emerge - this may embrace a variety of targets, financial, environmental and social. Since financial markets may prove slow to develop such a broader base of corporate accountability, it is not unreasonable to suggest that governments and political institutions need to monitor developments in environmental performance reporting and accountability with a view to introducing mandatory environmental and social reporting tools if necessary.

C. The objectives of financial statements and the relevance of non-financial data

In exploring the role that environmental data could or might play in the minds of users of financial statements, it is first of all necessary to have a general understanding of what financial statements themselves are meant to achieve. According to the United Nations,

"the objective of financial statements is to provide information about the financial position, performance and changes in financial position of an enterprise, which is useful to a wide range of users in making decisions and is necessary for the accountability of management for resources entrusted to it." ("Conclusions on Accounting and Reporting by Transnational Corporations" UN 1994 P5).

This statement of objectives is slightly broader than that used by the International Accounting Standards Committee:

"the objective of financial statements is to provide information about the financial position, performance and changes in financial position of an enterprise that is useful to a wide range in making economic decisions." ("Framework for the Preparation and Presentation of Financial Statements" - IASC 1995*)*:

The IASC approach appears to limit the usefulness of financial statements to the field of "economic" decisions and does not venture into any broader discussion of accountability or corporate governance. It is increasingly apparent, however, that the concept of corporate governance is actually wider than just financial accountability or regularity. Companies world-wide are beginning to accept that alongside their traditional financial responsibilities, they have also societal responsibilities (*inter alia* to behave ethically and to reduce their environmental impact).

"Usefulness", however, is an opaque term, with different meanings, interpretations and implications depending upon the perspective being adopted by the user. Of the many individual factors which have been argued to contribute towards the usefulness of financial statements, three characteristics in particular - relevance, objectivity and comparability (over time and between reporting entities) - are generally acknowledged to be central objectives of financial reporting and are incorporated into all recognized financial reporting frameworks (UN / IASC / FASB / ASB etc). It is probably inevitable that, in the presence of the these three characteristics, financial reporting adopts a largely quantitative perspective, with little space being found for non-financial or qualitative disclosures within the audited section of the annual report to shareholders.

The accounting and reporting format requirements of most accounting regimes world-wide tend to focus on financially quantifiable data, backed up by narrative /quantifiable/verifiable data vis a vis directors transactions in shares of the entity, significant events affecting the entity and the like. It is only relatively recently that the managements of public-interest entities have been required to add formal narrative/qualitative sections discussing the background to the reported results and the factors likely to be influential in terms of future developments - the Management Discussion and Analysis (MD&A - USA) or Operating and Financial Review (OFR - UK).

According to the Edinburgh-based survey company *"Company Reporting"*
"Information must be quantifiable in order for it to be of use in an objective appraisal of a company's performance and progress, and for comparison between companies. Nevertheless, it is undeniable that qualitative information will always assist in providing a context for raw but quantified information." ("Company Reporting Frontiers: non-financial performance and revenue investment measures in company annual reports" Company Reporting 1992 P1). The report goes on: *"Non-financial information is important because it can form the basis of, or contribute to, analyses of the nature and impact of investment and, more generally, performance measurement....."*.

Environmental data is usually (though not exclusively) non-financial in nature. It is also often qualitative rather than quantitative. There is great debate currently concerning the relevance of environmental data to financial decision makers.

D.   Shareholder value

The assumption throughout this paper is that we are considering the way in which financial *and* non-financial information concerning environmental activities and progress is communicated to the financial stakeholder group which is instrumental in affecting "shareholder value". "Shareholder value" is a concept which usually relates to the total market capitalisation of the firm (i.e. year end share price x number shares in issue, plus market value of long term debt).

An alternative approach to viewing shareholder value was provided in the 8 December 1996 issue of the UK *Sunday Times* newspaper (see Figure 2):

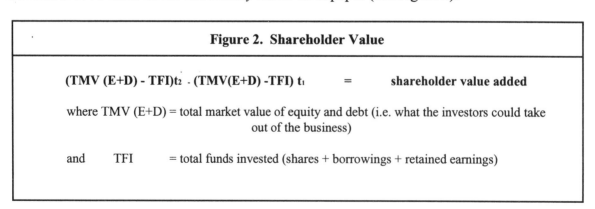

Figure 2. Shareholder Value

(TMV (E+D) - TFI)t_2 - (TMV(E+D) -TFI) t_1 =   shareholder value added

where TMV (E+D) = total market value of equity and debt (i.e. what the investors could take out of the business)

and   TFI   = total funds invested (shares + borrowings + retained earnings)

Therefore shareholder value increases when the total market capitalisation increases faster than the nominal value of the funds invested. Figure 3 below compares those UK companies which fared well in the Sunday Times "shareholder value added exercise" (see immediately above) with those companies which proved most successful in the recent Financial Times "Index of Corporate Environmental Engagement" (see Figure 1 above).

Figure 3: Shareholder value and environmental engagement						
Note: vertical axis: ranking in which quartile for environmental Engagement (1 = high 5 = low) horizontal axis: whereabouts in the top 120 UK shareholder value added companies list						
1				.Ent. Oil	.BA .Safeway	.Shell .SKB .Unilever .M&S .BT .RTZ
2		.Lasmo		.Smith & Nephew .Allied Domecq	.Asda .GEC .BAA	.BAT .BP .EMI .Grandmet .Sainsbury
3	.Tate & Lyle	.Courtaulds	.Blue Circle		.Boots .Argos	.Glaxo .Guinness
4			.RMC	.Dixons .Kingfisher	.Cadbury .Reckitt & .Colman	.C&W
5			.Burton	.TI .Burmah	.GUS .Tesco .S&N .Granada .Bass	.Reuters
	120	100	80	60	40	20
	Top 120 UK companies adding to shareholder value					

The conclusion from this rather unscientific exercise is that it is clear that some environmentally sound companies DO add value (8 out of the 14 best environmental engagers rank in the top 40 shareholder "value adders" - 6 in the top 20). It is equally clear that other environmentally praiseworthy companies are not adding shareholder value - at least not according to popular definitions of the term (6 out the 14 best environmentalists did not rank in top 120 "value adders").

In the above context non-financial data is important for allowing the outside observer to assess whether or not a company appears to have chosen the best available management strategies in order to achieve the twin goals of increased shareholder value and improved financial performance (i.e. a position in the top right hand corner of the table in Figure 3 above).

E. Finance and accountability theories in brief

In finance theory, all decisions are based on the premise that the over-riding aim of the organisation is to maximise shareholder wealth. Although short-term dividend decisions may affect shareholder wealth, it is the long-term capital growth in share values which is at the core of shareholder wealth. By introducing environmental and ethical/social considerations into this picture we complicate the (relatively) simple wealth maximisation rules of finance theory and begin introducing a new set of constraints, *subject to which* shareholder wealth can be maximised. Whether or not corporate management (or stock markets) can work happily or efficiently within this more constrained, yet still voluntary, arena is difficult to say.

The objective of providing corporate environmental performance data may go beyond simply enabling interested users to make economic decisions. Environmental data disclosure enables a company to demonstrate its *accountability* for its environmental activities. The act of disclosure may have economic consequences for the company making the disclosure: it may increase or lose sales revenue, it may invite lobbying or prosecution, it may serve to motivate the workforce or it may alarm local residents.

From the outset, the relationship between environmental performance and financial performance is unlikely to be positive and linear - there are too many other variables affecting shareholder value for this sort of relationship to hold true: share prices (and thus shareholder wealth) are vulnerable to short-term, market-wide influences. Consistently good environmental performance seems likely to be interpreted as one facet of good overall corporate management and thus seems likely to underpin long-term growth in shareholder value rather than affect it in the short-term.

F.   Environmental data and corporate financial reporting

Environment-related disclosures (of any description) through the annual report to shareholders are a relatively recent feature of corporate financial reporting. There are several reasons for this:

(i)   environmental issues as business issues have really only achieved wide discussion since 1990;

(ii)   the needs of stakeholders for environmental data and the value that they place on it is an under-researched area;

(iii)   environmental disclosures are not explicitly required by most statutes,national or international GAAPs - consequently measurement and disclosure techniques are currently only just beginning to be discussed by the accounting profession

(iv)   environmental issues - and particularly the benefits that *might* accrue from more environmentally sensitive methods of operation - seldom appear in the curricula of either prospective accountants or prospective business managers

(v)   environmental disclosures may be regarded (particularly in more litigious cultures) as providing a hostage to fortune

Such environmental data as is disclosed typically fall into three different categories:

Category 1   financially quantified data regarding environmental liabilities and provisions

Category 2   qualitative data regarding environmental policies, procedures and progress

Category 3   non financially quantified data regarding environmental performance

Whilst it is easy to see how Category 1 data meets user needs, the relevance, objectivity and comparability of data in Categories 2 and 3 is often less easy for outsiders to assess.

Figure 4 presents a possible hierarchy of corporate environmental disclosures via the annual report:

Figure 4: A possible hierarchy of current corporate environmental disclosures via the annual report to shareholders		
Category of disclosure	**Example of disclosure**	**Expected usefulness rating to financial community**
Category 1: financially Quantified data relating to environmental liabilities and provisions; exceptional environmental costs; green levies and taxes	Balance sheet provisions in respect of future clean-up costs	**High** - accounting standards and statutory requirements only require separate disclosure of material (significant) items. Disclosure is covered by audit opinion.
Category 2: qualitative data relating to (*inter alia*) environmental policies, procedures and progress; other environmental costs	Statement of corporate environmental policies; description of environmental audit procedures and coverage	**Moderate** - discretionary disclosure(s) are susceptible to PR hype and are not covered by any audit opinion - but they are evidence of corporate commitment. Cost identification and allocation may be problematic.
Category 3: non financial but quantified/verifiable data regarding environmental performance	Environmental performance data re emissions	**Moderate/low** - unlikely to be externally verified or (currently) comparable with other companies in same sector

The quantitative/qualitative focus of current environment related financial reporting practices is probably influenced significantly by the traditional requirements and positioning of the financial community itself.

Non-financial environmental information may not currently be useful to the financial community because the data is perceived to lack the primary characteristics of comparability and consistency. It is also normally unverified. A major concern is to ensure that such data obtains a higher "usefulness rating" in the future.

In the UK, the financial community is regarded as short-termist and infatuated with "the bottom line". Qualitative data (non-financial or environmental) which does not obviously meet the markets requirements for relevance, objectivity and comparability is likely to be considered of relatively little use (see results of the 1994 BiE/Extel survey discussed below). As a result, much value is placed upon research activity carried out by the investment community itself.

In countries less equity-market focused (obsessed?) than the UK, however, in Germany for example, the position is almost reversed, with German companies supplying a lot of qualitative (narrative) information but less quantified financial data. Figure 5 illustrates the environmental disclosure imbalance from a European perspective:

Figure 5: Environmental disclosures in the financial statements of the 25 largest companies in each of 6 countries							
	Neth	**Swe**	**Swit**	**Fran**	**Ger**	**UK**	**Tot**
Number of companies giving any information	16 or 64%	22 or 88%	19 or 76%	14 or 56%	25 or 100%	20 or 80%	116 or 77%
Notes to the accounts	3 or 12%	nil	1 or 4%	1 or 4%	nil	4 or 16%	9 or 6%
Policy statement	13 or 52%	12 or 48%	9 or 36%	10 or 40%	20 or 80%	14 or 56%	78 or 52%

Environmental impacts	6 or 24%	10 or 40%	6 or 24%	4 or 16%	14 or 56%	7 or 28%	47 or 31%
Targets and standards	3 or 12%	5 or 20%	2 or 8%	3 or 12%	9 or 36%	4 or 16%	26 or 17%
Product information	4 or 16%	11 or 44%	8 or 32%	8 or 32%	18 or 72%	6 or 24%	55 or 37%
Expenditures incurred	2 or 8%	3 or 12%	4 or 16%	1 or 4%	9 or 36%	3 or 12%	22 or 15%
Length (mean pages)	0.45	0.85	0.60	0.71	1.61	0.59	0.85

Source: *"Environmental, Employee and Ethical Reporting in Europe"* Adams, Hill & Roberts

G. Reporting of environmental issues in 1996

A good summary of the current international situation with regard to environment reporting and the disclosure of environmental data in company annual reports and stand alone environmental reports is presented in the KPMG *"International Survey of Environmental Reporting 1996"*. With regard to stand alone environmental reports it is worth remembering that, pre-1990, such stand alone reports simply did not exist. The 1996 KPMG finding that 23% of companies surveyed (up from 13% in 1993) produce corporate environmental reports, in addition to their annual report to shareholders, in itself represents a fairly sizeable revolution in corporate accountability.

Environmental issues/performance are reported to stakeholders through an ever expanding variety of different media: the annual report to shareholders (in the audited and in the unaudited sections), in stand alone environmental performance reports at the corporate, site or summary corporate levels, via employee newsletters, via press releases, the internet, computer disc, or via disclosures made direct to environmental regulators which remain on the public record.

Figure 6 presents the findings of the 1996 KPMG survey. The survey covered the 100 leading companies (in terms of market capitalisation) in each of 12 countries (the United States of America, Canada, Australia, New Zealand, the United Kingdom, the Netherlands, Belgium, Switzerland, Sweden, Denmark, Norway and Finland). The results are drawn from the 804 annual reports received (out of a possible 1150) and the 192 environmental reports also received.

Figure 6: KPMG survey of international trends in environmental reporting
• *annual reports*
Overall, 556 (69%) of companies surveyed mentioned the environment in their annual reports - a dramatic increase over the 37% found in the previous (1993) survey.
• *country differences*
95% of Norwegian companies mention the environment in their financial statements - [US = 86%]. New Zealand [39%] is the only country in the survey where the figure falls below 50%.

- *reporting on environmental costs and environmental policies*

18% of companies either include environmental costs in the financial statements or the notes to the financial statements, and/or set out an accounting policy on the environment. In the USA, 70% of companies surveyed include financial information on the environment - disclosures driven by the requirements of the Securities and Exchange Commission for disclosures of environmental contingencies and liabilities.

KPMG suggest that "for the most part Europe is far behind North America ..... however this may change when the initiatives currently underway regarding accounting requirements for environmental issues result in legal requirements and/or accounting guidelines.

- *position of environmental disclosures in annual reports*

31% of companies mention the environment in the equivalent to the director's report or management's discussion and analysis.

- *references to environmental report in annual report*

KPMG note the surprising finding that, of the 556 companies mentioning the Environment in their annual report only 85 referred to separate environmental Publication. This means that less than half of the 192 companies that submitted an Environmental report for the purposes of the survey mentioned the fact that they had issued such a report in their annual report to shareholders.

- *environmental reports*

192 (23%) of the companies surveyed produce some kind of environmental report (compared with 13% in the 1993 survey) - reasonably enough, and reflecting actual practice, KPMG include in their definition of environmental report a separate section of 3 pages or more dealing with environmental issues within the annual report itself).

- *industry environmental reporting*

more than 70% of the companies in the chemical industry publish environmental reports - forestry, paper, pulp, and oil and gas are the next best represented sectors.

It is also worth noting at this point, however, that such environmental reporting as there is going on at end 1996 is largely restricted to multi-national companies and developed countries. Extending the size range of companies when looking for environmental disclosures can produce dramatically different results as the 1996 annual survey by the UK based *"Company Reporting"* shows (see Figure 7):

Figure 7: Environmental reporting by company size		
KPMG 1996 Survey	69% of top 100 companies surveyed in 12 countries report on environmental issues in the annual report	up from 37% in 1993
***"Company Reporting"* (May 1996) - based on 1995 UK survey**	29% of 682 UK companies surveyed report on environmental issues within the annual report	down from 32% reported in the *CR* 1994 survey (although the CR survey does not necessarily review the same sample of companies each year)

The EU Eco-Management and Audit Scheme (EMAS) has provided an incentive for SMEs to become involved in environmental reporting but the overall take-up rate differs dramatically between EU member states (with over 800 registrations as at end April 1997, there were only 23 UK companies registered as opposed to some 350 German companies as at the end of 1996 - ENDS January 1997 P 7) and little research seems to have been done into the motivations behind EMAS registrations.

The KPMG survey provides reassurance that large companies world-wide have now adopted the reporting of environmental issues - whether through the annual report to shareholders or through a separate, free-standing environmental report - as a part of their normal day to day corporate governance/corporate reporting mechanisms. As will become evident, however, environmental disclosure data is not the subject of mandatory disclosure requirements anywhere in the world save in a number of restricted situations (e.g. USA - TRI disclosure requirements; Denmark - mandatory environmental reporting for particular industry groups; Thailand - Bangkok Stock Exchange listing requirements). Elsewhere, environmental disclosures in annual reports vary widely in scope and quality, as do stand alone environmental reports: there is little consistency and not much scope for inter-company comparison or benchmarking.

H.   What environmental information do financial stakeholders want from companies?

If it can be plausibly argued that improving environmental performance can improve the bottom line, then it is reasonable to go on and ask what sort of environmental performance information companies should disclose and how this information is or could be transmitted to relevant financial stakeholders. The minimum present disclosure requirements are summarised and reviewed in the forthcoming UN paper *"Accounting and Reporting for Environmental Costs and Liabilities Within the Existing Financial Reporting Framework" (UN 1997)*.

The review of non-accounting based literature presented below, however, suggests that many financial stakeholders regard the conventional financial accounting and reporting framework an inadequate or incomplete base on which to make decisions given that many (most?) issues relating to environmental risk and corporate environmental performance and strategy are wholly ignored by recognised GAAP frameworks. Amongst those who have exhibited an interest in environmental data for use in financial decision making are:

- lending bankers for credit risk minimisation purposes
- property insurers
- investment analysts in general, fund managers of green/ethical funds in particular
- lawyers and reporting accountants in due diligence / take-over / listing situations

Some companies - a very few - have undertaken the task of identifying stakeholder information / accountability needs by setting up stakeholder consultation exercises. But this process is not widely undertaken and the role of different stakeholder groups will vary from company to company. In the UK for example, IBM UK carried out a major stakeholder consultation exercise in 1995. But IBM UK is a wholly owned subsidiary of IBM Inc and therefore financial stakeholders played little or no part in this otherwise excellent exercise. The opposite experience holds true at BP, where the excellent level of environmental disclosures in the company's UK annual report to shareholders was admitted to have been prompted by a high level of US Securities and Exchange Commission interest in environmental matters contained in the company's US filings.

I.   Stakeholder surveys

In the last two or three years, however, there have been a number of major surveys which have attempted to "tease out" the needs of various categories of stakeholders, including financial stakeholders. These surveys include:

- The UK BiE/Extel survey (1994)
- The IRRC focus group research (1995)
- The UNEP/SustainAbility work (1996)
- The EMAS study (1996)

A summary of the outcomes - as regards financial stakeholder attitude to, need for or use of environmental data - is provided in Figure 8 below.

Figure 8. Surveys of (financial) stakeholder needs	
Survey	**Finding: financial stakeholders require**
1. BiE/Extel (UK 1994) "City Analysts and the Environment"	Factors of importance when assessing a company include: • quality of management (87% Very) • bottom line data (76% (Very) • environmental policy (4% Very) Generally these UK respondents did not feel that the absence of standardised reporting practices, the scientific uncertainty of environmental problems or the lack of availability of established environmental performance indicators were a barrier to their assessment of companies (P34)
2. IRRC (US 1995) "Environmental Reporting and Third Party Statements"	• Financial stakeholder focus groups emphasised their need for: • environmental liability data (backed up by compliance data) • a balanced tone of reporting • evidence of application of US standards to international operations • quantitative trends (e.g. TRI) • details of organisational commitment and strategy on the environment • more meaningful verification of environmental data/reports • increased standardisation in the reporting of environmental data
3. UNEP/SustainAbility (Global - 1996) "Engaging Stakeholders" Vol 2 P27)	Companies believe financial stakeholders want: • to gain confidence in the company's ability to manage environmental issues and liabilities • data to assist in the pricing of capital • data to assist in the assessment of environmental risks and liabilities The financial stakeholder groups want environmental data: • to help select sound investments • to benchmark and rank corporate environmental performance • to help screen investments "The new trend in shareholder information needs is in relation to the economic or financial consequences of environmental performance -there is a growing pressure to supply more investor - and insurer - related information and a growing interest in the correlation between environmental spending and shareholder value." (P29)
4. EMAS/Imperial (Europe 1996) "The Environmental Statement"	EMAS reports currently lack sufficient data on overall company environmental management and performance - also on level of environmental capital expenditures and financial. impact (i.e. overall consequences of the environmental effects and performance on the company as a whole)

The evidence of these surveys is mixed. UK financial analysts appear not to be particularly concerned about environment issues (costs or performance). In the USA, financial stakeholder focus groups respond to direct questions about their preferences in a logical and rational way - yes, if we are to have the information we'd like it meaningfully audited, comparable etc.

The most recent UNEP work (*"Engaging stakeholders"*) deals with specialist investors whose focus is on environmentally / socially sensitive companies. This last group of investors clearly wants - not just as much data as possible - but data of a relatively sophisticated sort, data which links financial inputs with environmental outcomes. Environmental Statements as required by EMAS are at a relatively early stage - the first reports were only issued in 1995 - but early research carried out on behalf of the EC Commission seems to point to some information short-comings in the site-based environmental reporting regime.

J.   Financial sector stakeholder initiatives

In addition, a number of financial sector user groups have begun to formalise their requirements for environmentally related disclosures. This is an important development because, hitherto, evidence of stakeholders requirements was either anecdotal, assumed or survey based. At least three major financial sector stakeholder groups have specified their demands to date:

(i)   the European Federation of Financial Analysts Societies (EFFAS- 1996);

(ii)   a group of five major Swiss banks who have issued a consultation paper dealing with environmental reporting disclosure (1997); and

(iii)   the UK Governments Advisory Committee on Business and the Environment

These sets of disclosure requirements are summarised below (paras 1.48 -1.57)

K.   The views of the European Federation of Financial Analysts Societies

The European Federation of Financial Analysts Societies (EFFAS) has published two significant reports (1994 and 1996) dealing with the informational needs of financial analysts vis a vis environmental issues. In contrast to the rather hazy views expressed by analysts in the BiE/Extel survey reported in Figure 8 above, EFFAS is extremely clear at articulating its demands for improved development of improved techniques for linking environmental and financial issues. The EFFAS recommendations fall broadly into two sections:

(1)   recommendations for improved financial disclosures in the financial statements and the annual report to shareholders these recommendations are summarised immediately below (in Figure 9)

(2)   recommendations for developing "eco-efficiency" indicators, through which a company's progress towards sustainable modes of operation may be judged. Eco-efficiency and the views of EFFAS are dealt with in Section 7 below.

Whilst there may be some overlap between the various demands for more data, the EFFAS "wish list" is at least a tightly argued and (for the most part) deliverable list of questions. As a result it could form a central part of any proposed expansion of the conventional accounting framework. Potentially "undeliverable" elements of the EFFAS "wish list" are indicated by an asterisk and explained in Para 1.50 below.

Figure 9. EFFAS catalogue of requirements for consolidated financial and environmental accounts	
Section	**Requirement**
Notes to the a/cs	1. Comments on the scope and methods of consolidation of the annual environmental report - what is not in the consolidated figures?
	2. Clear statements on how the different items are treated (expensed or capitalised) and on a consistent application (annual report and annual environmental report)
	3. Last historical data and targets
P& L Account	1. Energy costs
	2. Waste costs: disposal and treatment
	3. Costs of environmental protection and safety
	4. Costs of: remediation, abatement, clean-up
	5. Costs of environmental impact reductions (*)
	6. Other costs: communication, staff training
	7. Depreciation (presumably of environmental capital assets) (*)
	8. Environmental savings (undefined) (*)
Balance Sheet	1. Provisions for environmental liabilities
	2. Provisions to fully comply with environmental laws and regulations
	3. Contingent liabilities (off-balance sheet)
Cash Flow	1. Environmental capital expenditures (*)
Other	1. Does the company have an environmental policy and targets?
	2. Content of the environmental policy?
	3. Does the company publish an annual report?
	4. Does the company have a system to collect environmental data on a local and group level?
	5. Does the company discuss the main environmental problems? What does the company regard as its main environmental challenges?
	6. Does the company comply world-wide with existing laws and regulations, and if not, what are the costs and expenditures to reach full compliance?
	7. Has the company signed the ICC-Charter for Sustainable Development?
	8. Does the company have special insurance cover for environmental risks?
	9. Are legal sanctions pending?
	10. Do environmental audits exist?
Source: *"Eco-Efficiency and Financial Analysis - the Financial Analyst's Views"* EFFAS Commission on Accounting 1996	

L.   The "undeliverables" on the EFFAS wish list

In a well organised accounting system many of the financial disclosures sought by EFFAS could be recorded relatively easily (waste and energy costs for example). The main difficulties arise in connection with capital expenditures where it may not be possible to make consistent judgements as to how much capital expenditure constitutes environmental capital expenditure and how much is "ordinary" capital expenditure. It follows that a depreciation disclosure related to environmental capital expenditure may also be difficult to estimate with any degree of certainty. Environmental savings may be difficult to estimate and may not always be consistent from company to company. Environmental benefits other than savings are not addressed in the EFFAS "wish-list". It is not clear what "costs of environmental impact reductions" is supposed to mean - but it is quite likely that it may be difficult enough to agree on the physical nature of the environmental impact reductions themselves, even before progressing to estimate the costs to the reporting of achieving those reductions.

M.   The Swiss banking initiative

In mid-1997, five Swiss banking organisations issued a draft discussion paper *"Swiss Bankers' Association's (SBA) Environmental Reporting Requirements"* subtitled "Integrating company-specific environmental information into investment business". The banks identify two ways in which environmental information is useful for them:

(i)   it enables them to identify risks which arise from a company's business and to interpret those risks in their political context;

(ii)   an increasing number of investors also ask for environmental information on the companies in which they invest. banks can only meet this demand if the companies provide them with this sort of information themselves.

A standardised set of figures, say the Swiss bankers, makes assessing a company's environmental performance much easier.

Based on a four industry sector review (chemicals/pharmaceuticals, electronics, food and engineering) the SBA sets out disclosure recommendations under three broad headings (see Figure 10 below):

1.   Key environmental figures
2.   Relevant financial figures
3.   Relevant management information

Figure 10. Environmental disclosures recommended by the Swiss Bankers Association

Key environmental figures	Relevant financial figures	Relevant management information
Energy use	Energy costs	Strategy: what are the three most important environmental issues affecting the company's bottom line in the next 5 - 10 years?
CO2 and equivalents	Raw material costs (renewable and non-renewable)	EMS (ISO 14001/EMAS, BS7750 certification or company's own similar system) with special focus on risk management and legal compliance
CFC-11 and equivalents	Waste disposals	Communication: knowledge of most important stakeholders. Type of communication on environmental matters?
NOx emissions	Depreciation on environmental investments	Description of measures taken to improve eco-efficiency of processes and products
SO2 emissions	Depreciation or provisions for environmental liabilities	
VOC emissions	Quality assurance costs	
Waste (including special waste)	Environmental investments	
Additional sector-specific data	Environmentally-motivated provisions	

It is clear that the (environmental) information requirements suggested in the SBA draft are very similar in content to the disclosure requirements suggested by the European Federation of Financial Analysts. The contrast between the "pro-active" demands of the SBA and EFFAS are in stark contrast to the (almost disinterested) views expressed by UK financial analysts in the 1996 BiE/Extel survey described in Figure 8 above. The demand by the bankers and the analysts for hard environmental data (not just for financial data and soft management information) suggests a growing sophistication on the part of some financial sector users of corporate data, which other market participants would do well to note.

N.   The "Best Practice" recommendations of the UK Governments Advisory Committee on Business and the Environment - ACBE (1997)

The UK government established the Advisory Committee on Business and the Environment (ACBE) in the wake of the Rio Summit. A new report from ACBE (1997) "Environmental Reporting: An Approach to Good Practice" was authored by representatives from *inter alia* the accounting, banking, insurance and investment industries. The objective of the paper is to "propose an approach to good practice for businesses to follow in reporting on their environmental performance *to financial audiences*." (emphasis added). It may be argued that there are any number of environmental reporting guides or codes of conduct available - PERI, UNEP and the UK CBI spring to mind - why is another environmental reporting code necessary?

The aim behind the ACBE Code was, as stated above, to address financial audiences. One of the major shortcomings of previous environmental reporting codes was that the financial audience was that most often overlooked. The new ACBE Code re-iterates the environment related disclosures commonly captured by international GAAP and, in addition, recommends the disclosure of the items shown in Figure 11.

Whilst not going quite so far as some of the EFFAS and SBA recommendations, the proposed ACBE Code does represent the first UK attempt to step beyond the sometimes claustrophobic confines of the conventional financial reporting regime. The Code goes on to recommend the publication of a stand alone environmental report, as a complement to, and not as a substitute for, the inclusion of environmental information in the annual report to shareholders.

Figure 11: UK Advisory Committee on Business and the Environment – recommendations on discretionary environmental disclosures	
Discretionary financial data	**Discretionary non-financial data**
• the amount of environmental expenditure charged to the profit and loss account	• the policy that has been adopted by the enterprise in respect of environmental protection issues and managing environmental risks
• the amount of environmental expenditure capitalised, to the extent that it can be clearly differentiated from other capital expenditure	• the extent to which environmental protection measures, arising from changes in future legal requirements that have already been enacted or substantially enacted into law, are in the process of implementation
• the amount of costs incurred as a result of fines and penalties for non-compliance with environmental regulations, and compensation to third parties, where material	• reference to other quantitative or qualitative environmental information provided in a separate environmental report

• related accounting policies and comparative data	• descriptive and quantitative details of the environmental risks faced, environmental expenses incurred, and environmental initiatives undertaken (for listed companies - in the Operating and Financial Review/OFR)
• where environmental issues are relevant to a complete understanding of the financial position and performance of the reporting entity, a description of the issues	• whether or not a formal environmental management system is in operation (listed companies - OFR)
•	• compliance with environmental requirements (listed companies - OFR)

Much of the material contained in the UK ACBE recommendations is common to the guidance issued by the EU Accounting Advisory Forum in early 1996. The Forum has attempted to explore the conventional framework of accounting and financial reporting as contained in the EC 4th Company Law Directive (which nowhere mentions environmental issues explicitly) and identify those areas where environmental concerns are relevant and should be reported. That guidance, like the later guidance from ACBE in the UK, has no mandatory force.

O.   Conclusion

There does appear to be some degree of consensus emerging that the conventional annual reporting is too narrow and, in failing to address environmental issues explicitly, is enabling reporting enterprises to by-pass disclosure of environmental issues which might be considered relevant to the financial community. There is also evidence that some financial sector groups are beginning to use their market position to demand environmental performance data from companies as a pre-requisite for a credit or investment transaction.

The common core of environmental disclosures apparently demanded by external financial sector groups includes:

- *disclosure of policies, strategies and environmental management standards achieved*
- *data re key emissions related to environmental impact (esp. global warming)*
- *details of contaminated land held*
- *industry specific environmental performance indicators to facilitate benchmarking*
- *details of the degree of consolidations and completeness*
- *segmented details where possible*
- *financial data on waste, energy and other environmental operating costs; capital expenditure; provisions and liabilities*
- *impact of green taxes and levies*
- *impact of environmental issues on future earnings and cash flows*

**Appendix to Section I:
A core of environmental disclosures for annual reporting purposes**

In the past three or four years a number of companies have experimented with placing an environmental report within the annual report to shareholders. This report does not form part of the audited financial statements, but at least two companies (Coats Viyella -UK; and Danish Steelworks - Denmark) have had these voluntary environmental reports certified by an independent expert.

The advantages attached to such a reporting procedure can be summarised as follows:

- inclusion in the annual report means that the environmental data is more likely to be read by users of the financial statements than if it were only included in a completely separate report
- even if not independently audited the very fact that the data is presented formally in the annual report will add to its credibility
- the environmental message may be sharpened by being condensed into only a few pages – lengthy reports are often unfocused
- companies in the early stages of environmental reporting may find this reporting route more convenient than trying to produce a fully fledged, free standing environment report
- given the likely size of the print run for the annual report, this short form report is likely to be more cost-effective than producing a separate environmental report

The table below sets out the annual report environmental disclosures either suggested or required by a number of bodies:

- the European Federation of Financial Analysts' Societies (1996)
- the Swiss Bankers Association (1997)
- the UK Government's Advisory Committee on Business and the Environment (1997)
- the Hundred Group of UK Finance Directors (1992)
- the UN Expert Group on International Standards of Accounting and Reporting (1989)
- the EC 4th Directive on Company Law and the EC Accounting Advisory Forum (1996)

The table presents a recommended framework for environmental disclosures within the annual report to shareholders. The usual caveats apply in respect of separately identifying environmental investments and disclosing industry accepted EPIs. For the most part, however, the framework provides a minimum core of deliverable but not mandated disclosures - disclosures which can be demonstrated to flow from clearly expressed wishes of the financial sector user community, rather than being demanded by overly enthusiastic academics or lobby groups.

Figure 12. An environmental reporting framework for the annual report (based upon the suggestions and recommendations made by: EFFAS, SBA, ACBE, 100 Group, ISAR and ECAAF)		
Annual report element	**Recommended Environmental disclosure(s)**	**Required by law / standard?**
Chairman / CEOs report	corporate commitment to continuous environ-mental improvement	No
	significant improvements since last report	No
Business segment review	segmented environmental performance data (if not provided in the environmental review (see below)	No
	improvements in key areas since previous report	No
Environmental review	• scope of the review	No
	• corporate environmental policy statement	No
	• extent of world-wide compliance	No
	• key environmental issues facing the company	No
	• organisational responsibilities	No
	• description of environmental management systems and international standards (e.g. ICC/ISO/EMAS)	No
	• segmental performance data based around: energy use, materials use, emissions (CO2, NOx, SO2, CFCs etc) and waste disposal routes	No
	• sector specific data including industry agreed EPIs (including eco-efficiency based EPIs)	No
	• financial data on environmental costs (energy, waste, remediation, staffing, exceptional charges and write downs, fines and penalties, green taxes paid, capital investment)	No
	• financial estimates of savings and benefits flowing from pro-environment efforts	No
	• cross-reference to other environmental reports	No
	• independent verification statement	No
Operating & financial review /MD&A	• key environmental issues facing the company in the short to medium term and plans for addressing these • progress in addressing changes required by future legal requirements • actual and projected levels of environmental expenditure • legal matters pending	Yes "ish" - the UK OFR requirements are not explicit and refer to only very general aspects of environ-mental risk that faces the entity
Report of the Directors	• environmental policy statement (if not provided elsewhere)	No
Accounting policy disclosure	• estimation of provisions and contingencies • capitalisation policies • impairment policies • de-commissioning and land remediation policies • depreciation polices	Yes - if significant to a proper under-standing of the financial state-ments
Profit & loss account	• exceptional environmental charges (e.g. for remediation, de-commissioning or impairment charges) • other environmental costs and benefits (if not disclosed in separate environmental review - see above)	Yes - if meeting criteria for excep-tional item No - disclosure not required unless material
Balance sheet	• environmental provisions • de-commissioning provisions • environmental costs capitalised	Yes - if material Yes - if material Possibly - if separate class of asset
	• expected recoveries	Not unless material

Notes to the accounts	• contingent environmental liabilities plus explanations	Yes
Cash flow statement	Suggested by EFFAS but seems unnecessary if some of the forgoing information on costs is provided	No
Other	Environmental data can also be put in the summary financial statements (e.g. Body Shop 1996)	No

(schedules detailing the full analysis of the EFFAS, SBA, ACBE, 100 Group, ISAR and ECAAF suggestions are provided at the end of Section VI)

SECTION II: A REVIEW OF CURRENT ENVIRONMENTAL PERFORMANCE REPORTING TECHNIQUES AND ATTEMPTS AT FINANCIAL LINKAGE

A. Introduction

This section reviews the various techniques which are currently being utilised to measure and communicate corporate environmental performance. This section goes on to look at the issues involved in attaching financial numbers to environmental costs and benefits - a number of practical examples are provided which demonstrate some of the measurement and estimation difficulties involved. .

B. How is environmental excellence measured and communicated?

Environmental issues have really only begun to force their way onto the corporate communication agenda since 1990, when the first comprehensive corporate environmental reports appeared. Because of the novelty of the exercise, both environmental performance evaluation AND communication are at relatively early stages of development, even though it could probably be truthfully asserted that the pace of development in the area of environmental accountability in the 1990's is far faster than was the pace of development of financial accountability in the 19th century.

Environmental performance communication is primarily a "company to stakeholder" process through the medium of:
- Formal periodic statutory financial statements
- Formal but unregulated periodic environmental reports (except in Denmark where environmental reports are now required by law)
- Formal periodic reports to environmental regulators - these reports being available on a public register

In addition, the financial community itself will undertake less formal and almost certainly continuous "search / monitoring procedures" in order to identify and evaluate one-off pieces of data regarding corporate environmental activity (e.g. the implications of a chemical spill or the likely impact of proposed new EU environmental legislation on EU based companies and their non-EU competitors).

The financial community will usually also engage in periodic face to face meetings with the company itself (often known as "brokers meetings" - though fear of being accused of insider dealing has made this process less productive than of yore). Both in the USA (through bodies such as the Investor Responsibility Research Centre/IRRC) and in the UK (through the Ethical Investor Research and Investment Service/EIRIS and in-company research units - e.g. NPI and Jupiter) the financial community undertakes in-depth research into questions of environmental and ethical excellence.

Commenting on environmental excellence has become a "mini-industry" in its own right. By the end of 1996, there were perhaps half a dozen award schemes in existence for environmental reporting (UK, Canada, New Zealand, Denmark, Norway, the Netherlands and South Africa). In addition each major industry has its own environmental technology based award scheme (e.g. the Norsk Hydro Water Awards).

As well as regular award schemes, there are a number of regular rankings of corporate environmental performance - the newly launched *Financial Times* "Index of Corporate Environmental Engagement" (mentioned in Section I Para 5 of the introduction) is an example.

In attempting to establish whether or not environmental performance and financial performance can be linked in some way, we cannot ignore the fact that when discussing corporate *financial* performance we often fall back on a number of widely recognised performance indicators. These include:

- gross and net margins
- earnings per share
- dividend cover
- interest cover
- liquidity ratio
- debtor/creditor/stock turnover ratios
- return on capital employed
- return on shareholders funds
- capital gearing or leverage
- free cash flow

Although there is no one single quantitative measure which it is agreed is able to encapsulate overall financial performance, it is generally agreed that cash flow information is the primary input to the share valuation exercise: estimates of future profits and future free cash flows underpin all share valuation exercises and are therefore the primary determinants of shareholder value.

The diversity of financial performance measurements available means that it is premature to believe that the environmental performance of a major industrial concern can be summarised in a single number. A number of "environmental performance indices" have been developed at the corporate level - these are discussed briefly below (with several examples provided in Ch 6) - but they tend to be firm specific and are often constructed upon relatively subjective judgements about environmental impacts and priorities/key issues.

C.   Measuring environmental performance

Different approaches to determining environmental performance include:

- *Toxic Release Inventory data* (USA) - will usually be absolute physical quantities of particular emissions as specified to be disclosed by the appropriate regulator. Improved environmental performance implies a reduction in the output of such toxics when compared to changes in relevant output product quantities. Some agencies (e.g. IRRC in the USA) relate TRI disclosures to financial variables such as turnover or operating profit and use the resultant measure to benchmark across an industry sector or to chart performance over time.

- *Company specific indices* (see Ch 5) - are usually based upon a number of firm-specific characteristics (or upon an industry model such as that provided for the chemical industry by the UK Chemical Industries Association (CIA). The index is set at 100 in the selected base year and progress monitored and reported in subsequent years. The main criticisms of such index models are that (i) it is seldom possible to carry out inter-company comparisons, and (ii) the choice of environmental impacts reflected in the model(s) and the weightings used to prioritise particular environmental impacts are subjective and at the discretion of the entity.

- *Self-selected emissions targets* - usually with reference to a base year. This is probably the most common method of environmental reporting and performance measurement used in the UK, Western Europe and North America. Companies itemise their emissions (including wastes) and/or their environmental impacts and set reduction targets - progress against which is reported back in subsequent years. In the absence of formal industry reporting / impact guidelines this method of reporting is understandably popular, although it has proved difficult to carry out inter-firm comparisons with any degree of reliability due to the firm-specific nature of the parameters selected. No attempt is made to consolidate these separate performance measures into a single index measure of environmental performance.

- *Compliance with regulation/permit (externally determined)*: many industries are subject to external constraints regarding their ability to pollute. Reporting actual performance as against external granted consents or limits imposed is a common method of reporting environmental performance (especially in the water industry or where the reporting entity is subject to some sort of statutory integrated pollution control legislation). Reporting compliance in this way does not necessarily reflect underlying environmental performance, nor does it encourage the notion of continuous improvement.

- *Environmental Performance Indicators (EPIs) and Eco-Efficiency measures*: specific measures used by companies to monitor and report different aspects of their environmental performance are described later in this section. An example would be "eco-financial" indicators which seek to relate one particular aspect of environmental performance (e.g. packaging quantities) with a familiar financial attribute (e.g. per $1m turnover).

- *Environmental Burden* (EB : the EB method of evaluating corporate environmental performance is a relatively new technique. The European Federation of Financial Analysts Societies (EFFAS) outlined the methodology in its 1996 report "Eco-efficiency and Financial Analysis" (EFFAS term the methodology "The Classification Method" and say that it originally developed and refined at the University of Leiden). The EB method involves the identification of a number of environmental impact categories: these include - global warming / ozone depletion / smog creation / acidification / nutrification potential / human and eco toxicology / waste problem / biodiversity / other (e.g. noise, odour, light pollution) / world carrying capacity.

Under the EB approach the reporting entity selects a number of what it classifies as priority environmental impact categories from the above list, identifies the emissions relevant to each category, estimates their relative toxicity and computes a weighted environmental burden for each category. The organisation will then set progressive reduction targets. (A case study example of the ICI Environmental Burden approach is provided in Section VI).

It appears that there is no one accepted way of defining environmental performance. A minimum measure is obviously compliance with statutory permits. Under the most conventional approach one can monitor reductions in absolute discharges or success in achieving emissions targets. Under the emerging "environmental burden" approach one can relate emissions to significant environmental impacts.

Once measured, environmental performance can be communicated via a number of different media - and some companies use two, three or four different avenues to convey their environmental performance record to interested stakeholder groups. Amongst the most frequently used communications channels are the annual report to shareholders (or an abbreviated version), a stand alone environmental performance report, an internet web site and corporate videos/CD Roms etc..

D.   Linking the financial and the environmental

"They're looking for a P/E ratio where E stands for the Environment" (Noel Morrin - AEA Technology Plc).

If environmental performance cannot be encapsulated in a single figure then the existence of a relationship between environmental and financial performance may be hard to establish. The probable difficulty of establishing a link does not stop the search however.

In the recent UNEP/SustainAbility report *"Engaging Stakeholders"* (Vol 2) the following assertion was made concerning the needs of financial stakeholders:

"The new trend in shareholder information needs is in relation to the economic or financial consequences of environmental performance - there is a growing pressure to supply more investor - and insurer - related information *and a growing interest in the correlation between environmental spending and shareholder value."* (P29 - emphasis added)

If there is, as many would like to believe, a "correlation between environmental spending and shareholder value" it is necessary to point out immediately that the direction of the causal relationship could be either way. Environmental expenditure might create efficiencies and opportunities which boost shareholder wealth (this is the "being green is good for the bottom line" argument). Or, alternatively, enhanced shareholder wealth may provide management with the opportunity to spend more on the environment and thus further improve the corporate image and underpin or reinforce the shareholder wealth already created.

In the research paper *"Environmental and Financial Performance: Are they Related?"* (Chen, Fenn & Naimon, IRRC 1995) the authors address both the question of causality and the need of the financial community for information as to the effectiveness of corporate management. The detailed issues raised by this paper, along with other similar papers researching the relationship between the results of environmentally or ethically screened portfolios and the overall market index, is discussed in more detail in Section IV.

The IRRC research reported in Figure 13 is discussed in more detail below. Nevertheless it is important at this stage to note the conclusion of the researchers that, it may be difficult to establish a direct causal relationship between environmental performance and financial performance. The call here is obviously for more and better designed research.

Figure 13. the IRRC view

"The fact that greener firms are doing as well or better than their more pollution-intensive counterparts may be due to the fact that firms with more efficient manufacturing processes also pollute less. On the other hand, firms that pollute less might do so because they can better afford to invest in pollution control or pollution prevention technologies. Put differently, high pollution firms might simply be those that are less able to make the investments needed to comply.

Whatever causal mechanism is at work, this study suggests that the increasing attention being paid to environmental management issues by both corporations and the investment community may well be warranted from the perspective of financial self-interest. The effectiveness of a company's environmental management may provide insights into both its overall management effectiveness and its financial performance". *"Environmental and Financial Performance: Are they Related?"* (Chen, Fenn & Naimon, IRRC 1995)

However, the IRRC statement that "the effectiveness of a company's environmental management may provide insights into both its overall management effectiveness and its financial performance" is important because it draws the link closely between the BiE /Extel research into the views of financial analysts and the IRRC/GEMI work on 3rd party attestation statements, both reported in x.3 above. Both pieces of research focused on the beliefs of users that it was quality of management generally that mattered most to them as financial stakeholders.

E. Relating environmental expenditure to outcome

The question of relating environmental expenditure with, firstly, environmental effect and secondly financial outturn is further complicated by the interpretations which can be placed on the disclosure of raw data. At the outset of the environmental reporting debate, many commentators (this author included) argued strongly for enhanced financial disclosures - particularly in respect of environmental operating expenditure and environmental capital expenditure. Whilst the general principle of greater transparency is still valid, several problems have emerged with the concept of pure, unencumbered disclosure:

(i)   defining environmental expenditures;

(ii)   distinguishing between environmental capital expenditure and ordinary (non-environmental) capital expenditure;

(iii)   measuring environmental benefits;

(iv)   interpreting the significance of the level of operating and capital expenditures on environmental issues in the absence of clear measures of overall corporate environmental performance.

Each of these three problem areas is discussed briefly below.

F.   Defining environmental expenditures

As yet there are no widely recognised definitions of environmental expenditures. The forthcoming UNCTAD position paper *"Accounting and Financial Reporting for Environmental Liabilities and Costs* " will provide some much needed guidance in this area. The tentative definition of "Environment Costs" suggested in the paper is as follows (see Figure 14 below):

Figure 14. **"Environmental costs** include the costs of steps taken to prevent, reduce or repair damage to the environment which results from an entity's operating activities, or to deal with the conservation of renewable and non-renewable resources. They include, inter alia, the disposal and avoidance of waste, the protection of surface and ground water, preserving or improving air quality, noise reduction, the removal of contamination in buildings, researching for more environmentally friendly products, raw materials or production processes etc. Costs incurred as a result of fines or penalties for non-compliance with environmental regulations, compensation to third parties as a result of loss or injury caused by past environmental pollution and similar environmentally related costs are excluded from the definition of environmental costs, but should still be disclosed as a separate classification".

The US Environmental Protection Agency (1995) has provided some insight into the types of costs which might be categorised as environmental costs - (see Figure 15 below) - but this complex representation of potential environmental costs is not going to have a broad corporate appeal unless it can be shown that some predictable financial benefit will accrue from the process of reorganising the internal accounting systems that would be necessary to implement such a detailed environmental cost recording system.

In this context it is useful to quote the experience of British Telecom who, in 1995, commissioned Coopers & Lybrand to report upon the feasibility of installing environmental accounting systems within BT. When reading the conclusions of the consultants report it should be remembered that BT is generally regarded as a leading edge environmental reporter - and is the first major non "values based" company which has committed itself to a social audit.

BT concluded that, although there may be opportunities to make better use of existing financial control systems to collect information on environmental performance where this could be clearly defined and related to existing ledger codes, to generate more comprehensive data would require major, costly and often unproductive, changes to both the structure of BTs accounting systems and the way in which the systems are used by staff at group, business and operational level. (*"Environmental Accounting in Industry: A Practical Review" BT 1995 - P 12*).

<table>
<tr><td colspan="3" align="center">**Figure 15: EPA Environmental Cost Breakdown**</td></tr>
<tr><td colspan="3" align="center">**Potentially Hidden Costs**</td></tr>
<tr>
<td align="center">Regulatory</td>
<td align="center">Upfront</td>
<td align="center">Voluntary
(Beyond Complinace)</td>
</tr>
<tr>
<td>

- Notification
- Reporting
- Monitoring/testing
- Studies/modeling
- Remediation
- Recordkeeping
- Plans
- Training
- Inspections
- Manifesting
- Labeling
- Preparedness
- Protective equipment
- Medical surveillance
- Environmental Insurance
- Financial assurance
- Pollution Control
- Spill response
- Stormwater mangement
- Waste ,management
- Taxes/fees

</td>
<td>

- Site studies
- Site preparation
- Permitting
- R&D
- Engineering and procurement
- Installation

Conventional Cost
  Capital equipment
  Materials
  Labour
  Supplies
  Utilities
  Structures
  Salvage value

Back-End
- Closure/decomissioning
- Disposal of inventory
- Post closure care
- Site survey

</td>
<td>

- Community relations/outreach
- Monitoring/testing
- Training
- Audits
- Qualifying suppliers
- Reports (e.g. , annual environmental reports
- Insurance
- Planning
- Feasibility studies
- Remediation
- Recycling
- Environmental studies
- R & D
- Habitat and wetland protection
- Landscaping
- Other environmetnal projects
- Financial support to environmental groups and/or researchers

</td>
</tr>
<tr><td colspan="3" align="center">***Contingent Costs***</td></tr>
<tr>
<td>

- Future compliance costs
- Penalities/fines
- Response to future releases
-

</td>
<td>

- Remediation
- Property damage
- Personal injury damage

</td>
<td>

- Legal expenses
- Natural resource damages
- Economic loss damages

</td>
</tr>
<tr><td colspan="3" align="center">***Image and Relationship Costs***</td></tr>
<tr>
<td>

- Corporate image
- Relationship with customers
- Relationship with investors
- Relationship with insurers

</td>
<td>

- Relationship with professional staff
- Relationship with workers
- Relationship with suppliers

</td>
<td>

- Relationship with lenders
- Relationship with host communities
- Relationship with regulators

</td>
</tr>
</table>

G. Distinguishing between environmental capital expenditure and ordinary capital expenditure

Even if it is possible to identify certain operating expenditures which are clearly environment driven, there remains the difficulty of separately identifying environmental capital expenditure. The difficulty here relates to the tendency for companies to move *away* from so-called "end of pipe" solutions to pollution prevention, and *towards* integrated lower-pollution/emission technologies. Instead of simply bolting a piece of pollution prevention equipment onto the end of an existing dirty piece of technology, companies are re-investing in new capital equipment which brings lower pollution and emission levels as an integral part of the design. This makes it difficult to apportion the capital expenditure between "environmental" and "non-environmental" for public reporting purposes.

Once again, the UNCTAD position paper *"Accounting and Financial Reporting for Environmental Liabilities and Costs* " provides some definitive guidance in this area (see Figure 16 below):

Figure 16: "Environmental costs should be capitalised if they are incurred to prevent or reduce future environmental damage or conserve resources, and if they are intended for use on a continuing basis for the purpose of the undertaking's activities, provided one of the following two criteria are met:

(a) they relate to anticipated environmental benefits and extend the life, increase the capacity, or improve the safety or efficiency of assets owned by the company, or

(b) they reduce or prevent environmental contamination that is likely to occur as a result of future operations.

They should also be capitalised if they are incurred to prepare an asset or activity for operation and, in doing so, damage is done to the environment that cannot be avoided and that has to be rectified at some future point in time."

Useful though the definition might appear at first sight, it is clear that the "end of pipe" vs. "integrated" expenditure dilemma has not been satisfactorily resolved. In fact the position paper on to recommend that "when an environmental cost that merits recognition as a capital asset *is related to* another capital asset (emphasis added), it should be included as an integral part of that asset, and not recognised separately".

From an accountants perspective this is a neat and tidy solution. From the perspective of someone trying to establish a relationship between the level of environmental expenditure and resultant corporate financial performance it is no solution at all, the more so because of the absence of any statutory or accounting standards requirements to disclose environmental expenditure in the financial statements. As companies move increasingly to integrated pollution control investments and away from end of pipe solutions environmental expenditures will be harder to measure and increasingly difficult to identify from the published financial statements.

That said, there are numerous examples of companies attempting to provide this sort of information - if not in their annual report to shareholders, then in their annual environmental report. Yorkshire Electricity Plc, a UK regional electricity distribution company, is one of these. YE has taken a conscious decision to design its annual environmental report so as to focus on the specific needs of particular stakeholder groups. For the purposes of this paper, the following extract from its 1995/96 environmental report is very relevant and hence is reproduced below (Figure 17)

The YE extract is notable for three things:

(i)   as noted above it is designed specifically for the financial community (including turnover and profit figures as well as environmental expenditure estimates and statements on insurance and contingent liabilities);

(ii)   there is no attempt to compute or present financially linked environmental performance indicators, even though the financial data is presented in more detail than for the vast majority of environmental reporters; and

(iii) the financial disclosures underline the need for:

(a) hard and fast rules on disclosures of environmentally related operating and capital expenditure, and

(b) the need for the involvement of accountants in the environmental reporting process - the expenditure categories disclosed by YE under the heading "Capital Spending" appear, on the surface, to be rather dubious. Had these disclosures been made within the annual report to shareholders the financial statement auditors would have been under a duty to ensure that the information was in conformity with established GAAP.

Figure 17. Environmental Expenditure Case Study - Yorkshire Electricity **[Environmental Performance Review 95 - 96 P 8]**	
Financial Analysis **4.1 Overview of Group Financial Performance**	**Fig 4.F1** **Group turnover and profit before tax**
This section seeks to provide a brief overview of the financial aspects of the Group. The Group turnover and profit before tax for each of the last three years are given in Figure 4F1	**Year Turnover (£m) Profit Bef/Tax (£m)** **1993/94** 1,307.9 149.0 **1994/95** 1,459.3 217.0 **1995/96** 1,332.3 219.3

4.2 Environmental Spending

Steady progress is being made towards identifying environmental spending in more detail. For this year, however, the information provided is limited to what we can currently readily provide for expenditure completely or almost completely identifiable as environmental. Most figures given in Fig 4.F2 are approximate.

Fig 4.F2

Capital spending included	£(,000)	Revenue spending included	£(,000)
Oil bunding programme	1,285	Energy Efficiency Standards of	
Operational building enhancement	172	Performance	2,050
Community relations sponsorship	51	Land management (operational buildings)	550
Research on environment related issues	48	Repairs and clean-ups	479
A1/M1 link environmental impact		Salaries and administration	215
Assessment	30	Waste management	190
Ground investigations (non-operational sites)	19	Seconded staff costs	108
Noise measurement instruments	18	Removal of deleterious buildings	34
Bird diverters	4	Production costs of video on environmental	
Glanford Brigg generating station audit	2	issues	10
		Landscaping (non-operational buildings)	10
Total	**£1,629**	**Total**	**£ 3,646**

There was no environmental contingent liability or liability with respect to land contamination provisions made in 1995/96

4.3 Insurance: we were able to secure insurance protection to levels which in our assessment minimised the risk exposure. In line with the general position, gradual pollution is excluded from our insurance.

H.   Accounting for environmental benefits

A problem for those advocating broader financial environmental disclosure is that companies usually only present the financial implications of their environmental activities from a cost perspective and seldom if ever address the actual (or potential) benefits which accrue to them. There are very few companies who have tried to report publicly on the financial benefits of their environmental activities. A number of examples are set out below (in Figures 18, 19 & 20) along with brief commentaries.

Figure 18. Brodene Hartman A/S (Denmark)

In its 1995 Environmental Accounts, Hartman presents a section called **"Environment-Related Income"**.

"As part of the Hartman Group's overriding strategy, a steady reduction in energy and resource consumption is pursued through investment in cleaner technologies. In both 1994 and 1995, Hartman obtained financial support from the Danish Energy Agency. The bulk of these subsidies totalling DKK 15.8 million, was used by the CHP (combined heat and power) plant.

"Hartman's long-term goal is to be able to account for environment-based income as well, for example in the form of higher market share or improved earnings due to optimized environmental conditions".

Comment: Hartman's clearly stated long-term goal is very unusual - it is not apparent that accounting and estimation techniques exist which could easily achieve the companies aims, although it MIGHT be appropriate to start regarding environmental activity as an intangible asset, similar to internally-generated goodwill and, possibly, look to create a "brand value" based around the "green credentials" of the company

---

Figure 19. SAS (Scandinavia)

The first environmental report (1995) from the airline SAS contains a commendable amount of financial data (for a first time reporter). The "benefit-related" elements of the disclosure are reproduced below:

Environment-related revenues

Reduced environmental charges through phasing out Chapter II aircraft	>100 MSEK
Reduced packaging charges through improved routines for choice of and source separation	5 - 10 MSEK

Environment-related investments
Various disclosures (including new aircraft and "hushkits")(*)

Financial consequences of future measures
Most environmental projects are planned to be profitable within 1 - 2 years. SAS assumes that the system of charges will include environmental charges to an increasing extent, without this resulting in a rise in the total amount of taxes and charges. Stricter environmental restrictions and certification requirements may affect the second-hand value of the MD80s.

Comment: SAS are reporting at least three unusual finance related issues: savings based on current investment strategies; future investment strategies (detail not provided above*); and the financial consequences of future environmental measures which it is anticipated will affect the company. Each of these disclosures should be of interest to the financial community.

Figure 20. Baxter Healthcare (U.S.A)			
Estimated environmental costs and savings world-wide ($ millions)			
Environmental costs	**1994**	**1993**	**1992**
Costs of pro-active programme			
Corporate environmental affairs	1.4	1.6	1.5
Auditors' and attorneys' fees	0.6	0.3	0.9
Corporate env. engineering / facilities engineering	0.8	0.9	0.8
Division/facility env. professionals/programs	7.0	6.5	5.0
Packaging professionals /packaging reduction programs	2.1	2.0	1.8
Pollution controls, operations and maintenance	2.5	2.7	2.0
Total costs of pro-active programme	**22.2**	**21.5**	**19.0**
Remediation and waste disposal costs			
Attorneys' fees for clean-up claims etc..	0.3	0.2	0.2
Waste disposal	2.8	3.4	3.8
Remediation / clean-up on site	1.2	0.8	5.0
Remediation / clean-up off site	1.1	0.3	0.0
Total remediation and waste disposal costs	**5.4**	**4.7**	**9.0**
Total environmental costs	**27.6**	**26.2**	**28.0**
Environmental income, savings and cost avoidance			
Associated with environmental initiatives in report year			
Ozone depleting substances cost reductions	1.8	1.2	1.4
Hazardous waste disposal cost reduction	0.9	0.6	0.6
Hazardous waste material cost reduction	0.5	0.5	0.5
Non-hazardous waste disposal cost reductions	0.5	0.5	0.5
Non-hazardous waste material cost reductions	5.4	1.3	3.7
Recycling income	3.5	2.7	3.2
Green lights energy conservation - cost savings	0.3	1.1	0.4
Packaging cost reductions	10.5	6.3	5.4
Total income, savings and cost avoidance for report year's initiatives	**23.4**	**14.2**	**14.7**
(As a percentage of the costs of the proactive program	105%	66%	77%)
Total income, savings and cost avoidance from report year's initiatives	23.4	14.2	14.7
Cost avoidance in report year from efforts initiated in prior years back to 1989	51.2	38.4	166.3
Total income, savings and cost avoidance p.a.	**74.6**	**52.6**	**31.0**

Comment: the Baxter methodology is a sophisticated internal management tool, one which adds new dimensions to our concepts of how financial aspects of environmental activity might be controlled and reported.

I.   Interpreting the significance of the level of environmental expenditures

Interpretation of financial numbers such as have been illustrated or described above remains a controversial topic. Companies, understandably, are reluctant to spend considerable time and effort collecting financial data only to see it mis-interpreted, or perhaps worse, ignored, by the financial stakeholders to whom it was intended to be addressed. The possibilities for misinterpretation have been well rehearsed. They are summarised in Figure 21:

Figure 21: interpreting environmental expenditure disclosures		
Possible user interpretation	High environmental spend	Low environmental spend
Good interpretation	The company is committed to reducing still further the environmental impact of its activities	The company has invested in pro-environment technology in the past and its need to invest further is therefore reduced
Bad interpretation	The company has neglected environmental issues in the past and now has to spend heavily to catch up with competitors	The company either does not believe it has an environmental impact which needs addressing or it does not care

Companies can only go so far in trying to minimise the possibility of such misinterpretations occurring. They can provide:

- the raw financial data together with narrative explanations for significant year on year variations
- a historical trend record of that expenditure
- quantified estimates of financial benefits flowing from their pro-environmental behaviour (though experience shows that disclosures of environmental costs are more common than disclosures of financially quantified benefits)
- a measure (or measures) of actual environmental performance (however defined)
- a narrative description of their own interpretation of the linkage between financial spending and environmental outturn
- financially based environmental performance or eco-efficiency indicators which demonstrate the relationship between spending and environmental performance and, if possible, the reverse relationship: the relationship between improved environmental performance and improved bottom line impact

J.   Conclusion

The section has identified in general terms some of the difficulties inherent in trying to link environmental and financial performance. In the first instance it is argued that - despite guidance from sources such as the US EPA and the United Nations - there are still considerable accounting difficulties involved in identifying environmental costs. The issue of identifying and disclosing the financial benefits of good environmental performance has hardly yet begun to be addressed - although some interesting experiments are reported.

Secondly there are some doubts about how environmental expenditure levels might be interpreted by prospective users. Notwithstanding the difficulties these two hurdles embrace, there is a growing number of companies apparently willing to attempt definitions of environmental expenditures and disclose them in their environmental reports.

SECTION III: *ENVIRONMENTAL PERFORMANCE INDICATORS (EPIS)*

A.   Introduction

The next section considers in some detail one of the most popular ways of measuring and communicating environmental performance - the environmental performance indicator (or EPI). A fairly recent development in the area of EPIs is the construction of "eco-financial indicators" - these indicators are often argued to be one of the most powerful and useful ways of linking environmental and financial performance for the sort of short-term decision making that financial markets demand.

In the same way as corporate management sets financial performance targets, and constructs financial performance indicators, so management also uses environmental performance indicators (EPIs) to monitor and evaluate progress on the environmental front. The important issue is that EPIs, like their financial counterparts, must be seen to be indicative of something significant - a change in a normally steady trend or relationship, an adverse variance, an unexpected impact on the quality of the environment.

B.   External publication of environmental performance indicators

The International Standards Organisation (ISO) define an EPI as a *"specific expression that is used to provide information about environmental performance"*. (ISO/TC 207/SC4 ISO WD 14031.5)

Bartolomeo (1995) provides more background:

"(EPIs) can be defined as the quantitative and qualitative information that allow the evaluation, from an environmental point of view, of company effectiveness and efficiency in the consumption of resources. EPIs consist of process, system and eco-financial indicators".

There are no requirements forcing companies to make public that environmental management data that they use for internal control purposes. Nevertheless, in their stand-alone environmental reports, many companies have chosen to publish one or more EPIs. The selection of which EPIs to make public is entirely up to the company and, rather like the research which shows that financial graphs are more common when financial performance is positive (Beattie & Jones 1992), there must be a suspicion that the selection of EPIs for publication purposes is a selective and self-serving process. The EC EMAS regulation, although requiring the publication of an environmental statement, does not require the publication of any specific EPIs. ISO 14000 does not require even the publication of an environmental statement.

C.   Classifications of environmental performance indicators

Several different classifications of Environmental Performance Indicators are available, and it is inevitable that, in the absence of any agreed industry bench-marking regimes, that companies will choose amongst the available options to design that set of internal EPIs which best fits corporate environmental objectives. Two different sources of EPI design are cited below.

James & Bennett (1994) provide one fairly generic framework for EPIs (Figure 22):

Figure 22. EPIs - Categories and examples (James & Bennett 1994)	
Categories of EPIs	**Examples of EPIs**
1. measures of ultimate environmental *impact*	• species diversity around plant • noise levels at specified points • ratio of actual to sustainable discharges
2. *risk* measures of potential impact	• usage of high risk chemicals/materials • risk of fatalities to exposed populations • risk of damage to ecosystems
3. *emissions/waste measures* (of mass and volume of emissions and wastes)	• emissions to air: TRI toxics, sulphur dioxides, nitrogen oxides, CO2 etc • waste to landfill: hazardous, non-hazardous • waste water discharges
4. *input* measures (of the effectiveness of business process)	• measures covering people, equipment, materials, physical setting, internal support
5. measures of *resource* consumption	• measures of energy, materials, water, etc • electricity, gas, oil consumption • natural resource (paper/minerals/water) consumption)
6. *efficiency* measures (of energy and materials utilisation)	• energy: ratio energy used/wasted • ratio actual/theoretical energy use • materials: percentage utilisation • equipment: percentage utilisation
7. *customer* measures (of satisfaction and behaviour)	• level of approval • number of complaints • product related environmental awareness • % adopting desired behaviour
8. *financial* measures	• cost of environment related cap. Expenditure • direct environment related operating costs • regulatory compliance, fines and penalties • costs of energy/materials • avoided costs plus measurable benefits

All internally directed management information shares many common qualitative characteristics with financial information routinely communicated outside the organisation: i.e. it must be relevant, timely, objectively determined, accurate, understandable and verifiable. In addition (or possibly as a subset of relevance), EPIs must also contain information or must be designed in such a way as to shed light on the success that has been achieved in meeting

- organisational environmental objectives
- regulatory constraints or limits (CICA "Reporting on Environmental Performance" 1994)

The International Standards Organisation (ISO) has incorporated many of the qualitative considerations into its draft guidance on environmental performance evaluation. According to the draft ISO guidance on EPE, the following data types and qualities should be recognised (Figure 23):

Figure 23. Types of EPI and criteria for selection	
Types of data and indicators	**Criteria for selecting indicators**
• absolute: basic information with little interpretation or manipulation	• representative: of the environmental performance of the organisation
• relative: scaled to, or relative to, another parameter (e.g. tonnes of SO2 emitted per tonne of primary product)	• responsive to change: sensitive to changes and trends in performance
• indexed: such as baseline year = 100%	• helpful to prediction: should be able to assist in predicting future trends
• qualitative: unquantifiable data placed on a value scale	• understandable: simple, clear, meeting the needs of users. the significance of the indicator should be understandable
• financial: costs or benefits associated with environmental performance	• relevant: to the needs of management and interested parties
• aggregated: similar indicators aggregated e.g. by product group or over time	• cost-efficient: with respect to data collection and data use
• weighted: judgmentally weighted to reflect priority attached to the information	• target-related: related to internal management performance targets
	• comparable: as appropriate - over time, between facilities or sites, ideally between companies

ISO further suggests that EPIs should be designed to cover three broad areas of concern:

1. *Management issues*: environmental management indicators in the management area should provide information on the organisation's capability and efforts in managing matters such as training, legal requirements, resource allocation, documentation, and corrective action. (ISO14031.5 Section 4.1.2.1)

2. *Operational issues*: environmental performance indicators for the operational area should provide management with information on the environmental performance regarding:
    (a) consumption of goods, services, resources and energy on the input side of the operational area; and
    (b) products and waste streams (e.g. air emissions, water discharges, solid waste, noise, heat, odour, vibration, light or radiation) on the output side of the operational area (ISO 14031.5 Section 4.1.2.2)

3. *Environmental issues:* the environmental area includes air, water, land, plant and animal life, other natural resources, and human health. Environmental indicators for this area may address the local, regional and global environmental conditions. Evaluation of the condition of the environment is not expected by all organisations because many are not able to determine their impacts on the environment. (ISO 14031.5 Section 4.1.2.3)

A recent review of EPIs by Ditz & Ranganathan (WRI 1997) recommends that development and use of publishable EPIs be focused on four core areas:

(i)	materials use	quantities and types of materials used
(ii)	energy consumption	quantities and types of energy used or generated

(iii)   non-product output

quantities and types of waste created before recycling, treatment or disposal

(iv)   pollutant releases

quantities and types of pollutants released to air, water and land.

According to Ditz & Ranganathan, these four key areas "focus manufacturers, customers and others on products, processes and services that prevent pollution and boost resource efficiency".

In contrast to James & Bennett and the authors of the draft ISO guidance - whose focus is almost entirely *internal* in nature - Ditz & Ranganathan further argue that development of EPIs around these four key areas should be encouraged by national governments: "National governments should link these EPIs at the facility, industry and sector level with national and global environmental goals. Merging EPIs at the micro and macro levels allows firms, officials and the public to judge for themselves the contribution of individuals (i.e. firms) toward overall environmental goals and the effectiveness of environmental policy".

Figure 24 presents an illustrative example of how EPIs might be designed, bearing in mind both organisational control objectives and the need to monitor compliance with external regulations, and Figure 25 presents an extract from the Bosch Siemens Environment Report with some examples of output based EPIs.

Figure 24: **Example of EPI design for both Internal and external reporting purposes**			**Reporting Level and Frequency**		
Policy / Principle	**Proposed targets and undertakings**	**Proposed performance indicators**	**Senior Management**	**Middle Management**	**Included in Environmental /annual report**
Comply with environmental laws and regulations	100% compliance	• percentage compliance	Annually		Yes
		• total no. of violations	Quarterly	Monthly	Yes
		• total no. of spills and volumes involved	Quarterly	Monthly	Yes
		• total no. and $ value of fines levied	Quarterly	Monthly	Yes
Source: James & Bennett					

Figure 25. Environmental Performance Indicators at Bosche Siemens			
Environmental indices (production)	**1993**	**1994**	**Units**
Energy utilisation per appliance	62.9	55.4	kWh/appliance
Raw materials per appliance	-	26.3	kg/appliance
Packaging per appliance	5.6	4.7	kg/appliance
Waste per appliance	7.1	6.4	kg/appliance
Proportion of valuable substances = waste for recycling/waste	88	90	%
Effluent per appliance	181	151	litres/appliance
CO2 emissions per appliance	21.8	20.1	kg/appliance

In its 1994/95 Environmental Report Bosche-Siemens published a set of environmental indices related to production activities. The indices give information on the basis of each appliance produced and can be traced back to the detailed "input / output balance sheet" also produced by the company.

Producing EPIs against a constant per unit denominator seems to be an ideal way for a manufacturer such as BSHG to proceed. The possibilities for both intra- company comparison and sectoral bench-marking seem fruitful. Doubts exist as to the precision of the disclosures - is the level of aggregation simply too high? Should all EPIs be produced on a segmental basis? Presumably the company utilises a more detailed set of EPIs for internal purposes to cover different product lines. If it is considered valid to present EPIs in this manner it would also seem appropriate, year on year, to apply environmental operating or monitoring costs on a per unit of output basis.

D.   Financially related environmental performance indicators

The literature cited above covers a wide range of environmental performance indicators. Such detailed "scientific" or "management" data may, however, often prove to be of little use and even less interest to external financial stakeholder - banks, insurers, shareholders, financial analysts or fund managers. Figure 26 below highlights a number of financially related environmental performance measures found in the EPI literature. A brief review of these EPIs will lead us to a deeper consideration of "eco-efficiency measures".

Figure 26 examples of financially relevant environmental performance Indicators	
Possible indicator	**Comment**
1. Cost of environment related capital expenditure	Disclosure recommended by EFFAS, ECAAF, ACBE, SEC amongst others. Definitional problems are involved , but disclosure is essential if realistic portfolio based studies are to be carried out
2. Direct environment related operating or management costs as % of sales, value added, net earnings, divisional earnings or other unit of output costs e.g. production cost or site cost of sales	Ditto - widely recommended and possibly easier to determine since the definitional problems are not so great. Note cost/benefit issues arising however - companies may have to redesign internal accounting systems
3. Total costs of regulatory compliance	Subset of 2 above - can be related to other variables: total environmental costs, total site operating costs etc
4. Fines and penalties, damages and remediation costs	Disclosure recommendation based on straightforward need for accountability - can be expressed as % of total environmental costs, % of industry total etc
5. Cost of waste and waste disposal charges to costs of materials	Absolute costs not particularly useful- need to be related to output or activity levels - perhaps total costs of materials throughput in various processes or used on site

6.	Avoided costs / benefits of pollution prevention measures/ reduced costs of purchased materials resulting from recycling or reuse	For both internal and external purposes - the environment is not always regarded only as a cost - some companies(e.g. Baxter Healthcare) track cumulative benefits, or waste handling costs, or environmental performance improvement investments per tonne of release reduction
7.	Marginal cost of environmental protection measures	Can be used when "low hanging fruit" have already been picked (water utilities use to justify not improving 99.5% water purity rates)
8.	Insurance premiums as measures of the effectiveness of risk management activities	Reduced premiums result from reduced environmental risk - e.g. following EMAS or ISO 14000 certification. Expressed per $ of turnover or per $ of tangible assets employed
9.	Emission reduction / expenditure	For specific operations - relate emissions or reductions in emissions to environmental costs associated with the activity (if separately identifiable)
10.	Average environmental expenditure per ...	Unit of natural gas or energy transported or building volume served
11.	Environmental investments / total investments	Assuming environmental expenditures are separately identifiable: needs to be bench-marked from site to site or firm to firm
12.	Cost of energy or fuel consumption or packaging costs	Against turnover, cost of sales, units of output, number of employees, miles driven / flown etc
13.	Donations and other voluntary environmental costs	As % of total environmental operating costs and as % of turnover
14.	TRI emission per $m turnover	IRRC aggregate indicator

E.   Eco-Efficiency and eco-efficiency indicators (EEIs)

If there is to be a linkage found between financial and environmental performance then the answer may lie in the relatively new concept of "eco-efficiency". Eco-efficiency is about three things:

- making more product (or the same as we do at present)
- with less input materials (or relatively less input per unit of output)
- and therefore creating less environmental impact

A formal (but rather unhelpful) definition is provided by the World Business Council for Sustainable Development (WBSCD 1996):

"Eco-efficiency is reached by the delivery of competitively priced goods and services that satisfy human needs and bring quality of life, while progressively reducing ecological impacts and resource intensity throughout the (product) life cycle, to a level at least in line with earth's estimated carrying capacity".

The definition is unhelpful mainly because it is phrased at the "aspirational" level for the economy as a whole - rather than at the "practical" level with which an individual company can engage. Too many "meta-concepts" are involved all at once

- competitive pricing at the company level
- quality of life

- environmental impact and resource intensity throughout the life cycle
- the earth's carrying capacity

for any company to more than scratch at the surface of the concept. A number of more practical assertions have, however, been made about so called "eco-efficient" companies:

Figure 27. Advantages of eco-efficiency
•   they use less resources and cause fewer emissions to soil, water and air
•   this leads to an increase in the operating margin due to lower costs
•   this can lead to higher sales due to an enhanced value of the products to the customer
•   the risk of environmental liability decreases leading to a lower discount factor
•   higher margins and lower discount factors create greater financial value
Source: *"Eco-Efficiency and Financial Analysis: the Financial Analyst's View"* - The European Federation of Financial Analysts ' Societies (1996)

It is argued that eco-efficient companies, or companies which can demonstrate their eco-efficiency, should be of great interest to the financial community in general and financial analysts in particular. In a sense, therefore, eco-efficiency is an extension of "resource efficiency" - taking into account a slightly broader selection of value creating parameters - product value added, lower insurance premiums, reduced environmental costs and reduced environmental liability risks.

F.   How to measure and communicate eco-efficiency

When discussing the various approaches to defining EPIs above it was noted that the ISO recommendations provide the flexibility for EPIs to appear in various different formats:

Absolute	relative	indexed	qualitative	financial	aggregated	Weighted

Eco-efficiency indicators may only be a special sub-category of "Environmental Performance Indicators" ("eco-financial" Bartolomeo 1994 - or see Figure 25 above, financially relevant environmental performance indicators). Thus common eco-efficiency indicators might take an **absolute** emission quantity (e.g. tonnes) and express it **relative** to a recognised financial total or other industry recognised performance measure (e.g. turnover, number of staff, sq. metres etc). In Figure 28 below, a short selection of eco-efficiency measures identified by the European Federation of Financial Analysts Societies as being potentially useful for the purposes of financial analysis are set out:

Figure 28. Examples of eco-efficiency measures		
Consumption of energy	•	per employee or
	•	per $ value added
CO2 emission in '000 of tonnes	•	per employee or
	•	per $ value added
Total waste in 100s or 'ooos of tonnes	•	per employee or
	•	per $ value added
Company: Landys & Gyr, Switzerland.		
CO2 emissions in tonnes	•	per $m turnover or
CFC usage	•	per segment
Company: Thorn EMI, UK.		
Fuel consumption	•	per available seat kilometre ('000)
SO2 emissions	•	per available seat kilometre ('000)
Company: British Airways, UK.		
Source: all above examples cited by EFFAS "Eco-efficiency and financial analysis" (1996)		

G.   From company specific measures to industry wide bench-marks

Any resource input or emission can be defined in eco-efficiency terms (rawmaterials, packaging, water, fuel, gaseous emissions, VOCs, hazardous/non-hazardous wastes, landfill/incinerated/recycled) and compared with some widely recognised indicator (sales, value added, operating profit, staff costs, etc. EFFAS also suggest some interesting parallels to conventional financial reporting strategies:

-    report EPIs by operating segment (recognising that many companies are multi-product, multi-sector operations)

-    report EPIs by geographical segment (acknowledging the international / regional diversity of operations)

Although any resource input or waste output can be compared relative to some other measure, this information does not automatically flow OUTSIDE the company. Rather like the complex (150+) set of EPIs recommended by an early ISO 14031 draft, these measures are often meant for internal (management) consumption only. As with profitability, environmental progress can be either positive or negative, and the extent of disclosure depends on pressures on the reporting entity. These pressures to disclose may include:

- statutory requirements to disclose
- generally accepted accounting practices
- industry body recommendation e.g CEPHIC
- pressures from stakeholders (including financial stakeholders)
- competitive/best practice pressures (>>> adoption of ISO/EMAS type environmental management standard)

But, as of late 1997, these particular pressures do not seem to have resulted in widespread, comparable eco-efficiency disclosures.

The World Business Council for Sustainable Development (WBCSD) has accepted it is

124

vital to communicate eco-efficiency concepts to the financial community and has published a guide for financial analysts - "Environmental Performance and Shareholder Value" (WBCSD 1997). The guide is based around a series of case studies which, as well as focusing on isolated instances of financial benefit flowing from environmental initiatives, include company wide case studies also, following through from initiatives to bottom line effect.

This brings us back nearly full circle to repeat that, in accounting terms, it is axiomatic that savings and efficiencies in the environmental area will have a beneficial impact on the bottom line. But in the short term, it may not always be possible to correlate bottom line benefits from environmental sources with share price movements which outperform the market as a whole. The next section review a selection of the work that has gone into reviewing the link, if any, between positive environmental performance and positive share price movements.

H.   Actual implementation of EPIs

Recent research in this area suggests that companies are at very different stages of implementing environmental performance measures - as the results shown in Figure 29 and the analysis contained in the Appendix to this section demonstrate:

Figure 29. Company implementation of environmental performance indicators			
Q: Do you have environmental performance measures in place for the following categories?			
	Comprehensive	*Some*	*None*
Resource measures	46%	50%	4%
Solid waste measures	39%	54%	7%
Efficiency measures	27%	46%	27%
Financial measures	15%	77%	8%
Source: James & Bennett (1998)			

These research findings would seem to suggest that even if the financial   community could clearly articulate its needs for financially linked environmental performance indicators, industry as a whole would have difficulty in responding, at least in the short term, since less than 50% of companies appear to have comprehensive indicators for resources, waste and efficiency.

In the Appendix to this section, environmental performance reports published by companies operating in six industries are studied. These industries are: oil and gas, paper and packaging, the water industry, the motor industry, chemicals and pharmaceuticals and electricity generation and distribution. For each of the industries reviewed, an analysis sheet has been prepared structured as follows:

- business segments disclosed or otherwise identified
- environmental impact categories reported
- EPIs or industry benchmark identified

No attempt is made to interpret the EPIs discovered through this review. The analysis is simply presented as a contribution to further developmental work being undertaken by ISAR (and others) to derive generally accepted sets of industry (sector) relevant environmental performance indicators.

I.   Conclusion on EPIs: do financially linked EPIs matter?

At this time it a matter of conjecture (i.e. for further research) whether or not the financial community would automatically prefer financially linked environmental performance indicators or, given the right circumstances - consistent industry wide definitions, verified data etc - whether they would be willing (and able) to accept and assimilate strictly non-financial data. The existence of a well-recognised body of academically credible (preferably market based) accounting research demonstrating positive relationships between environmental and financial performance would probably demonstrate the importance of EPIs in the corporate environmental evaluation and reporting process. Some examples of such research are considered in section IV below.

Speaking to the US environmental newsletter "Business and the Environment" (January 1996) a representative on the ISO 14031 working group said "standardised EPIs could be a useful tool in external communication on an organisation's environmental performance and could improve the comparability of information given in environmental reports of different companies".

Standardised EPIs might be attractive to users of environmental information but they might not be necessarily so attractive to preparers. In the same issue of BATE another ISO delegate was quoted as saying that "countries with a strong litigation tradition may not be interested in using the results of the EPE (EPI) process for external reporting purposes ..... companies are likely to view the selection of EPEs (EPIs) as a very idiosyncratic, company specific exercise that need not be geared toward making comparisons between companies".

Various factors will determine the pace of development of EPIs (both financial and non-financial) as regularly used tools for inter-firm comparison. These factors include:

- *the speed of take-up of EMAS, ISO 14000 and related environmental standards*
- *the willingness of companies to voluntarily enter into a sector-wide public reporting of (potentially substandard or legally embarrassing) environmental performance results*
- *the extent to which the financial sector increases pressure on companies to make such disclosures*

The most important issues with regard to the public reporting of environmental performance indicators are intra-sectoral agreement on which EPIs are most important and year on year consistency in application of the measurement techniques.

Appendix to Section III
A six industry review of published EPIs

Note re geographical selection of companies

The selection of companies within industries was influenced more by the practicalities of what reports were immediately available than by the need to ensure an international spread of good examples. As it is the companies selected represent the following 11 countries: Denmark,

Finland, France, Germany, Italy, Norway, South Africa, Sweden, Switzerland, United Kingdom and USA.

In fact the "euro/us- centric" nature of the selection is probably a fair reflection of where environmental performance reporting is occurring in 1997. With advantage of hindsight some Asian and southern hemisphere companies such as Tokyo Electric and Sony (Japan), and BHP and WMC (Australia) could have been added into theanalysis.

The sectors reviewed are as follows:

- *Oil and gas (Figure 30)*
- *Paper, printing, pulp and packaging (Figure 31)*
- *Water utilities (Figure 32)*
- *Automotive (Figure 33)*
- *Chemical and pharmaceutical (Figure 34)*
- *Power generation (Figure 35)*

Figure 30. OIL AND GAS (British Gas, BP, Exxon, Neste, Shell UK, Statoil		
A. Business segments disclosed or otherwise identified:	**B. Environmental impact categories reported:**	**C. EPIs or industry benchmark identified:**
Upstream	*Water emissions (oil to water)*	Emissions as a % of production/sales *(upstream activities/per emission or tonnes in total . Per $1m revenue)*
	Air emissions (SO2/NOx/CO2/VOC)	Emissions as a % of throughput *(downstream activities/as above)*
Downstream		Emissions as a % of revenues *(downstream activities / per emission or tonnes in total)*
	Normal waste	Chemicals segment: emissions as a % of production *(per emission or tonnes in total)*
Chemicals	*Hazardous waste*	spills: total reportable & total tonnes spilled > 1 barrel< (number and volume
Other (e.g. shipping)	*Spills (No./Vol.)*	Hazardous waste *(per 1,000 tonnes product)*
	Energy use (including flared gasses)	energy use *(per unit of product- barrel?* flared gas volume *(cu.ft. per day)* Investment costs *(as % of segment Turnover)*
	Finance (investment costs vs. operating costs)	Operating costs *(per unit of Throughput or production)*
Minimum conditions for analysis: (1) completeness (e.g. UK or US vs. world-wide disclosures); (2) Segment definition and breakdown (e.g. geographical or class of business); (3) common units of measurement within firms in same industry; (4) accounting policies employed		

Figure 31. Paper, print, pulp and packaging (Aylesford Newsprint, The Beacon Press, Brodrene Hartman, Inveresk, James Cropper, MoDo)		
Business segments identified in reports issued:	**Environmental impact categories reported:**	**Environmental performance indicators (EPIs) identified:**
Paper production	*Resource use: - water*	- water use (absolute) - water use relative to tonnes production
	- energy	- energy use (absolute) - energy use (therms?) relative to tonne of production or £'000 sales - balance of electricity vs. natural gas
	Emissions to water: *- suspended solids* *- BOD* *- COD* *- PCPs*	- % compliance with consents - Av. Tonnes / day - Av. Tonnes / day - Av. Tonnes / day - Av. Gram / day also compare emissions relative to production
	Emissions to air: *- sulphur di-oxide* *- oxides of nitrogen* *- sulphur dioxide* *- CO2*	- tonnes (absolute) or per day - tonnes (absolute) or per day - tonnes (absolute) or per day also compare emissions relative to production - tonnes (absolute)
	Emissions to land: *- various categories of waste*	- process (or solid) waste to 3rd party landfill (tonnes) or % of process or solid waste) - solid waste recycled as % of total also compare waste relative to production
Distribution / transportation	*Emissions to air* *- CO2*	- tonnes of finished product per road delivery - road vs. rail deliveries (tonnes) - mpg per vehicle power than published urban driving standard

Figure 32. Water Utilities		
Business segments identified:	**Environmental impact categories reported:**	**EPIs identified:**
Water supply and effluent treatment	*Water resources management*	- water resources: reservoirs, abstraction, ground water - no. of prosecutions (per year, per regulatory agency) - av. daily supply (megalitres p/day) - leakage rate (megalitres p/day + as % of av. daily supply)
	Drinking water quality	- overall compliance with (% samples meeting) drinking water standards
	Waste water & sewage treatment (+ sewage sludge use/disposal)	- av. daily waste water rec'd - no. of sewage treatment works - equivalent annualised population - non-compliant treatment works - as % of all works + equiv. ann. pop - % samples meeting standards - as % of total population served - total vol. Sludge produced - % recycled: farmland, disposed to landfill, incinerated, sea disposal, treated - flooding incidents
	Coastal waters / beaches	- no. of bathing waters - no. of bathing waters non-compliant - % of bathing waters non-compliant
	Resource use (energy + transport + procurement etc)	- natural gas - electricity use (MWh or Gwhs) - electricity generated - generated as % of used - business mileage (private + commercial) - fleet size + % diesel
	Emissions *Waste*	- CO_2/Nox/SO_2/HC/HCFC - general solids + VOCs
Waste disposal business	*Emissions*	- CO_2, NO_x, SO_2, HC
	Energy use	- natural gas / electricity
	Landfill	- waste inputs ('ooo tonnes): special, industrial, domestic, construction, liquid waste treated - methane emissions ('000 tonnes pa) - waste inputs ('ooo tonnes): special, industrial, domestic, construction, liquid waste treated - methane emissions ('000 tonnes pa)
Consultancy services and general administration	*Corporate ecology*	- energy use (see above) - wastes generated - recycling - emissions (see above)
Indicators of sustainability (see also ICI "Environmental Burden" approach (see Chemicals analysis sheet) for another alternative to standard EPI disclosures)	***Severn Trent Plc -*** *the EPIs identifies above in Col. 3 above are restated under the headings shown to the right which accord with the UKs sustainable development strategy*	*- Global atmosphere* *- Air pollution* *- Fresh water protection* *- Depletion of non-renewable resources* *- Land and soil protection* *- Biodiversity* *- Local environmental issues*

Companies reviewed (all UK unless otherwise stated): Anglian Water , Northumbrian Water, Severn Trent, South West Water, Thames Water, Umgemi Water (South Africa))

Figure 33. Automotive [Daimler Benz (Germany); Fiat (Italy); Rover (UK); Volkswagon (Germany) ; Volvo (Sweden)]		
Business segments identified:	**Environmental impact categories reported:**	**Environmental performance indicators (EPIs) identified:**
*Reports to date appear to focus mainly on **production issues** for data disclosure purposes (although the narrative parts of the reports do cover life-cycle and product stewardship issues - see Volvo below)*	*Energy (equiv.tonnes of oil, Gwh,*	- absolute quantities used - % per energy source - externally vs. internally generated - fossil energy vs. dist. heating - **specific energy consumption measures:** 　(Fiat = TOE/billion lire of manufacturing cost) 　(Rover = Av. Kwh per vehicle)
	Water use ('ooos cu.m/pa)	- absolute quantities used - recirculation index (Fiat = Total re-cycled / total used) - **specific water consumption measures** 　(Fiat = cu. m / million lire of manufacturing cost)) 　(Rover = cu.m per vehicle)
	Waste (tonnes, cu.yards)	- absolute quantities generated, split between sources inc. special waste - disposal routes: incineration, treatment, recycled, controlled landfill - solid waste re-cycling index (Fiat = re-cycled waste / total solid waste - **specific waste generation measures:** 　(Fiat: = tons waste per billion lire of manufacturing costs) 　(VW = kg per vehicle produced)
	Productions emissions (tonnes)	- solvents (Fiat & D/Benz) - dust, SO2, NOx - hydrocarbons 　(quantity per vehicle produced = VW & Volvo)
Life cycle issues	*Resource use*	- % of re-cycled material used per vehicle
	Vehicle emissions	- comparison with statutory limits (Volvo)

Figure 34. Chemicals and Pharmaceuticals		
Business segments identified:	**Environmental impact categories reported:**	**Environmental performance indicators (EPIs) identified:**
These appear to differ from company to company but can be summarised as: *(i) raw materials supply* *(ii) manufacturing operations* *(iii) product distribution* *(iv) waste disposal* *however there is little evidence that life-cycle issues have been taken into account (except where - see ICI - an environmental burden approach is computed*	***Resource consumption:*** *Materials (tonnes)* *energy (giga or tera joules)* *water (cu. m)* *packaging ('ooo tonnes)* ***Waste** ('ooo tonnes solid or cu.m. liquid)* ***Emissions*** ***Transportation*** ***Compliance***	 - absolute quantities - eco-productivity (N/N = indexed turnover / indexed resource consumption - same for * below) - absolute quantities and different sources - energy efficiency index (ICI = energy consumed / index of volume of production) - energy consumption index (N/N = *) - per employee and per metric ton of end product (Roche Energy Rate) - absolute consumption - water consumption index (N/N = *) - absolute quantities - packaging consumption index (N/N = *) - absolute quantities: hazardous vs. non-hazardous; solid vs. liquid - process vs. non-process related - disposal route(s) and relevant %'s - % recycling - VOC's / CO2 / SO2 / solid particulates as absolute quantities - priority to air, land etc (Dow) - volume/tonnage transported - prosecutions and complaints
	***"Environmental Burden"** - a new approach being tested by ICI - based on various environmental impact categories – see right and section X of main report for more detail*	**Roche:** global warming contribution - metric tons CO2 equivalents per million Sw. Francs.

Companies reviewed: Dow Europe, Elf Atochem * (France), Henkel (Germany), ICI (UK), Monsanto (USA), Novo Nordisk (or N/N: Denmark), Rhone Poulenc ** (France), Roche (Switzerland),**

**** note: like many other chemical companies Rhone Poulenc also utilises an independently verified set of "environmental indices" which tracks emissions to water, air and waste to land.**

***** ditto Elf Atochem which has separate water and energy indices - but these are not directly comparable with other companies which use the indexation approach**

Figure 35. Power generation, transmission and distribution		
Business segments identified:	**Environmental impact categories reported:**	**Environmental performance indicators (EPIs) identified:**
Generation	*Emissions:* *Global warming* *Acid rain* *Resource consumption*	CO_2 – tonnes per Gigawatt or Grammes per kWh - SO_2 – ditto - NO_x – ditto - fuel: % from renewable vs. non-renewable sources - compliance with air quality consents
Transmission and distribution	*Energy losses* *Visual effects*	- % total electricity transmitted - % loss on distribution - underground cables as % of total transmission/distribution (miles)
Systems maintenance	*Oil leaks* *PCBs in transformers*	- reduction in pumping of oil filled able circuits - leaks vs. volume of oil pumped - elimination
Other	*Waste (tonnes/ cu.m)* *Noise* *Corporate ecology* *Transportation* *Procurement* *Customer energy efficiency*	- generators: ash produced and how disposed of - absolute volume: breakdown and proportion recycled/sent to landfill - recycling/re-use of oil - no. of complaints/street excavations - absolute energy consumption (kWh) - reduction in associated emissions - fleet size/breakdown/fuel type/fuel used tc - reduction in CO_2 emissions - reductions in CFCs and halons - educational programmes - consumer statistics: costs per unit consumed - target energy savings (absolute GWh) -

Companies reviewed: all UK unless otherwise stated: The Eastern Group, Eskom (South Africa), London Electricity, National Grid, National Power, Northern Electric, Scottish Power, Yorkshire Electricity

Note: whereas with the water utilities the issue of leakage is usually both identified and addressed, with the electricity companies the issue of "electricity loss" is sometimes identified but rarely, if ever, dealt with in any degree of detail.

SECTION IV: *ENVIRONMENTAL PERFORMANCE AND THE INVESTMENT COMMUNITY*

A.   Introduction

It has been mentioned several times in the foregoing sections that although environmental cost avoidance, reduced waste, new recycling revenues etc will automatically be good for the bottom line of the entity, it will not automatically follow that these benefits will be reflected in share price - that being dependent on and responsive to a wider range of variables than simply environmental factors.

This section reviews some evidence of (i) the way in which the investment community interprets and uses environmental data and (ii) the success or otherwise of investment portfolios which are voluntarily limited to environmental or socially responsible investments. Several different approaches are described including the emergence of environmental risk rating methodologies (which mimic the work of the well-established credit ratings agencies such as Standard & Poors) and the screening and "best in class" methodologies of investment managers concerned with environmentally responsible investment. A number of different academic research findings are cited which seem to indicate that although corporate environmental concern cannot be positively correlated with superior stock market returns, voluntarily limiting an investment horizon to environmentally responsible companies need not automatically incur the investor a penalty terms of lower than average returns.

B.   External assessment of environmental performance - "risk rating exercises"

Rightly or wrongly, some sections of the investment community have begun to view environmental performance in general - and environmental risk in particular - as something capable of being summarised or compressed into a single figure, a rating similar to that used for credit rating purposes by companies such as Standard & Poors. Several environmental risk rating methodologies are being developed.

Risk rating methodologies seldom address actual environmental performance, although the strengths and weaknesses of the environmental management systems are evaluated. A rating reflects an outsider's perception of the environmental risk to which a company is exposed. In all the methodologies seen by this author, the financial strength of the company plays a major part.

There are a number of environmental risk rating methodologies being developed at present by the financial community. Whilst the search for the Holy Grail of a single figure risk rating is understandable, the biggest problem of such techniques appears to be that they all used (sometimes strikingly) different methodologies - and as a result it is difficult for any of them to claim to be more reliable than any of their competitors

---

Figure 36. Environmental Risk Rating - an Example

The SERM model measures a company's environmental exposure in relation to its financial strength. It does this through the following steps:

1. Direct risks are assessed in financial terms (e.g. cost of clearing up a spillage, fines for breaching permitted emission limits)

2. Indirect risks are also assessed in financial terms (e.g. loss of sales resulting from tarnished reputation

3. Direct risk and indirect risk for each area of concern are added to provide a combined total

4. the combined total is adjusted by a probability factor for each area of concern, based on size and diversity of operations and the probability of such an incident occurring assuming average management systems and implementation

5. Management systems and their implementation are evaluated and given scores

6. The product of the management systems and implementation scores is used to derive a residual risk figure from the adjusted total risk for each area of concern

7. A total residual risk figure is calculated which provides an estimate of the company's exposure in any year

8. Total residual risk is calculated as a percentage of market capitalisation, and the resultant figure is converted into the rating on a 27 point scale.

Where a company is not quoted, or the rating applies only to a division of a quoted Company, the rating panel makes an estimate of the financial strength to use in place of Market capitalisation.

Source: Safety & Environmental Risk Management Rating Agency Ltd (SERM) 1996

A number of other environmental risk ratings procedures are being developed, both in the UK and elsewhere. The Business in the Environment/Financial Times "Index of Corporate Environmental Engagement" described in Section I has been described by its authors as a "reaction" to the more quantitative forms of environmental risk rating such as offered by SERM. A related but separately derived rating process has been developed by the Centre for Studies in Financial Innovation (UK). The CSFI approach has been piloted on a major UK power generator. An outline of the CSFI process is presented below (see Figure 37). CSFI suggest that their rating scale might be interpreted as follows:

Figure 37. the CSFI environmental risk rating model	
CSFI rating scale	**Examples of applied ratings**
AAA: a company in excellent financial condition with minimal, well-identified environmental liabilities, and with a strong ability to meet any losses that might materialise. Also well placed to handle any foreseeable tightening of regulatory requirements.	
AA: as AAA but with larger environmental liabilities	**Megawatt Plc**: is a power generation company, and most of its capacity is coal-fired. the company is large and financially strong, and has invested a certain amount in equipment to reduce pollution. At the moment, its gaseous emissions are within permitted limits. But the government has subscribed to an international agreement to tighten emissions targets over the next decade, and the company now faces large additional, anti-pollution investments. The chairman has warned that while the company can afford the expenditures, other investment plans might be affected. **Rating AA**: With its heavy dependence on coal, the company clearly has large potential environmental liabilities, and the chairman's warning indicates that these will be costly. However the size and strength of the company, plus the long time scale for the investments suggests no major cause for concern.
BBB: a company in a strong financial with good business prospects, but one where environmental liabilities are a potential source of loss, though not on any material scale	
BB: as BBB, but where environmental losses could become material	
B	**Happy Food Inc.** is a small manufacturer of frozen foods. A new anti-waste ordinance will oblige it to take back all its packaging for recycling, or pay for the work to be done by the municipality. The company hopes to be able to pass this considerable cost on to its customers, but competition is intense and there must be doubt as to whether this is possible. **Rating B**: Happy Foods is in the unpleasant position of being caught in a regulatory vice. It is a small company in a tough market, and the frozen food business does not offer much scope for reducing packaging. The company will probably survive, but it faces a very difficult period. The fact that it allowed itself to get into what must have been a foreseeable predicament also reflects badly on management.

Risk assessment ratings take a broader view of corporate environmental performance by assessing such issues as the strength of internal environmental controls. At present, however, most environmental risk rating methodologies are still at the developmental stage, with no public dissemination of results. It is not clear whether finalised assessments will be in the public domain or will be used by the companies concerned in negotiations with their bankers, insurers and other finance providers

C.   Portfolio screening for environmental (and related social) concerns

If the objective of financial reporting up until the 1990s has been "to provide information about the financial position, performance and changes in financial position of an enterprise that is useful to a wide range in making economic decisions" (IASC 1995), it is legitimate to ask what should happen to corporate reporting practices when the expressed needs and desires of external users change.

In the United Kingdom funds invested in a "socially responsible" manner (i.e. in ethically or environmentally screened investment trusts) have grown from approximately £400m in 1993 to over £1.3 bn as of November 1996 (EIRIS estimate). In the USA it was estimated that in

1995, some $639 billion was invested in socially responsible assets of one sort or another (Social Investment Forum 1995). That sum represented approximately 10% of all funds under management in the US. In total the Forum estimated that $162 billion was directly invested in socially screened portfolios, the balance ($473 bn) was controlled by investors who either sponsored shareholder resolutions or who voted their proxies on the basis of formal policies embodying socially responsible goals. Of the $162 bn directly invested in screened portfolios the Social Investment Forum estimate that the funds are sourced roughly equally by religious institutions (30%), individuals (23%), institutions other than government pensions funds (24%) and government pension funds (23%).

If 10% of all US investors want their funds to managed in more socially responsible way it follows that those responsible for managing the funds must have access to information which reports comprehensively on the social as well as the financial performance of the enterprise. Companies should thus be reporting on the presence or absence of morally reprehensible activities: detrimental environmental activity, involvement in ethically unacceptable trading (tobacco, alcohol and weapons being those activities most commonly identified by the Social Investment Forum). That is why the conventional financial reporting framework, defined and designated by the IASC, is too narrow and requires augmentation.

To support the environmental / ecological investment industry a number of different organisations have set up "screening" procedures, either to help themselves select potential investment opportunities for the funds they manage, or to advise clients on the ecological / ethical merits of particular companies. These are in addition to the environmental risk rating methodologies described above. It should be noted that screening normally encompasses at least two distinct stages:

- environmental or ethical screening (which may be either positive or negative in nature), and
- financial screening.

In "positive screening" the fund manager or client specifies the positive attributes they are looking for and constructs a portfolio from those companies that match these attributes. In "negative screening" the fund manager or client automatically rules out certain categories of investment (tobacco, alcohol, etc). Examples of positive screening include:

- products and services of long term benefit to the community
- a record of suitability, quality and safety of products and services
- involvement in environmental improvement and pollution control
- involvement in conservation of natural resources
- openness with regard to its activities
- open approach to the management of staff, customers and public affairs/issues

(Positive criteria of Friends Provident, largest UK ethical investment manager: source *"IsThere a Cost to Ethical Investing"* WM Company 1996)

One of the agencies that provides advice to others rather than managing its own portfolios directly is the US-based Investor Responsibility Research Centre in Washington DC. IRRC articulates the need for its services as follows:

"Environmental issues are increasingly relevant to the financial performance of major corporations and the portfolio decisions of investors. In the US, widespread public interest, constantly changing environmental regulations, growing enforcement of a variety of environmental statutes that govern the handling of hazardous substances and the discharge of pollutants and proliferating legislation over who should pay for environmental liabilities related to past waste disposal practices have brought environmental issues to the attention of management at corporations in a broad spectrum of industries.

And while many countries currently lack the broad array of environmental laws that exist in some of the most industrialised nations, environmental protection is rapidly becoming a global issue, as environmental regulations emerge from international treaties and become critical elements in trade negotiations and policy. With growing frequency, huge international business deals, ranging from hydroelectric projects in Canada to paper mills in South East Asia to oil field developments in Russia, are coming unhinged as a result of environmental concerns.

As environmental concerns move from being "a cost of doing business" to being a potent market force in their own right, the risks and rewards associated with a corporation's environmental performance are growing. ....(it is) possible to monitor the environmental practices of large companies using information from government environmental enforcement databases and other sources, and to distinguish between the performance of companies within industry groups".

(Source: *"Corporate Environmental Profiles Directory 1996"* - Executive Summary - IRRC Environmental Information)

D.   Examples of screening / analysis in action

Environmentally derives examples of these screening activities / advisory services include:

Figure 38. Examples of environmental screening	
Investor Responsibility Research Centre (IRRC/USA)	Corporate profiles directory - covers S&P 500 including data on: • liabilities resulting from past contamination of specific sites • permits denies or temporarily restricted because of inadequate environmental safeguards • estimates of routine emissions of toxic chemicals • reports of significant accidental spills of oil or chemicals • environmental enforcement actions that could lead to monetary penalties • environmental disclosures in securities filings • companies descriptions of their environmental policies, management practices and programs

Jupiter Asset Management (UK)	Set environmental criteria for green investment under • Processes: policy publication, environmental management structure, monitoring of environmental impact, disclosure of environmental data, trading partner assessments, energy efficiency, legal compliance • Products and Services: environmental impacts, R&D, packaging and labelling
National Provident Institution (NPI/UK	"Best in Class" questionnaire approach covering: • Environmental performance Indicators: policy, annual report disclosures, board level responsibility, EMS and scope (answers graded) • Industry specific questions: (see Section B for full list of questions covering 16 industry sectors) Summarised by ranking as "best in industry class"
Swiss Info Centre (SIC/Switzerland)	Regular publication of individual company "Economic, Environmental and Social Analysis" fact-sheet. (See also Section B for example of "Environmental criteria and Key data" analysis sheet - including eco-efficiency data)

E.   Market Based Portfolio Research

Successful portfolio diversification is at the heart of all investment management. Diversification reduces risk and the volatility of returns and a well-diversified portfolio should enable the investor to at least earn returns on a par with the market portfolio (i.e. the average return for the market as a whole). Market based accounting research involves comparing the actual returns of a specific sample of companies with the return earned on the so-called "market portfolio". Researchers seek to identify those events which can be shown to explain significant differences - either positive or negative - between the sample return and the market return.

As investors become more sophisticated (perhaps "demanding" or "choosy" would be better words) about where their money goes, they begin to place constraints on fund managers: DON'T invest in - tobacco companies, arms manufacturers, alcoholic drinks makers, the sex industry, companies known to exploit labour markets in less developed countries, companies with poor environmental performance records. DO invest in well managed, ethically managed, environmentally pro-active companies.

Such demands place the fund manager in a dilemma because the available pool of investment opportunities from which to select the required investment portfolio shrinks the moment such constraints are imposed. The outturn is likely to be either that the resultant portfolio will under perform the market or that it will have an unacceptable risk profile.

In his book (*"The Ethical Investor" Harper Collins 1995*) Russell Sparkes of the Central Methodist Finance Board approaches the topic under the broad heading of "The Rewards of Virtue" and states the central problem facing fund managers:

"The question of investment performance is a key one for ethical investors. If, as opinion polls show, 35% of investors in socially responsible funds are willing to do so in the expectation of receiving a lower rate of return, this is not true of the other 65%".

Thus it is important to know whether or not it is possible to select investment opportunities which meet strict environmental criteria and at the same time do not penalise the investor by providing lower returns or increased risk. If it can be shown that better environmental accountability and improved environmental performance have the effect of suppressing conventional financial returns then there is a real danger that major companies will choose not to become as environmentally or ethically sound as they might otherwise have become. Research which reviews the financial returns provided by specialist environmental or ethical funds is therefore crucial to the future of this sector.

F.   A review of the main research outcomes

Such research as there is on the outturn from environmentally and/or socially responsible investment is not at all comprehensive. The differences between investment funds themselves (environmental, dark/light green, ethical - all with varying exemptions, means that they are often not directly comparable: it may be OK to compare them individually against the market return, but it may not be legitimate to compare them one against the other. In the rest of this sub-section the outcomes of two major pieces of research are described:

1)   the US research carried out by the Investor Responsibility Research Centre (IRRC) **which concludes that investors in managed screened funds should not have to pay a penalty for making such positive (active) investment decisions, and**

2)   some UK work performed by a private sector financial adviser WM Markets, **which again concluded that ethical investments (embracing environmental within ethical) can provide competitive returns.**

G.   An overview of the IRRC research (see Figure 39 below)

The 1995 IRRC study examined the relationship between environmental and financial performance using a new objective data set detailing the environmental performance of the Standard and Poor's 500 companies. The environmental performance data was compiled by IRRC using government data that had not been previously available to researchers. Industry-balanced portfolios were constructed and the financial returns of "high-pollution" portfolios were compared with those of "low-pollution" portfolios. The study also examined the stock market reaction to new information on the environmental performance of individual firms, and provided a preliminary analysis of which comes first - good financial performance, or good environmental performance.

Overall, the study found no penalty for investing in a "green" portfolio and, in many cases, low pollution portfolios achieved better returns than high pollution portfolios and the S&P 500 index. The study suggests that "the increasing attention being paid to environmental management issues by both corporations and investors may well be warranted from the perspective of financial self interest."

Figure 39. Technical details of the IRRC research		
Environmental Performance Variable Definitions	*Selection of Portfolios* Two portfolios were constructed	*Financial Performance Variable Definitions* Accounting returns:
1. Number of Super Fund sites 2. Number of compliance penalties 3. $ value of compliance penalties 4. Volume of toxic chemical releases 5. Number of oil spills 6. Volume of oil spills 7. Number of chemical spills 8. Volume of chemical spills 9. Number of environmental litigation proceedings	(1) with low values of the environmental measure of interest and (2) with high values. The S&P 500 was sorted into 85 different industry category groupings Dummy variable = 0 if environmental measure is lower than median for industry group (= 1 if measure is higher than median)	(1) Return on assets (ROA) (2) return on equity (ROE) (3) unadjusted total return to stockholders (4) risk adjusted total return to stockholders

"Environmental and Financial Performance: Are they related?" **Investor Responsibility Research Centre 1995**

Notes to the IRRC example

(a)   in the context of this particular paper, which is seeking to explore the possibility (or perhaps the necessity) of expanding the corporate financial reporting framework, it is perhaps worth noting the IRRC comment that of the 9 environmental performance variables used in their research, 8 were drawn from official US government statistics and 1 came from the SEC 10-K filing (which may or may not be classified as a piece of information typically required by US GAAP). This does put into sharp focus the suitability of conventional financial reports for extracting environmental data required for analysis purposes.

(b)   IRRC conclude their research by saying: "This study has presented new evidence on whether or not so-called "green" investors need to pay a premium for their convictions. The answer appears to be no. Investors who chose the environmental leaders in an industry-balanced portfolio were found to do as well, and sometimes better, than those choosing the environmental laggards in each industry. One could construct a well-balanced index fund,with superior environmental performance characteristics, that closely tracked the S&P 500 index or other comparable market measures."

(c)   This conclusion can be linked to the "best in (industry) class" researched used by UKs NPI for their Global Care Fund. Positive screening of this sort involves going beyond simply vetoing all stocks in a particular industry category - instead it implies seeking out the industry environmental leaders. As already intimated, however, this information may not be readily apparent from the audited financial statements (or indeed the annual report *in toto*) as currently presented.

H.   A review of the WM UK based research (see Figure 40 below)

The WM research, published in late 1996, is an investment industry based research exercise.(hence perhaps the rather tasteless headline applied in the press release - "You can have your ethical cake and eat it"). The research focuses on the ethical investment industry in the UK generally rather than on environmental investment in particular.

Figure 40. The WM Research

The result of the research is summarised as follows: *__competitive returns are achievable but at the cost of some extra volatility.__* Three separate strands of research constituted the WM work and led to the following conclusions:

1.   an "ethical charity universe", set up for the purpose of the analysis, had, in the four years 1992-95, an identical UK equity return to that of unconstrained funds, 15.5% per annum. This suggests, say WM markets, that the exclusion of certain stocks did not appear to have a major impact on equity return.

2.   the second approach covered the FTSE All Share Index "ex-Vices" and it showed that since January 1992, annualised rolling three-year returns up to May 1996 were on average about 1% per annum better than the FTSE All-Share Index. Further, the associated increase in volatility was (only) 0.2% per annum. This, according to WM Markets, if sustained, would represent a good return-to-risk trade-off.

3.   the third approach examined the FP Stewardship managed Fund, the largest pool of ethically managed assets in the UK - valued at £218 million at the end of 1995. A close study of this fund's results reveal a good relative performance, 2% above the WM All Funds Universe weighted average of UK equities over the 10 years to end 1995. The comprehensive screening process adopted by the fund's managers, involving both negative and positive (*) screens, resulted in a portfolio of stocks very different to the All Share Index. Consequently, say WM, over annual periods, performance may diverge widely from the All Share Index and also the typical equity portfolio of a UK Fund.

(*)   it appears that the "positive" screening methods employed by Friends provident DO capture environmental as well as ethical constraints (see 12.4 above for details of the positive criteria employed by Friends Provident.

Source: "Is there a Cost to Ethical Investing?" WM Research 1996)

I.   The Kleinwort Benson (RSA) Tomorrow's Company Fund

The results of the two research exercises described above are promising from the perspective of the aspiring "green" or "clean" company. These results are substantiated on the broader more popularist canvas by the backers of the recently launched " Tomorrow's Company Investment Fund" (Kleinwort Benson 1996). The "Tomorrow's Company" ideal is a concept launched by the UK Royal Society of Arts (RSA) - an agenda for "sustainable business success". In the UK the RSA has a serious, ultra-Establishment reputation. The (very successful) results of the exercise described below should therefore not be dismissed immediately as pre-fund-launch PR!.

In RSA terms, sustainability does not refer only to the inter-generational equity concept which lies at the core of the environmental debate, rather to a broader set of criteria for judging business success. Among the Tomorrow's Company criteria are:

- development of a unique success model
- communication of a clear sense of purpose and values
- seeing relationships as the underlying foundation of business competitiveness
- providing a clear "performance measurement" framework
- demonstration of leadership and ability to inspire through their actions

There would appear to be some correlation between the RSA Tomorrow's Company criteria and some of the positive screening criteria used by Friends Provident .

A 30 share experimental portfolio was selected according to the Tomorrow's Company criteria (the shares received the highest rankings on the Tomorrow's Company "inclusive assessment process"). The portfolio results were "back-tested" against the FTSE All Share Index from December 1992 through June 1996. Using December 1992 as the base year the FTSE All Share Index achieved a 35% increase. The "Tomorrow's Company" portfolio achieved a 90% growth over the same period.

J.   Academic research studies

Summarised in Figure 41 below is a selection of academic research into the question of whether or not good environmental performance leads to improved shareholder value through stock price increases.

Figure 41. Environmental screening research exercises: a summary
Hart & Ahuja (1994) "Does it pay to be green?". Abstract: "Anecdotal evidence can be marshalled to support either the view that pollution abatement is a cost burden on firms and is detrimental to competitiveness or that reducing emissions increases efficiency and saves money, giving firms a cost advantage. This paper examines empirically the relationship between emissions reduction and firm performance for a sample of S&P 500 firms using data drawn from the IRRC Corporate Environmental profile and from Compustat. Results indicate that efforts to prevent pollution and reduce emissions drop to the "bottom line" (ROS, ROA, ROE) within 1 - 2 years of initiation and that those firms with the highest emission levels stand to gain the most.
Snyder & Collins (1993) "The performance impact of an environmental screen". Abstract: this paper reports results of the backtest of an environmental equity screen over 20 years. The screen leaves a sufficiently large universe of stocks for practitioners to build diversified portfolios, and the universe of "passing" stocks shows total returns slightly higher than the parent universe, with only slightly higher volatility.
Hamilton (1995) "Pollution as news: media and Stock Market Reactions to the Toxics Release Inventory Data". Abstract: "This study investigated whether pollution data released by the EPA in the June 1989 TRI were "news" to journalists and investors. The results indicate that the higher the pollution figures (such as air emissions or offsite shipments of toxic waste) were in a firm's TRI reports, the more likely print journalists were to write about the firm's toxic releases. Investors also found this information of interest, since nearly three quarters of the TRI pollution releases came from publicly held companies. Stockholders in firms reporting TRI pollution figures experienced negative, statistically significant abnormal returns upon the first release of the information. These abnormal returns translated into an average loss of $4.1 million in stock value to TRI firms on the day the pollution figures were first released."
Repetto (1996) "Diversification and the alleged costs of environmentally screened portfolios". Abstract: "Aside from the possibility that pollution-intensive industries might have differing betas, a portfolio that excluded or under-weighted stocks in these sectors should have the same expected returns as a portfolio that included them. There should be no "diversification risk" from limiting portfolio choices in such a way."
DiBartolomeo (1996) "Socially screened portfolios: an attribution analysis of relative performance". Abstract: "Equity portfolios whose selection of securities is subject to social responsibility screening represent different sets of economic opportunities from, and hence generally produce different returns from,. those of more broadly based market indices. This paper uses multi-factor models to demonstrate that these differences in return probably do not arise from the socially responsible behaviour of the included companies, but rather from economic and sector exposures which are the implicit result of social screens. It also demonstrates that the usage of such multi-factor models can reduce the difference in cumulative return between screened and unscreened index portfolios to almost nothing, also while meaningfully reducing the differences in month to month performance".

> **Diltz (1995) "Does social screening affect portfolio performance?"**. Abstract: "we find that social screening has little impact on portfolio returns. We view our results to be good news for investors who desire to invest in socially screened portfolios and for the portfolio managers who are required to apply social screens".

> **Johnson (1995) "An analysis of the relationship between corporate environmental and economic performance at the level of the firm"**. Abstract: "the study determines that superior environmental performance is related to superior economic performance only for certain types of environmental performance, and more particularly, certain types of environmental performance within certain industry sectors. On the other hand, in some cases, poorer environmental performance can be economically rewarded. For example, although oil spills negatively impact economic performance, poorer environmental performance (e.g. higher emissions) is actually consistent with better economic performance in the case of total toxic chemical emissions. These results suggest that the present US environmental regulatory system is not effective in creating consistent economic incentives for corporations to allocate resources towards the improvement of their economic performance, particularly with respect to toxic chemical emissions."

> **J S Toms (1996) "Enlightenment vs. self interest: financial performance Differentials of "ethically" managed companies"**. Abstract: A CSER (Community, Social and Environmental Responsibility) Index, which parallels a widely used measure in the USA, is applied to British companies, whose performances are compared by reference to differentials in accounting and investor appraisal measures. On both measures there are found to be significant associations between CSER and financial performance. There is tentative evidence to suggest that much of the enhanced profitability associated wit CSER is associated with marketing and superior profit margins. Other evidence suggests that an investor selecting high CSER company securities might achieve enhanced returns for no extra risk

K.   Conclusion

There seems little doubt that interest in "new" forms of investing will continue to grow. Whilst some investors will continue to be attracted to developing markets (Central and Eastern Europe, South America, China etc), many more will seek safer and more defensible homes for their savings. As ecological and social investment grows it will be joined by variants such as "the Tomorrow's Company" investment fund which is neither purely environmental nor purely ethical in nature but which seeks to identify "sustainable companies" and where non-financial data performance measures are regarded as indicators of long term business success.

A relatively small but growing section of the investment community is moving away from a quantifiable, bottom-line, earnings per share, gearing fixation and learning to demand and use non-financial measures. If this information is absent from the annual audited report to shareholders then the investors must seek the information elsewhere. As a result the value of the annual report itself could be downgraded and hence so will the value of the accountants contribution - other professionals will eagerly step forward to provide the information that accountants can't or don't want to reach.

The results reported above do not offer out the immediate hope that companies which have taken environmental initiatives are likely to reap any immediate economic rewards for their shareholders. The importance of the results lies in the almost unanimous findings that

(a)   pro-environment activities will not adversely affect share price and

(b)   that environmentally screened portfolios by and large achieve similar results to portfolios selected from the full universe of available stocks.

What the results seem to suggest is that improved environmental performance does not appear to act as a brake on either profitability or share price performance as compared with non (or less) environmentally conscious companies. Thus investors who make a deliberate choice to single out environmentally (or ethically) commendable companies will no longer have to feel that they are paying a financial penalty for doing so.

As a refutation of the argument that pro-environmental activities adversely affect bottom line performance, this is at least some positive ammunition for those who would wish to see companies generally improve their environmental performance.

SECTION V: SUMMARY AND CONCLUSIONS - HOW DO WE GET BEYOND THE CONVENTIONAL MODEL?

A.   Introduction

The conventional financial accounting model focuses primarily on the recognition, measurement and disclosure of assets, liabilities and provisions. To a lesser and somewhat unexplored extent, it also attempts to deal with risk issues, although reporting of risk is still at an early stage. The conventional model is directed towards supplying information to those requiring information for economic decision making purposes. Underlying that objective would seem to be a profit maximisation objective. But, as noted in Section IV, in the USA, nearly 10% of all investors either voluntarily impose social constraints on their investment activity or vote their proxies on the basis of formal policies embodying socially responsible goals.

Conventional investors and the new cadre of socially responsible investors would both appear to require environmental data in excess of that currently being delivered. The former (conventional investor) group would seem to need more data regarding the financial impact of potential environmental risks and the likely impact of corporate environmental strategies on future cash flow streams. The latter (socially responsible investor) group probably requires more data on environmental performance relative to other (potentially) acceptable investment opportunities.

B.   Recommendations for the annual report to shareholders

Accepting that all material environmental liabilities and contingent liabilities *are* recognised, *are* appropriately measured and *are* properly disclosed by the existing system, what sort of additional information could be delivered in the annual report to shareholders on a cost-effective basis? A wide range of suggestions has been identified in this paper. Possibilities include:

- a <u>separate environmental section</u> including a cross-reference to any separately published stand-alone corporate environmental report or separately available site reports
- the existence (and contents) of a <u>corporate environmental policy</u> (it is hard to believe that relevant companies - especially listed companies - do not have an environmental policy) and the extent to which such policy is applied on a standardised basis world-wide
- the <u>locus of responsibility</u> for environmental issues at Board level
- the extent of <u>compliance</u> with prevailing environmental legislation
- the <u>likely impact</u> of future environmental legislation - accepted but not yet enacted
- the extent to which the company is prepared to go <u>beyond compliance</u> (and its success in doing so)

- the existence (or otherwise) of a corporate commitment to have its environmental management systems certified to recognised international standards
- the current financial consequences of environmental compliance and corporate environmental strategy (e.g. compliance costs, other operating costs, fines/penalties paid, capital expenditures - if separately identifiable, environmental taxes/levies paid
- projected future environmentally directed expenditures
- the number of (significant?) complaints and the number of complaints upheld (quantified according to category of complaint), the number (and volume) of spillages
- financially quantified benefits flowing from pro-environmental activities: re-cycling revenues, taxes and levies avoided, operating cost savings achieved, insurance premiums reduced, new sales/contracts achieved/won
- industry relevant environmental performance indicators - preferably including eco-efficiency measures
- an external opinion on the credibility or otherwise of the environmental disclosures (whether in the annual report or a separate environmental report)and on the extent (if at all) to which the report is based on significant managerial assumptions

C. Recommendations for developmental future work in the area of annual report disclosures

The major issues to be resolved relating to the improvement disclosures of environmental data in the annual report and accounts would seem to be:

- agreeing **financial accounting definitions** in respect of environmental costs and revenues
- developing a widely accepted range of **standardised environmental performance indicators** suitable for external reporting purposes
- gaining acceptance for a **standardised format for external environmental reporting**: whether through the annual report to shareholders or through a stand alone performance report
- developing a **qualitative conceptual framework** to underpin corporate environmental reporting activity
- improving the credibility of corporate environmental reporting activities by **formalising the external attestation process**
- researching on an "events" basis the link between environmental performance and financial performance

D. Recommendations for stand-alone environmental performance reports

In stand alone environmental reports it seems that a number of innovations could be useful:

- clearer statements regarding the key environmental issues facing the reporting entity
- more use could be made of the sort of segmental reporting techniques used for consolidated financial reporting purposes
- a clear statement regarding the completeness of the environmental reporting should be made
- a statement of the number of contaminated sites, the current state of remediation at each

site and the likely timing and cost of future remediation procedures

— the provision of <u>industry relevant and industry accepted bench-marked environmental performance indicators (including experimentation with eco-efficiency indicators</u>

— the provision of <u>externally verified third party opinions based upon accepted and tested verification procedures</u> (though these may still be developing)

— increased experimentation with <u>development of sustainable development indicators</u>

E. Recommendations for the accounting profession

Responsibility for improving the quality of corporate environmental communications and establishing the financial / environmental transparency of organisations does not rest entirely with the accountancy profession. Nevertheless there are a range of developments where the accounting profession is probably better placed than other groups to launch initiatives. These include -

- press to have both disclosure and listing requirements in respect of environmental issues widened and strengthened: apply pressure at both IASC and IOSCO levels
- press for national auditing bodies to make explicit the environmental responsibilities of the external financial statement auditor - base on IAPC work
- focus on developing better measurement techniques to capture and report environmental benefits as opposed to only reporting costs
- develop environmental cost accounting case studies; present case studies at full company level rather than isolated instances of cost saving
- create a research focus on eco-efficiency methodologies
- review "boilerplate" nature of OFR/MD&A type disclosures and press companies to include more discussion of environmental risk and relative environmental performance in the annual report
- become more prescriptive concerning the non-financial issues to be presented in the narrative part of the accounting package
- encourage the development of environmental reporting across a wider range of companies and lobby to have such information externally verified
- explore how recognised accounting techniques - such as consolidated and segmental reporting - can be applied to environmental reporting issues
- conduct research into the long term returns earned by eco-efficient or ecologically friendly companies
- commission an internationally known research institute to carry out an annual survey of "the state of environmental investing"
- work with finance sector to identify eco-financial indicators on an industry by industry basis: form a high level steering group to produce "ISO" type standards on environmental performance disclosures
- green the accounting syllabus so as to integrate environmental issues and thinking into the everyday life of the accountant, in practice or in industry

PART II

RESOURCES

SECTION VI: *ILLUSTRATIVE EXAMPLES OF RECENT BEST PRACTICE IN ENVIRONMENTAL ACCOUNTING AND REPORTING*

This section contains a series of illustrative examples of recent "best practice" developments in environmental accounting, reporting and communications. The section is divided into the following sub-sections:

A. Environmental financial accounting and reporting

B. Environmental performance indicators

C. Environmental reporting and verification

D. Sectoral benchmarking

E. Other techniques:
  (1) environmental burden
  (2) sustainable cost calculations

F. Environmental reporting guidelines

A.   Environmental financial accounting and reporting

As discussed in the foregoing sections the conventional financial accounting and reporting framework has, until now, limited its recognition of environmental issues to those few mainstream matters that, usually because of their financial significance, demand both recognition and measurement alongside other, more familiar, non-environmental issues. Thus we would accept that issues such as:

- exceptional items
- information re impaired assets
- accounting policies regarding long-term de-commissioning or site restoration costs
- significant environmental liabilities and provisions
- material contingent liabilities
- environmentally derived risk data

all have their proper place in either the profit and loss account, the balance sheet or the MD&A/OFR discussion section.

Set out below, each with a short commentary paragraph are a series of illustrations taken from recent annual financial / environmental reports. The examples have been chosen either because they seem to exemplify current best practice within the conventional model, or because they are attempts (not always successful it should be noted) by the reporting entity to step outside the conventional model and provide more information than is traditional.

It should also be noted that even those companies producing interesting and novel examples of financial environmental data do not always explain WHY they are doing so! Often the information simply pops up in the corporate environmental report with no attempt to specify the user group towards whom the information is aimed. The Yorkshire Electricity financial analysis discussed earlier is an honourable exception to this rather depressing rule, since the company has taken a clear decision to set aside 2 or 3 pages or its annual environmental report and dedicate them to a financial stakeholder audience.

(Note: these "best practice" examples do not cover examples of non-financially-related reporting, thus no examples of pure environmental performance data are presented in this section.)

Environmental Financial Accounting/Reporting - Best Practice Examples

1.   Environmental financial accounting through the financial statements

---

Figure 42. The British Gas Plc Example (UK) Annual Report and Accounts 1995

Chief Executive's report
- cross reference to annual environmental report + tel. no.   P 18
  + very general comments

Financial Review
- "We have also re-appraised the level of remedial work requiredto clean up contaminated old gas manufacturing sites, whichhas necessitated an increase of £200m in the environmental provision set up in earlier years. the bulk of this provision relates to costs that are expected to be incurred as a result of the introduction of the Landfill Tax"   P 19

Principal Accounting Policies
- *"Land and buildings:* ....valuations take into accountestimated non-statutory decontamination costs"   P 34
- *"Abandonment costs:* provision is made for the estimated cost of well site restoration at the end of the producing lives of the fields, principally on a unit of production basis. The provision is calculated on proved reserves and price levels estimated at the balance sheet date. Changes in these estimates are dealt with prospectively"   P 35

Profit and Loss Account
- Turnover   £8,601 m
  Operating costs   (7,624) m
  Exceptional charges: environmental costs   (200) m   P 36

Notes to the Accounts
- *"Exceptional charges: environmental costs -*
  The 1995 results include a further provision of £200m for dealing with the Group's obligations with regard to contaminated old gas manufacturing sites. the bulk of this provision, estimated by the Group's surveyors, relates to costs that are expected to be incurred as a result of the introduction of the Landfill Tax. The further survey work, undertaken during 1995, coupled with theGroups increasing experience of remediation work undertaken to date, has also been taken into account. It should be noted that the survey work programme continues and that exact costs, nature and timing of the remediation work remains uncertain.In the future, changing environmental legislation will impact the final cost of remediation." (*)   P 46
- *Provisions for liabilities and charges: environmental costs*:
  B/fwd £233m + £200m P&L - 12m utilised = £421m in B/S   P 54

Comment: a good example of conventional financial accounting based environmental disclosures through the annual report. It is worth noting, however, that the comment regarding "changing environmental legislation" (*) did not appear in the financial review section

---

Figure 43. The British Petroleum Plc Example (UK)

The BP 1995 Annual Report and Accounts carried, as it has done regularly in recent years, a selection of environmental disclosures too lengthy to be repeated in full here. A summary of the disclosures is set out below:

- *Highlights inside front cover:* reduced emissions to air and water

- *"Business Operating Review"*: Health, Safety & Environment section

- *"Financial Review"*: Environmental expenditure section: -

Environmental expenditure	(£million)	
	1995	1994
Operating expenditure (*)	146	175
Capital expenditure (*)	160	230
Charge for environmental remediation	360	74
Charge for de-commissioning	62	42

(*) estimates because of difficulty of separate identification

Narrative explains accounting policies and reason behind high 1995 remediation charge.

- *Accounting Policies*: (1) de-commissioning provisions (2) environmental liabilities

Notes to the accounts:

- *Exceptional items*: include "refinery rationalisation costs" of £965 million of which £440 million represents environmental remediation and other costs.

- *Other provisions:* (1) de-commissioning (2) environmental (*)

  (*) B/fwd £383 m + £360 m (P&L) - £29m (utilised + £8m (exchange adj) = £722m all of which exclude the £440 charged as an exceptional item.

- Contingent liabilities: extensive note covering residual effects of Exxon Valdez disaster (1989) and reference to other ongoing environmental actions - none of which is expected to have a material effect on the group's financial operations

Comment: BP has always made fairly full disclosures of environmental costs and liabilities. It does come as a surprise, however, to disclose just how significant environmental costs can be - in 1995 ordinary charges to income plus exceptional charges amount to £800 million.

---

2.   Polluted land disclosures

Disclosures in this area are fairly rare at the best of times. The two examples selected below represent contrasting but nevertheless equally unsuccessful attempts to do justice to the topic of how to report on polluted or contaminated land in the corporate environmental report. In neither instance does the company make any attempt (in the environmental report at least) to financially quantify the potential cost of remediation. On reflection the British Gas example in Figure 43 above might be argued to provide a little more data - except that it too suffers from the problem of possible incompleteness (the "is that it?" feeling), not to mention the fact that taking a "big bath" and finally acknowledging all the potential losses is neither a systematic nor a sensitive way of accounting for potential environmental remediation liabilities.

Figure 44. The Novo Nordisk Example (Denmark

The 1995 Novo Nordisk Environmental Report, despite being a ground-breaking report in many ways (e.g eco-efficiency disclosures), contains few directly financial disclosures. The one exception - and even that is not stated in financial terms - is a schedule of "polluted sites in Denmark". The original disclosure contains details on 11 separate sites - the 3 replicated below are typical:

Site	Type of pollution	Registered/recorded in the Land Register as a waste dump?	Extent of pollution and remedial and control measures
8S, Laurentsvej 39, Bagsvaerd	Polluted by petroleum from former gasoline station	No	Seeped down to ground water level Clean-up to be paid for by the Danish Oil Industry Association for Remediation of Retail Sites has begun
4C Novo Alle Bagsvaerd	Polluted by acetone from own production	No	Seeped down to ground water Ongoing drainage of water from soil around tank pit and investigation of groundwater for acetone. Remedial pumping started 2nd quarter 1996.
FeF Chemicals Koege	Chemicals pollution from own production	Yes	Seeped down to groundwater level. Remedial pumping started

Comment: it is not immediately clear why Novo Nordisk makes such disclosures - unless it is forced to do so by the new (1996) "Act on Green Accounts". In other countries such disclosures would probably not be sanctioned by the corporate legal advisers for fear of offering up a hostage to fortune. As it is the disclosures are merely interesting: they do not cover countries other than Denmark (so perhaps there is some legal protection at work here), nor do the disclosures comment upon either (a) the likely costs of the clean-ups or (b) the likely time-scales involved, over which the clean-up costs would be spread. Sometimes more information is actually less!

Figure 45. The Monsanto Example (USA)

Bound by Superfund legislation in the USA Monsanto discloses the following in its 1995 Environmental Annual Review: named as a "potentially responsible party" at 92 sites in the USA - 8 at the preliminary phase (possible involvement only); 30 in the interim phase (necessary site studies or clean-up plans determined); 47 at the clean-up phase (active clean-up underway or funds provided to support clean-up); 7 where no further involvement with the site is anticipated.

Comment: rather like Novo Nordisk (see immediately above) Monsantos' disclosures in the environmental report tell only half (or perhaps only one third) of the story. the missing two thirds centres on (1) what is the situation elsewhere in the world where Monsanto has sites? and (2) what are the financial implications for Monsanto - both in the US and elsewhere? No doubt this information can be obtained by studying the small print of Monsantos US annual report but, in the absence of this data or a cross-reference to it, the section of the environmental report dealing with contaminated sites is very short on real meaning.

151

3. Long-term de-commissioning costs

Figure 46. WMC Resources Ltd (Australia)

WMC is a natural resource (minerals extraction) company based in Australia. Its first (1995) environmental report contained an excellent industry-relevant summary of the financial dimensions of its environmental activities:

Environmental Financial Reporting in WMC

Environmental expenditures fall into two categories:

– Current environmental protection and housekeeping
– Rehabilitation after production is completed

Current/continuous environmental protection and housekeeping costs are allocated to an environmental cost centre. Costs are incurred protecting native species, preserving habitat, and in education, training, communications, research, sampling, nursery plantations and general administration. Expenditure is also incurred in operating and maintaining equipment to control or contain emissions and spillages which would otherwise impact on the environment.

Rehabilitation is undertaken as production in a disturbed area is completed. During the area's productive life, costs for closing and removing equipment and foundations, digging up roads, contouring sites, rehabilitating soils, replanting/reseeding, monitoring sites etc are estimated. These estimates are progressively accounted for as part of production with a provision in the Balance Sheet. this approach ensures there is adequate provision in the accounts for rehabilitation by the time production ceases. While there is some rehabilitation expenditure during an area's productive life, most is incurred after closure.

WMC's environment accounting policy is under review and will be addressed more fully in future reports.

At 30 June 1995, WMC had accrued rehabilitation provisions of $105.8 million. the Company estimates that, as at 30 June 1995, the total rehabilitation costs that would be incurred upon the disposal or abandonment of its mineral and petroleum properties would be $244.5 million, resulting in a contingent liability of £138.7 million.

Comment: WMCs disclosures in its environmental report must be assumed to replicate and be consistent with disclosures made in its annual report. The disclosures are - in terms of the technical detail provided - well ahead of that supplied in most environmental reports (or even annual reports for that matter). There are still some "missing" disclosures, however, such as the accounting policy for distinguishing between capital and operating expenditures and discussion of the possibility of and financial impact of future legislative changes.

Figure 47. The Nuclear Electric Example (UK)

Nuclear liabilities and provisions as at 31 March 1996

	Total payable at 31.3.96		
	Undiscounted £bn.	Discounted £bn.	Provided to date £bn.
Spent fuel treatment and storage:			
AGR	4.4	2.8	1.8
PWR	0.3	0.1	0.0*
Total	4.7	2.9	1.8
Station decommissioning:			
AGR	2.7	0.5	0.5
PWR	0.3	0.1	0.1
Total	3.0	0.6	0.6
High level waste disposal:			
AGR	0.5	0.1	0.0
PWR	0.5	0.0*	0.0*
Total	1.0	0.1	0.0*
Intermediate level waste disposal:			
AGR	0.6	0.2	0.1
PWR	0.0*	0.0*	0.0*
Total	0.6	0.2	0.1
Share of de-commissioning of other facilities:			
AGR	0.6	0.2	0.2
PWR	-	-	-
Total	0.6	0.2	0.2
Total as at 31 March 1996	9.9	4.0	2.7

* Liabilities do exist for these categories, however, the amounts involved are not significant to £0.1bn.

Comment:
(1) the financial disclosures made by Nuclear Electric rank among the most technical made by any company, anywhere in the world, in a stand alone environmental report.
(2) It is worthwhile noting that the undiscounted amounts are stated at current prices and that the discount rate used is 3% per annum. There is also a cross-reference to the inclusion of such provisions in the financial statements, noting that it is the discounted amounts which are included in the accounts
(3) no explanation is given in the environmental report for the change from 31.3.95 to 31.3.96 - when the totals were £25.5 bn, £13.8 bn and £10.5 bn respectively.

---

4.   Internalisation of external costs

As noted above, one of the longest and most sophisticated discussions of financial issues in general, and external costs in particular, was found (perhaps unsurprisingly) in the environmental report of Nuclear Electric.

Figure 48. BSO Origin (The Netherlands)

The Dutch IT company BSO origin is notable for the "green accounts" included in the annual report itself. These green accounts attempted to place a price on the cost to society of cleaning up after BSO, and to compute a "net value added" by subtracting these externalities from the positive conventional "value added" extracted from the conventional financial statements.

BSO's net value added computation (extracts)

Impact category		Quantity	Unit cost	Total cost ('000 Dfl.)
Atmospheric emissions:				
natural gas	NOx	678 Kg	10 Dfl/kg	7
	C02	717t.	100 Dfl./T.	72
electricity				
road traffic	**for other detailed figures see BSO 1993 annual report**			
air traffic				
waste incineration				
Total				**3,502**
Waste:				
waste water	**for other detailed figures see BSO 1993 annual report**			
waste produced by company				
residual post incineration waste				
waste produced at power stations				
waste produced by water treatment				
Total				**206**

	Total cost		
Total costs of environmental effects	**3,708**	(1992:	3,555)
less: levies and other environmental taxes paid	**(452)**	(1992:	342)
Net value extracted	**3,256**	(1992:	3213)
Value Added (from P & L Account)	**456,334**	(1992:	411036)
Net Value Added	**453,078**	(1992:	407823)

Comment: BSO has been criticised because (a) of uncertainty over the accuracy of the damage unit costs and (b) it is not clear how the company uses the information once computed. Nevertheless as a model of how one might set about estimating a "green profit" it is a good start.

Figure 49. The Nuclear Electric Example - 2 (UK)

"If the "polluter pays" principle is to be applied fairly, it is necessary to quantify the environmental and health impacts of industrial activities and cost them. There has been a variety of studies of these "external costs" for electricity generation and estimates are presented in the adjacent table"

Table A: estimates of external costs for the main forms of UK electricity generation in p/kWh

	Old coal	New coal	Gas	Nuclear
Conventional air pollution	0.56	<0.23	0.03	neg
Global warming	0.48	0.41	0.19	0.01
Routine radiation	0.02	-	-	0.02
Disasters	?	?	?	0.02 - 0.27
Total	**1.06**	**0.64+**	**0.22+**	**0.05 - 0.30**

Inclusion of external costs, such as those associated with environmental damage or improvements, in prices charges for goods and services, is seen by the Government as an important part of the strategy for sustainable development. the fact that some forms of generation, such as nuclear power, do incorporate most of their environmental costs, and others, such as those involving the burning of fossil fuels, do not, currently distorts the electricity market. Table B uses these environmental costs to demonstrate the savings achieved during 1994/95 by the operation of Nuclear Electric's power stations. If the market is to play a positive role in protecting the environment, it must value these environmental benefits. On the basis of current estimates, this could be achieved by giving a credit for nuclear power or, alternatively, by imposing increased costs on fossil fuel generation through, for example, a carbon tax:

Table B: estimated external environmental costs saved by NEs operations 1994/95

	Av Unit damage costs (p/Kg)	Emissions saved by NE ops (mtonnes)	External Environmental cost saving £m
Sulphur Dioxide	22	0.54	120
Oxides of Nitrogen	19	0.17	31
Carbon Dioxide	1.4	13	182
Total saving			**£333m**

Comment: the debate on the internalisation of external costs centres on the twin problems of (1) obtaining adequate data on external costs and (2) affecting the existing structure of the marketplace. One may not agree with Nuclear Electric's arguments but the disclosure represents a graphic illustration of the issues involved.

The US EPA has recently (1996) published a lengthy case study "Full-cost accounting for decision-making at Ontario Hydro". The diagram below illustrates how Ontario Hydro are attempting to integrate full cost accounting into their internal decision making. The basis upon which externalities are costed has already been addressed in the two preceding examples and will not be covered again here. In the case of Nuclear Electric (see above) it would seem that a primary external use for them is propaganda. In the case of BSO Origin the application is difficult to determine. In the Ontario Hydro case (below) the company clearly has a range of applications in mind. It remains to be seen whether or not such techniques can have anything other than company specific applications however.

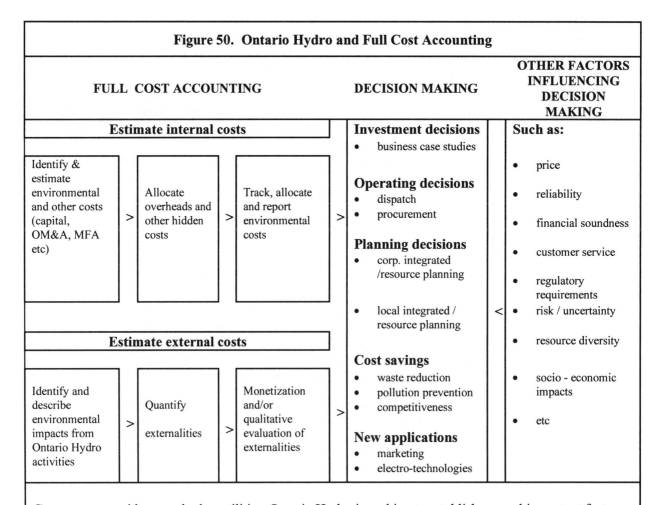

Figure 50. Ontario Hydro and Full Cost Accounting

FULL COST ACCOUNTING	DECISION MAKING	OTHER FACTORS INFLUENCING DECISION MAKING
Estimate internal costs	**Investment decisions** • business case studies	**Such as:**
Identify & estimate environmental and other costs (capital, OM&A, MFA etc) > Allocate overheads and other hidden costs > Track, allocate and report environmental costs >	**Operating decisions** • dispatch • procurement **Planning decisions** • corp. integrated /resource planning • local integrated / resource planning	• price • reliability • financial soundness • customer service • regulatory requirements < • risk / uncertainty • resource diversity
Estimate external costs	**Cost savings** • waste reduction • pollution prevention • competitiveness	• socio - economic impacts
Identify and describe environmental impacts from Ontario Hydro activities > Quantify externalities > Monetization and/or qualitative evaluation of externalities >	**New applications** • marketing • electro-technologies	• etc

Comment: as with several other utilities, Ontario Hydro is seeking to establish several important facts:

(1) is it possible to achieve any consistent or comparable estimates of external damage costs? research reported in the EPA case study suggest that estimates vary widely as between different fuel sources and different research subjects, and

(2) once estimates are available is it possible to use them, either for internal decision making purposes or for external reporting purposes?

5. Environmental costs breakdown

Some companies go to great lengths to provide details of the their environmental expenditures (see Baxter above and BC Hydro below), forgetting that in the financial reporting arena detailed cost breakdowns are hardly ever provided, the financial statements being primarily a set of (potentially) important sub-totals.

Figure 51. The BC Hydro Example (Canada)			
Statement of Environmental Expenditures **y/e March 31**	**1994** **C$**	**1993** **C$**	**1992** **C$**
Programmes and Initiatives			
Government, public and regulatory affairs	1,308	668	329
Project studies and co-ordination	4,256	2,463	3,083
Compensation programs	2,192	2,006	-
Management systems and plans	3,073	2,687	1,566
Electro-magnetic fields	527	343	329
	11,356	8,167	5,307
Air Quality			
Air emission reduction	150	322	n/a
Dust control	308	201	n/a
Thermal facility upgrade	1,701	-	n/a
	2,159	523	
Fish and Water Resources			
Fish protection and enhancement	565	209	n/a
Fish passage	1,637	2,648	n/a
Water quality	86	79	29
Programmes management	930	713	893
	3,218	3,639	922
Land and Wildlife			
Right of way maintenance	6,868	5,423	4,833
Land improvement	159	123	108
Pest management	456	453	n/a
Project administration	1,517	965	528
	9,000	6,964	5,469
Hazardous Materials & Waste Management			
Oil storage and containment	2,348	301	37
Contaminated sites	3.103	485	n/a
Hazardous goods storage	1,628	1,970	1,468
Waste monitoring and compliance	740	729	417
	7,819	3,385	1,922
Social Resources			
Beautification projects	1,289	484	320
Recreational sites	,650	1,829	1,108
Debris disposal	1,476	1,407	1,246
Security, safety and social issues	67	2	n/a
	5,482	3,722	2,674
Energy Management			
Conservation programs	1,631	880	547
Education programmes	101	102	134
	1,732	982	681
Total Expenditures for the Year	**$40,766**	**$27,392**	**$16,975**

n/a = data not available   **BC Hydro Report on the Environment 1994 P39**

Comment: allocating costs (whether capital or revenue in nature) between environmental and non-environmental categories seems to be popular at the theoretical level but harder to achieve in practice (see Nuclear Electric comment below). When it IS achieved, simple disclosure may, on its own, not be particularly useful . See also Yorkshire Electricity operating/capital expenditure split example (Figure 17) which, with the additional of annual trend patterns would be more useful but, but still would not tell much about the relationship between expenditure and environmental improvement.

Figure 52. The Nuclear Electric Example

"In theory, a company could report separately on all the costs associated with its environmental issues, from the resource used, the costs of environmental regulations, right down to how much is spent each year on environmental sponsorship. In practice, when we set out on this task, we found it difficult usefully to segregate environmental costs from the other costs of our business. We found that almost all our major activities and costs were related in some way to environmental protection and are already reported in our main accounts. Nevertheless, in response to the call for more financial information, this year for the first time we have included in the environmental report information on those of our costs most obviously related to environmental protection. "

Nuclear Electric Environmental Report 1994/95 P 12

6. **Other environmental disclosure (with financial reporting implications)**

Figure 53. WMC Environmental Corporate Governance Disclosures

Corporate Governance

Each month the Chief Executive Officer reports to the Board of Directors of WMC Ltd on environmental matters. A written report is circulated prior to the Board meeting. Updates on key developments are provided to the meeting.

Each quarter, the CEO submits a site-by-site review of environmental issues. The report includes "non-compliance" incidents, rectification programs (including target compliance dates and the officers responsible for the rectification activity) and progress on the implementation of the Environmental Management System. Full supporting documentation is provided to the Board, with a summary report to each Director. The Group Manager - Environment briefs the Board quarterly on significant developments.

The Chief Executive's quarterly report is compiles from compliance/non-compliance certificates prepared by each operation, reviewed and "signed-off" by the relevant line manager, and by the Corporate Environment department. The Board regularly visits sites to review operations.
WMC Resources Ltd: Environmental progress Report 1994-95 P 6

B.   Environmental performance indices

1.   "One- Stop" Environmental Performance Indicators

The possible range of individual environmental performance indicators was discussed in Section III. Despite - or perhaps because of - the views expressed by commentators (some for, some against) a number of companies have determined try to "wrap up" their environmental impact within a single statistic. The table immediately below identifies a number of such "one stop shop" examples (the list is not intended to be comprehensive - many of the indices are very similar). In the majority of cases the emissions or environmental issues taken into the index are selected because of their perceived importance or severity of environmental impact.

	Company	Sector	Index/EPI Description
	Figure 54. Composite environmental performance indicators		
1	Danish Steelworks (Denmark)	Steel-making **(Environmental declaration)**	Measures the net environmental impact of 1 tonne of steel, on a year to year comparative basis
2	Novo- Nordisk (Denmark)	Pharmaceuticals **("Eco-Productivity" Index -EPI)**	Separate indices for: raw materials, water, energy, packaging (*see example below*)
3	Rhone-Poulenc (France)	Chemicals **(RP Environmental indices)**	Calculated separately for water, air and waste (*see worked example below*)
4	Roche (Switzerland)	Pharmaceuticals **(Eco-efficiency rate)**	A ratio resulting from the comparison of: (i) sales per million Swiss Francs spent on environmental protection and (ii) a measure of environmental damage based on the sum of various "weighted pollutants"
5	Nortel (Canada)	Telecommunications **(Environmental Performance Index)**	Has 4 main categories: regulatory compliance, environmental releases, resource consumption and contaminated site remediation (25 separate parameters in all). Categories are weighted on the basis of: impact, financial and other risks, Controllability, adequacy as an environmental performance indicator. 1993 baseline = 100. Progress is upwards (1994 ,143 was OK but below target figure of 175). Detailed calculations not provided.

2.   Novo Nordisk (Denmark) - the "Eco-productivity index" (EPI)

According to Novo Nordisk their EPI "is our indicator of a trend towards more sustainable production. The index shows how much production has increased relative to consumption of a particular resource e.g. water. The higher the EPI, the better we are at utilizing our resources. Three of the 22 targets for 1994 were related to the EPI, but primarily due to the running-in of new plants we managed to achieve only one EPI target. The EPIs for 1993 have been revised due to a change in accounting principles"

	Figure 55 (1). The Novo Nordisk ECO-PRODUCTIVITY INDEX			
	REPORTED	**REVISED**	**TARGET**	**ACTUAL**
	1993	**1993**	**1994**	**1994**
Raw materials	119	122	126	123
Water	131	135	140	135
Energy	133	134	139	145

Novo Nordisk use their EPI to monitor year on year performance against previously set targets. The detailed explanation of the Novo Nordisk index system is provided in the glossary of terms at the end of their annual environmental performance report:

Figure 55 (2). The Novo Nordisk eco-productivity index: a detailed explanation

The EPI is calculated by dividing the amount of product sold by the inputs consumed - raw materials, water, energy and packaging materials - using 1990 as the baseline. The EPI goes up if we are able to produce more per unit of input. As a measure of the amount of product sold, we use turnover corrected for changes in currencies and prices For raw materials the index is calculated as follows:

		1990	**1991**	**1992**	**1993**	**1994**
A	Corrected t/over for enzyme. business- vol/mix		22%	21%	12%	14%
B	Corrected turnover index	100	122	148	165	188
C	Raw materials (1000 metric tons)	159	169	187	214	244
D	Raw materials index	100	106	118	135	153
E	Eco-productivity index = B x 100/D	100	115	125	122	123

Commentary: the Novo Nordisk eco-productivity indices appear relatively straightforward and could be combined into a single index figure should the company so wish. Although there is no direct financial input to the calculations it should theoretically be possible to map financial performance as reported in the P&L account against the various eco-productivity indicators.

3.   **Rhone Poulenc (France - chemicals)**

Figure 56 (1). Rhone Poulenc - the environmental performance index

Type of pollution	Co-efficient	RP publishes environmental
Water Chemical oxygen demand (COD) Inhibiting materials Materials in suspensions Nitrogen Phosphorus Soluble salts	1 15 0.3 1 0.5 0.001	indices for water, air and solid waste. Each index is based on six parameters, each corresponding to a type of pollution weighted by a specific co-efficient (see table 1). These co-efficients represent the Group's priorities. For example, priority is given to eliminating toxic elements in water, so toxic discharges carry 15 times the weight that is attributed to organic

Air Nitrogen oxide Nitrogen protoxide Volatile organic compounds Sulphuric acid Halogenated hydroxides Particles	5 0.5 5 3 1 2	matter (represented by COD). In each index, pollution discharged during the year (GEP) is measured by the sum of the quantities of the various pollutants, weighted by the corresponding co-efficients. Each yearly index shows the change in relation to the previous year, with a base of 100.
Solid waste *Landfill waste* Special industrial waste Ordinary industrial waste Inert organic waste *Incinerated waste* Incinerated halogenated waste (external) Incinerated non-halogenated waste (external) Incineration in Group facilities (internal)	 10 2 0.1 5 1 0.5	The results are not adjusted for variations in the volume of business. Changes in parameters are integrated by modifying the GEP for both the current and preceding years. The choice of pollutants used in the RP environment index is based upon the CEFIC defined standard format for gross pollution figures. **An example of the full calculation of the 1993 Rhone Poulenc Environment index is shown below:**

Figure 56 (2). Details of 1993 Rhone Poulenc Environmental Index Calculation

WATER	Emissions 93	AIR (*)	Emissions 93	WASTES (*)	Emission 93
COD SS NTK IM P Salts	1 x 42366 0.3 x 17880 1 x 7063 15 x 1469 0.5 x 1642 0.001 x 1080228	NOx N2O VOC SOx HX PART	5 x 9221 0.5 x 45360 5 x 8069 3 x 13405 2 x 441 2 x 1874	*Landfill:* special ordinary inert *Incinerated:* internal + ext. halogenated external non- halogenated	10 x 31044 2 x 77533 0.1 346689 0.5 x 275882 5 x 9559 1 x 36902
GEP 93	78729	**GEP 93**	153975	**GEP 93**	722813
Reminder GEP 92	 90631	Reminder GEP 92	 169672	Reminder GEP 92	 720468
Index 93	**87**	**Index 93**	**90**	**Index 93**	**100**

(*) the figures indicated for the calculation of the air and waste indices only concern the French facilities

Commentary:. RP has made its own selection of priority targets across the three emission routes. A problem of this approach is that each company will probably choose a different set of emissions and there is no guarantee that similar weightings will be given to similar emissions by differing companies. Under the RP approach it is even possible that different sites within the same company may choose different index components and weightings.

C. Environmental reporting and verification

Since this UN study was commissioned, a number of other studies have been published which focus upon the role of third party attestation of corporate environmental reports. These include:

(i)   the IRRC study
(ii)   the FEE study
(iii)   the SustainAbility / UNEP study

The "verification" studies summarized:

Figure 57. The role of 3rd party attestation statements	

The IRRC Study
 	
"Environmental Reporting and Third Party Statements"
 	
Investor Responsibility Research Centre 1996
 	
Conclusions:
	• None of the stakeholder groups participating in the study believed that recent third party statements added much, if any, incremental value to corporate environmental reports published in 1994
	• The conclusion of the participants was that without agreed standards of reporting, the third party statements are "meaningless"
	• In order to add substantively to the credibility of environmental reports at least three new attestation elements must be incorporated into 3rd party attestation statements:
	  (i) a statement that all major risks are included in the report
	  (ii) recommendations on performance improvements
	  (iii) a prioritization of outstanding environmental challenges facing the company

The FEE Study **"FEE Research Paper on Expert Statements in Environmental Reports"** **Federation des Experts Comptables Europeen 1996** **Conclusions on expert statements generally:**	• In the absence of generally accepted guidelines on how to perform an audit of an environmental report or how to report, the (expert) statement should include a description of the scope of the audit/audit objectives. A description of the nature of the audit procedures performed should be given to support the level of assurance that can be given • The conclusions in the expert statement must be carefully stated, particularly if the scope of the engagement is limited. Experts should reconsider their use of "true and fair" and similar phrases which may result in unreasonable expectations
The SustainAbility / UNEP Study **"Engaging Stakeholders - 2 The Case Studies"** **SustainAbility / UNEP 1996**	• Increasing requirement for environmental reports to be independently verified - particularly in countries where environmental reporting legislation is being introduced or where stock exchange listing requirements are starting to embrace environmental issues and disclosures

D. Sector specific questions asked by analysts using environmental screens

Nearly all the stakeholder groups responding to the SustainAbility / UNEP (1996) study "Engaging Stakeholders" reported that enhanced comparability and sectoral benchmarking of environmental performance was very high on their list of priorities.

Set out below are a series of sector specific questions which form the basis for the "best in class" analysis of potential investment opportunities by the UK NPI Global Care Fund research department. The questions represent those issues which the stakeholder considers *most* important to the industry in question.

Figure 58. The NPI "Best in Class" sectoral questionnaire	
Retail banks	
1. what steps have you taken to minimise the direct environmental impacts of the bank's activities? (energy conservation, waste paper recycling etc)	2. lending policy: (a) has the bank signed the UN Statement on banking and the Environment? (b) Do you have procedures to avoid lending to business causing significant environmental damage?
Building and construction	
1. what instructions are staff given on disposing of waste? Do you have targets to minimise or recycle waste?	2. what measures have you taken to ensure that all new and redeveloped buildings are designed for maximum conservation of energy and water?
Building materials and merchants	
1. what is your policy on selection of raw materials and environmental performance of suppliers?	2. what targets have you set for energy efficiency and air emissions (manufacturing and transport)?
Chemicals	
1. are environmental factors taken into account early in planning new products to reduce environmental effects throughout their lifetime (production, use and disposal)?	2. do you produce audited reports of hazardous emissions to air, water and waste to landfill which are available to the public, or do you intend to in the future?
Distributors	
1. what measures do you take to reduce energy use and in particular energy used for transport?	2. do you ask your suppliers for details of their environmental policies for production of their products print to marketing and distribution?
Engineering	
1. are environmental factors taken into account early in planning new products to reduce environmental impacts throughout their lifetimes (production, use, re-use and disposal)?	2. have you set targets for waste minimisation, particularly for hazardous waste?
Food producers	
1. what measures do you take to treat high BOD - effluents / wastes?	2. what is your policy on selection of raw ingredients (e.g. source and production) and environmental performance of suppliers?
Health care	
1. what procedures do you have to dispose of clinical and / or other hazardous wastes? 2. do you operate any targets, schemes or procedures to ensure that energy usage is reduced?	3. (nursing homes only). what initiatives do you take to enhance the quality of life for residents?

Household goods	
1. what is your policy on selection of raw materials and environmental performance of suppliers?	2. in what ways is your packaging designed to facilitate recycling, re-use or recovery?

Leisure and hotels	
1. how do you ensure that new developments / investments have no adverse effect on the (local) environment? are there different procedures for developing countries?	2. do you have targets / schemes to reduce energy, water use and minimise waste to landfill at your operational and office sites?

Paper, packaging and printing	
1. what environmental criteria do you use in the selection or production of paper, plastics and other raw materials? 2. In what ways are your products designed or labelled to ensure easy recycling?	3. what is your policy on potential health impacts arising from dioxins / phosphates/ oestrogenic compounds?

Pharmaceuticals	
1. what targets have you set to reduce emissions of hazardous waste? what procedures govern waste disposal? 2. do you produce a regular report on your emissions to air, water and wastes or do you intend to in the future?	3. what is your policy on animal testing? what steps have you taken to reduce animal testing?

Property	
1. what measures so you take to ensure adequate remediation prior to development of a new site?	2. when selecting and developing sites, what standards are set for (a) site section (brownfield, near to transport) and (b) building environmental efficiency (energy, water, waste)?

Retailers, general	
1. have you any initiatives to reduce energy use in (a) retail premises and (b) your distribution fleet? 2. what measures have you taken to reduce packaging waste and set up facilities for recycling in anticipation of the incoming packaging legislation?	3. when sourcing from developing countries (or from companies with facilities in such areas) what specifications do you have for overseas workers conditions? How do you ensure these are adhered to?

Textiles and apparel	
1. at your manufacturing sites, what measures have you taken to reduce effluents and set targets? 2. what is your policy on selection of raw materials and environmental performance of suppliers?	3. what is your policy on overseas workers conditions, in your own production facilities or those of your suppliers?

Transport	
1. what targets does your company set to reduce energy use, both in buildings and for transport? 2. what measures do you take to reduce noise and other disturbance to local communities?	3. does your company have a strategy on the long-term effects and organisation of transport in the UK?

Sectoral comparisons

Developing the approach set out in the above table, the analyst then compares the environmental data drawn from different sources to arrive at the "best in class" ranking:

Figure 59. Intercompany comparison (banking sector)						
Company	Env Policy?	Annual report?	Board response	EMS	Env rating	Ethical issue?
HBSC	Y good	Y	N	N	6	-
Barclays	Y good	Y	Y	N	3	-
NatWest	T ex	N	Y	Y	1	-
Lloyds TSB	Y av	Y	Y	N	4	-
Abbey National	N	N	Y	N	7	-
Standard Chartered	N	N	N	N	8	-
Royal Bank of Scotland	Y ex	Y	Y	N	2	-
Bank of Scotland	Y av	Y	Y	N	5	-

E.   Other techniques

1.   The Environmental Burden ("Classification Method") in more detail

The advantage of the approach to environmental performance measurement is that it appears to be a scientifically more acceptable version of the firm specific index approach described above in 6.2. The categories of environmental impact and the decisions concerning relative toxicities are derived from external debate and would be publicly available - thus enabling the development of an industry sector benchmark. The disadvantage appears to be that EBs for different environmental impact categories cannot be aggregated - this deprives the stakeholder of the much desired "single figure measure" of environmental performance - as a result it may also leave the stakeholder unclear as to how the reporting entity makes strategic choices between different categories when deciding on reduction targets.

The "Environmental Burden" approach recently announced by ICI is based upon the "Classification Method" described in the EFFAS report and is summarised in the form of a case study in Figure 53 below. ICI has announced that it intends to apply this new EB approach and extend its use in the future. Whether or not this approach has the potential for a scientifically acceptable chemical industry environmental performance benchmark remains uncertain - although the methodology would seem to be capable of widespread application. It does appear that Du Pont is also using a version.

Figure 60. Case Study: the ICI "Environmental Burden" approach to measuring environmental performance

Rather than simply focusing on the absolute nature of emissions, ICIs EB approach seeks to provide a way of ranking the potential environmental impact of various emissions. In doing so ICI believe that they will

- get a more meaningful picture of the potential impact of their emissions (as compared with the customary practice of merely reporting the weights of substances discharged;
- be able to identify the most harmful emissions and reduce these first;
- give the public a better understanding of the potential problems associated with emissions, as well as showing how ICI is continuing to reduce the potential impact of its wastes.

The EB approach involves three main steps:

Step 1: identify a set of recognised global environmental impact categories upon which its various emissions to air and water may exert an influence. The impact categories identified by ICI are: Acidity, Global warming, Human health effects, Ozone depletion, Photochemical ozone (smog) creation, Aquatic oxygen demand and Eco-toxicity to aquatic life

Step 2: a factor is assigned to each individual emission which reflects the potency of its possible impact (these factors are derived from the recognised scientific literature)

Step 3: a formula, based on the weight of each substance used multiplied by its potency factor, is applied in order to calculate the EB of the emissions against each environmental category

---

ICI also identify a number of other important factors concerning the EB approach:

- individual chemicals can be assigned to more than one environmental impact category
- each chemical has a specific potency factor for each category and these factors can differ
- each category has its own characteristics and units of measurement
- burdens for each category cannot be added together to give a total EB - it is not appropriate since they are as different as "chalk and cheese"
- EB assumes that all individual operations comply with local regulations
- EB does not address local issues such as noise and odour

The ICI "Environmental Burden" - a worked example

Environmental impact category = *atmospheric acidification*

1. Record the weight of each single substance emission which has the potential to impact on atmospheric acidification. In this case, the total weight is 32 tonnes.
2. Ascribe a potency factor (PF) to each emission:

	Weight	PF
Amonia	20	1.88
Hydrogen chloride	3	0.88
Nitrogen dioxide	3	0.70
Sulphur dioxide	5	1.00

(note: in each case, one substance is designated as the "baseline" or standard for each environmental impact category and is given a PF of ONE (1). In this example sulphur dioxide is the reference substance, so the units of the calculated burden are tonnes SO2 equivalent)

3. The EB = W x PF formula is applied to each substance and then aggregated to obtain the EB for atmospheric acidification:

	Weight x	PF =	
Amonia	20	1.88	37.60
Hydrogen chloride	3	0.88	2.64
Nitrogen dioxide	3	0.70	2.80
Sulphur dioxide	5	1.00	5.00
	32 tonnes or		48.04 units SO2 equivalent

4. The EB will change if the mix of substances emitted changes, even though the overall tonnage remains the same

ICI state that their intention is to use the EB approach to frame its emissions reduction strategy for the future. As a first step ICI says it will half its EB in four of the environmental impact categories (ecotoxicity, aquatic oxygen demand, acidity to air and water and potentially hazardous emissions (carcinogens) to air, by the end of year 2000, the baseline year being 1995. The results will be published in the annual group Safety, Health and Environment report.

2. Sustainable cost calculations - moving away from unsustainability?

In this section sustainable cost calculations are discussed. These will be necessary to account (in the literal sense) for realistic attempts to move away from unsustainable modes of operation.

Although not immediately directly relevant to the financial institution user, techniques such as full-cost accounting take us "beyond the conventional accounting model". Set out below is a schematic view of how accounting can respond to the sustainability issue both from within the conventional model and - by virtue of developing new and innovative techniques - from beyond it

---

Figure 61. Roles of accounting in the pursuit of sustainability

Improvement within current economic orthodoxy (reducing unsustainability/weak sustainability

ECO-EFFICIENCY ISSUES	ECO-JUSTICE ISSUES
• **EMAS accounting - for wastes, efficiency, energy, pollution etc ("Pollution Prevention Pays")** • **Reworking investment appraisal methods** • **Contingent liabilities, asset revaluations and other financial reporting issues** • **Tellus Institute methodology** • **Basic environmental reporting**	• **Employee and employment reporting, information for collective bargaining** • **Value-added statements** • **Bilan Social** • **Community reporting** • **Stakeholder analysis**

Recognition of the demands of sustainability (strong sustainability)

ECO-EFFICIENCY ISSUES	ECO-JUSTICE ISSUES
• **Sustainable cost calculation and reporting** • **Full cost accounting (EU's 5th Action Programme)** • **Advanced environmental and sustainability reporting (including Life Cycle Assessment and okobilanz** • **Accountability and transparency**	• **Full social reporting and social book-keeping systems** • **External social audits** • **Transparency on transfer pricing and resource acquisition issues** • **Accountability and transparency**

Source: from "Business Conceptions of Sustainability and the implications for accountancy" (Bebbington & Thomson, ACCA 1996)

An example of a sustainable cost calculation

On of the major obstacles seen to be preventing companies moving towards more sustainable methods of operating is the level of costs involved. the costs involve higher input costs, increased capital expenditure, increased remediation costs. Coupled with all that is the very real threat that such costs may not be able to be passed on to the customer because of the level of competitiveness in the market place for the goods in question. Bebbington and Thomson also present a brief overview of a so-called "sustainable cost calculation". Such a calculation would attempt to quantify the additional annual costs which it would be borne by an organisation if it were to remedy any environmental damage it created in the course of a year.

Figure 62. Stages in costing Environmental Sustainability			
------------------------>	------------------------>	------------------------>	--------------------->
(a) Present position	**(b) Most sustainable option currently available**	**(c) Zero environmental impact**	**(d) Past damage remedied**
Unsustainable operation	**More sustainable operations**		**Fully sustainable operations**

Notes:

(a)   is the present unsustainable position where many environmental impacts arising from the production of inputs to the organisation are not included in the input costs

(b)   is the most sustainable position which is currently attainable which imputes the cost of the most environmentally sound products and services that are available from the market. It is expected that those goods and services would cost more than those under (a) because some environmental externalities have been internalised in their production and are subsequently reflected in their financial cost

(c)   is a position where present operations would have a zero environmental impact in the current period. This requires two more cost elements to be calculated, which are:

    (i)   the additional costs required to ensure that inputs to the organisation have no adverse environmental impacts in their production. These are costs which arise in addition to those costs already internalised in the most environmentally sound products and services which are currently available; and

    (ii)   the costs required to remedy any environmental impacts that arise from an organisation's operations which would still arise even if the organisation's inputs had a zero environmental impact. For example, even if the generation of electricity has a zero environmental impact there may still be an environmental impact from an organisation's use of that electricity. This environmental impact would need to be remedied in the current period for the organisation to have a zero environmental impact.

(d)   is a fully sustainable position where an organisation has no adverse environmental impacts during the current period and has also remedied any adverse environmental effects arising from past operations.

The sustainable cost calculation is envisaged to take into account items (a) to (c)
.

Source: Bebbington & Thomson, ACCA 1996

Through the development of techniques such as Life Cycle Analysis companies are seeking to understand better the overall environmental impact or their operations. Techniques such as Design for Environment and Re-Use and Recycling are intended to move the business towards a more sustainable mode of operation. But if the picture in Figure 63 above is merely a reasonable approximation of what sustainability might mean in practice then there is little doubt that few (if any) organisations are even beginning to approach stage (b), let alone stage (c).

F.   Environmental reporting guidelines - environmental reporting through the annual report - a core framework

Element of the annual reporting package	European Fed'n of Fin Analysts Societies (EFFAS)(1996)	Swiss Bankers Association (SBA) (1997)	UK Advisory Committee on Bus. & Env'ment (ACBE) (1997)	UK 100 Group of Finance Directors (1992)	UN ISAR (1989)	EC 4th Co. Law Directive / EC Acc. Advisory Forum (1996)
Environmental Report	• scope and method of consolidation - what is excluded? • Content of env. policy & targets? • X-ref to other env. Report • env. Data collection system / group & local levels? • Discussion of main env. Issues & challenges • details as to extent of world-wide compliance - costs to reach full compliance • Signatory to ICC SD Charter? • Adequacy of env. Insurance cover • Legal actions pending • Environmental audit details	Physical / p'duction related data: • Energy use • CO2 & equivs. • CFC-11 & equivs • NOx emissions • SO2 emissions • VOC emissions • Waste (inc. special waste) • Sector specific data (e.g. noise in the airline industry) Management Information: • Strategy - 3 most important issues for next 5 - 10 years • EMS certification details • Commun'tion strategy steps (being) taken to improve eco-efficiency	• key impact areas & issues & company response • summary data of a non-financial data (physical & technical) • benchmarkable data • env policy & m'ment • monitoring systems & controls • improvements in key areas • fines & prosecutions • progress on implementing changes req'd by fut. legal req'ments • X-ref to other env. report(s) • Directors responsibility statement • independent review (voluntary)	• environmental impacts and risks of the business • environmental targets and priorities (segmentalised by business / country of operation) • environmental policy & guiding principles • implementation details • organisational responsibilities • monitoring procedures	• key impact areas targets and perf. relative to the targets • env. policy & programmes • improvements in key areas	• X-ref to other environmental information provided • policy improvements in key areas • government incentives • progress on implementing changes req'd by fut. legal req'ments

	(EFFAS)(1996)	(SBA) (1997)	(ACBE) (1997)	UK 100 Group (1992)	UN ISAR (1989)	EC AA Forum (1996)
Operating and Financial Review / MD&A		(see man'ment data above)	• descriptive / quantitative desc. of env. risks faced • env. costs incurred • initiatives taken • link to £'s charged or provided in accounts			• where relevant to fin.position, description of issues & the entity's response
Profit & Loss Account (& related notes)	• energy costs • waste costs disposal and treatment • env. Protect. & safety costs • remediation, abatement & clean-up costs • costs of env. impact reduction • other costs: e.g. training & communication & staff • dep. of env. assets • env. Savings	• energy costs • raw mats: renewable & non-renewable • waste disposal costs • dep. of env. Investments • exceptional charges • quality assurance costs	• env. expenses	• exceptional items	• env. operating expenditures split between: - liquid eff t'ment - waste gas & air - solid waste - monitoring - remediation - recycling	required: • extraordinary env'mental items recommended: • env. expenses charged to P&L on a segmental basis • fines & penalties for non-compliance, compensation costs
Balance Sheet (& related notes)	• provisions for env. Liabilities • contingent liabilities	• provisions for env. liabilities	• provisions for environmental liabilities and risks • contingent liabilities • prov. for LT de-com costs • env. costs capitalised • recovery offsets • asset impairments & provisions for repairs	• provisions • contingent liabilities	• liabilities, provisions & reserves • contingent liabilities • env. capital expenditures - dep. period - write offs	required: • "other" provisions separately disclosed if material • contingent liabilities recommended: • env.expenses capitalised

	(EFFAS)(1996)	S(SBA) (1997)	(ACBE) (1997)	UK 100 Group (1992)	UN ISAR (1989)	EC AA Forum (1996)
Accounting policies	• valuation / measurement methods		• valuation methods • accounting policies generally		• liabilities & provisions • catastrophe reserves • contingent liabilities	• valuation methods
Cash flow statement	• env. Capital expenditure					
Other				• high level commitment in CEOs report		

BIBLIOGRAPHY

The bibliography is divided into two parts:

Part 1:   **general reference sources (textbooks, research reports, refereed research papers, legislation etc)**

Part 2:   **corporate annual or environmental reports**

Part 1 General reference sources

Where appropriate - i.e. when the organisation concerned is normally known by its acronym (e.g. ACCA, IRRC, UNCTAD etc - acronyms have been used as first choice throughout, followed by the expanded proper name of the responsible organisation)

ACBE (UK Government's Advisory Committee on Business and the Environment) *"Environmental Reporting: An Approach to Good Practice"* (ACBE 1997)

ACCA (Association of Chartered Certified Accountants)
(1) *"Business conceptions of sustainability and the implications for accountancy"* (ACCA Research Report 48, Bebbington J & Thomson I - 1996)
(2) *" Environmental performance indicators"* (ACCA Research Report forthcoming, James P and Bennett M 1998)

Bartolomeo, Matteo *"Environmental Performance Indicators in Industry"* (FEEM Working Paper 41.95 - 1995)

Beattie V & Jones M *"The Communication of Information Using Graphs in Corporate Annual Reports"* , ACCA Research Report 31, London 1992).

Bebbington J & Thomson I - see under ACCA

Bennett M & James P *"Financial dimensions of environmental performance: developments in environment-related management accounting"* (unpublished conference paper 1996)

BiE (Business in the Environment)
(1) and Extel Financial *"City Analysts and the Environment: a survey of environmental attitudes in the City of London"* (BiE 1994)
(2) and AEA Technology *"The Index of Corporate Environmental Engagement: a survey of the FTSE 100 companies"* (BiE 1996)

BT (British Telecommunications) *"Environmental Accounting in Industry: a practical review"* (BT1996)

Canadian Institute of Chartered Accountants *"Reporting on Environmental Performance"*

Company Reporting Ltd.
  (1) *"Company Reporting Frontiers: non-financial performance and revenue investment measures in company annual reports"* (Company Reporting 1992)
  (2) *"Corporate Environmental Reporting in the UK"* (Company Reporting 1996)

CSFI (Centre for the Study of Financial Innovation)
  (1) *"Rating Environmental Risk"* by David Lascelles (CSFI 1993
  (2) *"An Environmental Risk Rating for Scottish Nuclear"* (CSFI 1995)

diBartolomeo D *"Explaining and controlling the returns on socially screened US portfolios"* (unpublished conference paper 1996)

Diltz JD *"Does social screening affect portfolio performance?"* (The Journal of Investing, Spring 1995 P64 - 69)

Ditz JD & Ranganathan J *"Measuring Up: Towards a Common Framework for Tracking Corporate Environmental Performance"* (World Resources Institute 1997)

ECAFF (EC Accounting Advisory Forum) "Environmental Issues in Financial Reporting" (DG XV. 6004/94)

EFFAS (European Federation of Financial Analysts' Societies) *" Eco-Efficiency and financial analysis: the financial analyst's views"* (EFFAS 1996)

EPA (Environmental Protection Agency - USA)
  (1) *"An Introduction to Environmental Accounting as a Business Tool: key   concepts and terms"* (EPA 1995 - also ACCA 1996 reprint)
  (2) *"Full Cost Accounting for Decision making at Ontario Hydro"* (EPA Environmental Accounting Case Study 1996)

Friends Provident *"Ethical Investment for Superannuation Funds"* (Conference presentation materials 1996)

Grayshott Corporate Finance *"Safety and Environmental Risk Management Rating (SERM)"* 1996 (unpublished)

Hamilton JT *"Pollution as News: media and stock market reactions to the toxics release inventory data"* (Journal of Environmental Economics and Management, 28, 98 - 113 (1995)

Hart SL & Ahuja G *"Does it pay to be green? An empirical examination of the relationship between pollution prevention and firm performance"* (Michigan Bus. School Research Paper 1994)

Hilton A *"A risky business for our favourite retailers"* (London Evening Standard February 20, 1997

IBE (Institute of Business Ethics) *"Benefiting Business & the Environment"* (London, 1994)

ICI Plc *"Environmental Burden: the ICI approach"* (ICI 1997)

INEM (International Network for Environmental Management) *"Case Studies in Environmental Management"* (Germany, 1996)

IRRC (Investor Responsibility Research Center)
  (1) *"Environmental Reporting and Third Party Statements"* (IRRC 1996)
  (2) *"Corporate Environmental Profiles Directory 1996: Executive Summary"* (IRRC 1996)
  (3) *"Environmental and Financial Performance: Are They Related?"* (Cohen MA, Fenn SA, & Naimon JS, IRRC 1996)

ISO (International Standards Organisation) *"Environmental Management - Environmental Performance Evaluation - Guideline"* (ISO /WD 14031.5 - working draft, forthcoming 1997)

James P & Bennett M
  (1) *"Environment-related performance measurement in business: from emissions to profit and sustainability?"* (Ashridge Management Centre AMRG 946)
  (2) see ACCA - forthcoming 1998

Johnson SD *"An analysis of the relationship between corporate environmental and economic performance at the level of the firm"* (abstract of doctoral dissertation; unpublished 1995)

Jupiter Asset Management Ltd *"The Assessment Process for Green Investment"* (1995)

Kleinwort Benson Investment Management *"Tomorrow's Company - The Investment Opportunity"* (fund press launch material - 1996)

KPMG Bohlins *"International Survey of Environmental Reporting"* (KPMG 1997)

NPI (National Provident Institution) *"Global Care Best in Class"* May 1996 (unpublished)

100 Group of Finance Directors *"Statement of Good Practice: Environmental Reporting in Annual Reports"* (Hundred Group, London 1992)

Repetto R (World Resources Institute) *"Diversification and the alleged cost of environmentally screened portfolios"* (unpublished discussion draft 1996)

Snyder JV & Collins CH *"The Performance Impact of an Environmental Screen"* (Winslow Management Company 1995)

Sparkes R *"The Ethical Investor: how to make money work for society and the environment as well as yourself)"* (Harper Collins 1995)

Sunday Times (UK) *"Creating value: the best and the worst"* (Sunday Times December 8, 1996 Business 2, P 4 -5)

SustainAbility/UNEP (see under UNEP)

Swiss Bankers Association " Draft discussion paper regarding the voluntary disclosure of environmental information" (SBA 1997)

Swiss Info Center *"Focus on Nestle: an economic, environmental and social analysis"* (1994)

Toms J S *"Enlightenment vs Self Interest: Financial Performance Differentials of "ethically" Managed Companies"* (University of Nottingham Discussion paper 1996.IX 1996)

UNCTAD/ISAR
   (1) *"Conclusions on Accounting and Reporting by Transnational Corporations" (UN Geneva, 1994)*
   (2) *"Environmental Financial Accounting"* - an accounting guideline   issued by the UN Intergovernmental Working Group of Experts on International Standards of Accounting and Reporting (ISAR)

UNEP
   (1) UNEP/SustainAbility *"Engaging Stakeholders"* Vols 1 & 2 (UNEP 1996)
   (2) *"Cleaner Production World-wide Vol 2"* (UNEP 1995)

WBCSD (World Business Council for Sustainable Development) *"Environmental performance and shareholder value"* (WBCSD 1997)

Weiss, Pierre *"Ethics and Investment: philosophy; examples and results"* (1996 unpublished conference paper)

WM Company *"Is There a Cost to Ethical Investing?"* (WM Research 1996)

Part 2 Corporate reports consulted

Anglian Water (UK)
Aylesford Newsprint (UK)
BA (British Airways) (UK) Annual Environmental Report 1996
BC Hydro (Canada) Report on the Environment 1994
The Beacon Press (UK)
British Gas (UK) Annual Report and Accounts 1995
BP (British Petroleum) (UK) Annual Report and Accounts 1995
Brodrene Hartman A/S (Denmark) Environmental Accounts 1995
BSO Origin (The Netherlands) Annual Report 1993
Chemical Industries Association (UK) Indicators of Performance 1990-1995
Daimler Benz (Germany)
Det Danske Stalvalsevaerke A/S (Denmark) Annual Report 1994
Eastern Group (UK)
Elf Atochem (France)
Eskom (South Africa)
Exxon (USA)
Fiat (Italy)
Henkel (Germany)
ICI (UK)
Inveresk Plc (UK)
James Cropper Plc (UK)
London Electricity (UK)
MoDo (Sweden)
Monsanto (USA) Environmental Annual Review 1995
National Grid (UK)
National Power (UK)
Neste Oy (Finland)
Nortel (Canada) Environmental Progress Report 1994
Northern Electric (UK)
Northumbrian Water (UK)
Novo Nordisk (Denmark) Environmental Report 1995
Nuclear Electric (UK) Environmental Report 1994-95 & 1995-96
Rhone-Poulenc (France) Environment Report 1994
Roche (Switzerland) Safety and Environmental Protection at Roche: Group Report 1995
Rover Cars (UK)
Scottish Power (UK)
Severn Trent Plc (UK)
Shell UK
South West Water (UK)
Statoil (Norway)
Thames Water (UK)
Umgemi Water (South Africa)
Volkswagen (Germany)
Volvo (Sweden)
WMC (Australia) Environment Progress Report 1994-95
Yorkshire Electricity Group Plc (UK) Environmental Performance Review 95-96

GUIDE TO ACRONYMS

ACBE   UK Government's Advisory Committee on Business and the Environment (UK)

ACCA   Association of Chartered Certified Accountants (UK)

BiE   Business in the Environment (UK)

CICA   Canadian Institute of Chartered Accountants (Canada)

CSEAR   Centre for Social and Environmental Accounting and Reporting (University of Dundee)

CSFI   Centre for Studies in Financial Innovation (UK)

ECAAF   EC Accounting Advisory Forum (Eur)

EFFAS   European Federation of Financial Analysts Societies (Eur)

EMAS   Eco Management and Audit Scheme (Eur)

EPA   Environmental Protection Agency (USA)

FEE   Federation Des Experts Comptables Europeens (Eur)

FEEM   Fondazione Eni Enrico Mattei (Italy)

ICAEW   Institute of Chartered Accountants in England and Wales (UK)

IRRC   Investor Responsibility Research Centre (USA)

ISAR   United Nations Intergovernmental Working Group of Experts on International Standards of Accounting and Reporting

ISO   International Standards Organisation (Int.)

NPI   National Provident Institution (UK)

UNCTAD   UN Conference on Trade and Development (UN)

UNEP   United Nations Environment Programme (UN)

WBCSD   World Business Council for Sustainable Development (Int.)

WRI   World Resources Institute (USA)

CONSULTEES

Jonathan Barber	SERM
Matteo Bartolomeo	FEEM
Jan Bebbington	CSEAR
Martin Bennett	University of Wolverhampton
Kelley Bernbeck	BiE
Daryl Ditz	WRI
Holly Elwood	EPA
Laura Gottsman	EPA
Professor Rob Gray	CSEAR
Chris Hibbitt	NIvRA
Professor Peter James	Sustainable Business Centre
Mark Mansley	Delphi
Susan McCloughlin	EPA
Noel Morrin	Bie / AEA Technology
Kaspar Muller	EFFAS/Ellipson
David Moore	CICA
Anne Marie O'Connor	NPI
Dave Owen	University of Sheffield
David Owen	Delphi
Janet Ranganathan	WRI
Lorraine Ruffing	ISAR
Russell Sparkes	Central Finance Board of the Methodist Church
Tessa Tennant	NPI

and the members of the following groups with which the author was involved:

- The ACBE financial reporting working party
- The ACCA environmental reporting award panel of judges
- The FEE environmental task force

CHAPTER IV

TRANSFER PRICING REGULATIONS AND TRANSNATIONAL CORPORATIONS PRACTICES: GUIDANCE FOR DEVELOPING COUNTRIES

SUMMARY

The transfer price is the price set by related corporations for the sale or other transfer of goods, services and/or intangible property between them. Due to the somewhat subjective nature of transfer pricing a number of different methods have been devised to determine the price which would have been negotiated in an "arm's length" sale. At times the transfer prices set by related corporations may differ from that which would have been negotiated on an open market in similar circumstances. This may occur through inadvertence or through intentional manipulation, e.g. to avoid taxes, import duties and restrictions on currency and profit repatriation. Transfer pricing can also be used as a restrictive business practice to eliminate competitors.

Governments have enacted legislation to determine the transfer price and prevent abuses in this area. These regulations are not wholly uniform, particularly in their disclosure requirements. Further, the current reporting requirements may provide insufficient information for users of financial statements. This chapter makes recommendations for improved accounting and reporting measures, which would make transfer pricing practices of transnational corporations more transparent for accounting purposes.

I. INTRODUCTION

This report was mandated by the Intergovernmental Working Group of Experts on International Standards of Accounting and Reporting (ISAR) in order to assist its members to analyse the various methods which have been devised to determine transfer prices, that is, the values at which associated parties exchange goods, services and intangibles. The Group is concerned that transnational corporations (TNCs) may use transfer pricing as a means to alter the allocation of profits between associated parties. Transfer pricing guidelines and practices used by TNCs are reviewed within the report in order to make recommendations for accounting disclosure rules which could guide both home and host countries.

The global economy is changing with the transition of eastern and central Europe and Latin American countries to more market-oriented economies, the maturation of many Asian economies and advances in information technology. The increasing sophistication and complexity of the economic, political, technological, legal and regulatory environments, especially in developing countries, are reflected in the rising number and types of cross-border transactions engaged in by TNCs.

Some countries avoid regulating transfer pricing due to fear of discouraging foreign direct investment, the existence of monopolies within the country, and a lack of adequate administrative infrastructure. Cross-border transactions, coupled with more countries engaging in transnational activity, are leading countries to insure that TNCs adhere to international tax regulations and treaty provisions in order to collect a fair share of taxes. The exploitation of differences in tax policies, transfer pricing regulations, import duties, withholding taxes, currency risks and profit repatriation restrictions encourage TNCs to shift subsidiary profits between tax jurisdictions in order to maximise global profit and/or minimise taxes, consequently depriving some countries of their proper tax revenue.

Developing countries and countries in transition are new to the international transfer pricing arena and are increasingly at risk until they adopt regulations which insure the equitable pricing of transferred goods and services. The economic consequences, most notably loss of tax revenue, of profit-shifting via transfer pricing manipulations are detrimental to a country's continuing development. These consequences are minimised through a transfer pricing regime which addresses administrative, accounting and tax requirements of these countries and reflects current global transfer pricing procedures, generally based on an arm's length principle. The regime must be viewed as practical and equitable by both tax authorities and TNCs to be successful.

II.   SUMMARY OF FINDINGS

Most tax authorities agree that the arm's length principle must be upheld when calculating transfer prices for both tangible goods and intangible property. Much work on the international level has been undertaken concerning the methods that best promote this principle. Are transaction-based transfer pricing methods, such as the comparable uncontrolled price (CUP), resale, and cost-plus methods, preferable or superior to profit-based methods (profit split and comparable profits method, CPM) or the newly minted transaction-profit hybrid methods, such as the transactional net margin method (TNMM)?

Many countries' tax authorities are uncomfortable with CPM due to its arbitrary nature, its dependence on comparisons of profits rather than price, and the question of whether it yields a true arm's length result. If CPM is based on an industry average rate of return, or on a rate of return for the TNC rather than for narrowly defined business activities, CPM is not acceptable, given the findings of this report. TNMM, as a hybrid transaction profit method using comparisons of net profit margins and specific-business-activity transactions, is still subject to many of the criticisms levelled at CPM, and must be allowed only as a second-best option.

Most current tax treaties include provisions which address double taxation of related parties, procedures for competent authorities to settle disputes involving two or more countries and provisions for a confidential exchange of information about TNCs. However, most treaties do not force a resolution of transfer pricing disputes between competent authorities or by binding arbitration. Thus, settlement of such disputes and relief from double taxation are not guaranteed.

TNC pricing methods for external reporting purposes are set according to host and home country regulations. However, there are transfer pricing methods which are permissible in one country but not another. Therefore, it is quite possible that a TNC may keep multiple sets of books, one for the tax authorities and one for management. This situation is the result of the conflict between the need of the fiscal authorities to meet budget targets and the need of the managers of TNCs to allocate profit in a way that rewards performance and risk-taking. Keeping multiple sets of books enables TNCs to dismiss the effects of government-mandated methods on subsidiary performance. Although in the first instance this practice may seem unorthodox, the management of a TNC is otherwise forced to deal with the distorting or complicating effects of particular transfer pricing methods. If not constrained by governmental regulations, some TNCs would choose one transfer pricing method which satisfied both management objectives and the regulations of both host and home legal jurisdictions. Multiple sets of books would not be necessary.

General guidance on the reporting of transfer pricing policies and related party disclosures is contained in Conclusions on Accounting and Reporting by Transnational Corporations (UNCTAD/DTCI/1), and in the International Accounting Standard (IAS) No. 24. "Related party disclosures", as well as Exposure Draft E51 and the proposed revision of IAS No. 14 "Reporting financial information by segment". However, the guidance in these pronouncements is so general that it does not achieve its objectives of identifying and discouraging transfer pricing manipulations.

Existing guidance on accounting disclosure should be revised so that relationships between parent TNC and its subsidiaries are clear as well as the specific transfer pricing methods used by geographic segments or subsidiaries. Furthermore, all disclosures by segments should be standardised by accounting principles, by presentation and by profit/loss reporting levels so that comparability and consistency exist across segments whether by country or by product and/or service.

III.   SELECTED TRANSFER PRICING METHODS

While the arm's length approach is the global standard, there are some proponents of other approaches, including formulary apportionment. A discussion of common transfer pricing methods and their strengths and weaknesses is necessary before assessing TNC practices. The definitions in this section are drawn from Coopers and Lybrand (1993), US Sec. 482 (1994), OECD (1996, 1995), and Price Waterhouse (1995).

A.   Arm's length approaches

The arm's length standard requires that the prices charged between related (associated) parties are equivalent to those which would have been charged between unrelated (independent) parties to the same transaction. Transactions between related enterprises are termed controlled transactions while transactions between unrelated enterprises are deemed uncontrolled. An arm's length price or range of prices may be determined using either transaction-based or profit-based methods. Transaction-based methods include the CUP, resale price, cost plus and other methods. Profit-based methods are based on the profits which arise from controlled transactions between one or more of the related TNCs and include the profit split method and CPM.

The method providing the best arm's length result is determined by comparing the degree of comparability between related and unrelated TNCs and by the completeness and accuracy of the data, the reliability of the assumptions and the effect of any problems with either the data or the assumptions on the derived transfer price. Comparability is determined by a functional analysis of activities performed by related TNCs in controlled transactions and by unrelated TNCs in comparable uncontrolled transactions. The analysis identifies the location of the function, resources used, risks undertaken and assets employed, both tangible and intangible.

The major problem with arm's length pricing is that it must be verified by comparison either directly using CUP, which requires readily identifiable comparable transactions between unrelated corporations, or indirectly using any other methods which compare transactions between unrelated corporations with similar functions. It is difficult to identify transactions that are sufficiently comparable to use the CUP method, so many TNCs use other methods that are less direct.

B. Transaction-based methods

Initial transfer pricing legislation equated transaction-based methods such as the comparable uncontrolled price (CUP) with "arm's length price". The CUP method compares the price charged for transferred goods between related TNCs in a controlled transaction to the price charged in a comparable uncontrolled transaction. If exact comparables exist, it is likely to be the best method. However, exact comparables are rare, and information about them difficult to gather. If inexact comparables are used, as is more common, there are difficulties in obtaining and adjusting the data for differences between the transactions compared. Results reached through a search for inexact comparables outside of the controlled group are often unacceptable due to lack of detailed information on specific business and geographic segments.

Later tax authorities also recognised that comparisons with gross profit margins (resale price margins or cost plus margins) could also be used to test whether pricing was arm's length. The resale price method is based on the price at which the product that has been purchased from a related TNC is resold to an unrelated TNC, less a percentage (gross profit) of the selling price. This method is generally limited to property which has not been substantially altered by the reseller. Difficulties arise from problems with the completeness and accuracy of both the data and the assumptions.

The cost plus method is based on the costs incurred by the manufacturer (supplier) in a controlled transaction to a related purchaser, plus a percentage (gross profit mark-up) of those costs. As with the CUP and resale methods, its accuracy as a best method is limited by data and assumption problems.

C. Profit-based and other methods

During the last few years these transaction-based methods have been supplemented by profit-based methods, see figure below. This is, in part, due to the difficult, in finding comparables. Profit-based comparisons can be made on either a transaction basis or a company wide basis. There is no firm division between transaction-based methods and profit-based methods. Most important, the OECD Guidelines were developed on the basis that the only admissible methods whether traditional methods or profit-based methods, are transaction-based. The profit split method divides profits between related enterprises using an economically valid basis that approximates the division of profits that would have been anticipated and reflected in an agreement made at arm's length. A fair profit split should reflect the arm's length principle and result from a functional analysis of the TNC's transactions and operations.

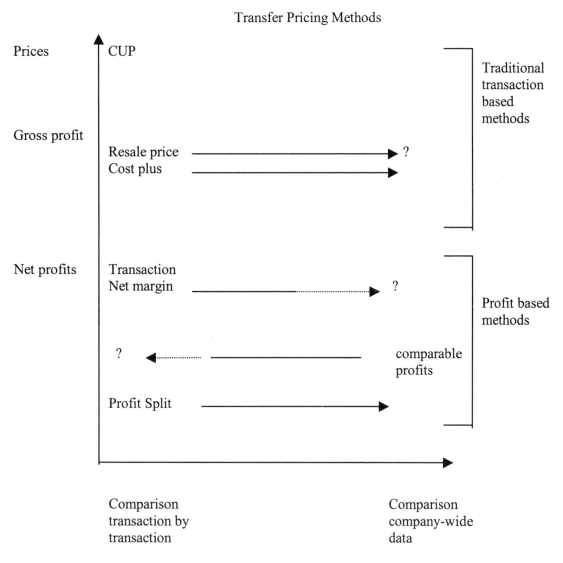

Transfer Pricing Methods

Source: T.A. Symons, Profit Overhead versus Transaction Based Methods, Price Waterhouse, London 1996

A profit split may be calculated using contribution analysis, where the combined profits of the transaction are divided on the relative values of the functions performed by each company. It may also be derived using residual analysis, where a basic return is allocated to each party based on market returns, ignoring any unique and/or valuable assets, with a subsequent division of the residual profit (or loss) based on an analysis of facts and circumstances.

CPM determines the level of profits that would have resulted from a controlled transaction if the net return on the transaction, as indicated by various objective profit measures (such as the return on assets, operating income to sales and other suitable financial ratios), was equal to the return realised by a comparable independent enterprise. There is some debate over the arm's length nature of CPM, in that it depends on profit comparisons rather than price and/or transaction comparisons and functional analysis.

The advantage of the profit split method over CPM is "that a profit split is based on the commercial activity of the entity under examination itself and its related parties and inevitably is related to their economic success or failure and is closely connected to the actual transactions of the group. It thus avoids a major criticism of CPMs, which is the tendency to penalise the commercially unsuccessful by seeking an adjustment to profits based on the results of their more successful commercial rivals" (OECD response to the United States of America's Internal Revenue Service, OECD, 1993, p. 23). The International Chamber of Commerce has criticised CPM, stating that it can only lead to arbitrary outcomes and presents a seriously flawed view of the arm's length principle.

The OECD now classifies the profit split and its newly created TNMM as "transaction profit" methods. TNMM "examines the net profit margin relative to an appropriate base (e.g. costs, sales, assets) that a taxpayer realises from a controlled transaction (1995). The OECD Guidelines apply the net margin method to single transactions or to controlled transactions that can be grouped. The method follows these steps:

- set one (or more) measures of operating profitability (operating return on sales, operating return on assets, gross profit; operating expenses ratio);

- identify appropriate comparable uncontrolled arrangements;

- establish operating profitability using chosen method, based on information derived from comparables;

- apply to a measure of financial performance of tested party not affected by related party arrangement;

- derive arm's length pricing for tested party using basic arithmetical techniques. (Symons, 1996)

By using net profit margin rather than profits, TNMM resembles resale price and cost-plus methods and the narrower US definition of CPM. According to some practitioners the use of net margin methods is, in one way or another, "extremely commonplace" in almost all countries. In the United States, the use of CPM has become almost mandatory. The reason for its growing popularity is that it is extremely difficult to find comparables for the traditional transaction-based methods. This is because given the nature of a TNC group, many of the transactions within it would never occur among independent enterprises. Also reliable pricing information on external comparables is increasingly withheld as commercial pressures lead to greater business secrecy. If company-wide information is used in applying the net margin method, then there is a large amount of information on net profit comparables because published, audited company data are available and reliable. Hence, the increased use of net margin methods could be due to the availability of such information (Symons 1996).

OECD Guidelines recognise that such practical considerations may cause enterprises to chose transactional profit methods. In practice given the lack of comparables, no one method alone can provide a complete arm's length answer. Therefore, enterprises may find themselves using several methods (Symons 1996).

The major non-arm's length approach is global formulary apportionment which is the cause of much discussion and controversy. Formulary apportionment and its unitary variation are based on an allocation of the global profits of a TNC group on a consolidated basis among the associated enterprises in different countries. This approach uses a predetermined formula to allocate profits, treating all TNC affiliates the same in terms of generating revenues and costs. While the appeal of this method is the consistent application of a predetermined formula, major difficulties with this method are the danger of double taxation, lack of agreement among countries on the predetermined formula, the universal application of the formula to dissimilar TNCs across industries and countries and the non-arm's length results produced. Global formulary apportionment is rejected by both OECD and the United States.

IV.   CURRENT REGULATIONS, AGREEMENTS, TREATIES AND PENALTIES

A.   Current regulations

TNCs headquartered in developed countries have been very active in transferring goods and services between the parent company and subsidiaries, both domestic and foreign. As a result, these countries have developed transfer pricing regulations for inbound and outbound cross-border transfers. Whether the burden of proof falls on the tax authority or the TNC varies by country, as shown by a Coopers and Lybrand study (1993).

COUNTRY	BURDEN OF PROOF
Australia	Is on the taxpayer.
Belgium	Varies. It is for the tax authorities to prove that an abnormal advantage has been granted to a foreign affiliate, but in the case of deduction of expenses generally and payments made to tax-favoured entities, the burden of proof is with the taxpayer.
Denmark	Lies firmly with the tax authorities.
France	The allocation of the burden of proof depends on which legal rule/principle is in dispute.
Japan	Is on the taxpayer to show that the price set by the revenue authority is incorrect.
Sweden	On the tax authority.
United Kingdom	On the taxpayer.
United States	On the taxpayer to show that the Internal Revenue Service has acted in an arbitrary and capricious manner or has abused its discretion. Is on the tax authorities if the IRS asserts criminal fraud.

Source: Coopers & Lybrand, 1993, p. 113.

OECD

The OECD published in July 1995 its report on <u>Transfer Pricing Guidelines for Multinational Enterprises and Tax Administrations</u>, which was approved by its Committee on Fiscal Affairs. It is both the only international guideline available and the most widely accepted guideline and has been developed over a number of years. As it represents an international consensus of OECD countries and is a flexible instrument, it could be taken as a starting point by countries developing their regulations for establishing prices for transferring goods, services and intangibles across national frontiers within the same group of companies.

The guidelines also address documentation requirements, application of the guidelines to intangible property and services, and administrative rules regarding mutual agreement procedures, simultaneous examination, safe harbours, advance pricing agreements (APAs) and arbitration issues. Further guidance on permanent establishments, thin capitalisation and cost sharing issues, should be available for comments in mid-1996. The participants of the 7th meeting of the UN ad hoc group of experts on international Cupertino in tax matters, argued that the group should take OECD's work as a starting point and identify areas in which work needs to be done by the group. They felt that the basic problem - enforcing the arm's length principle - is faced by all countries. Thus, there was a certain acceptance of the general applicability of the guidelines to developed and developing countries.

The OECD prefers the transaction-based methods as the best ways of applying the arm's length principle. CUP should be used whenever possible; otherwise, the resale and cost-plus methods are equally acceptable. There is no rigid hierarchy, however. Profit-split and TNMM should be used only as a last resort.

The OECD applies the same methods to tangible and intangible goods. The OECD offers specific guidance on how to determine transfer pricing for intangible property when valuation is difficult at the time the transaction is executed. If unrelated parties would have been willing to accept the risk of unforeseen subsequent developments without a future adjustment to the price, related parties are permitted to do the same.

B.   Advance pricing agreements

A provision which allows a TNC to enter into a pre-transaction agreement with the tax authority(ies) of its home and/or host countries can reduce audit and litigation costs and time. It is termed an advance pricing agreement (APA) in the United States, an advance pricing arrangement (APA) by the OECD and part of a pre-confirmation system (PCS) in Japan. The OECD defines an APA as an arrangement which determines, in advance of controlled transactions, an appropriate set of criteria (e.g., method, comparables and appropriate adjustments thereto) for determining the transfer price for those transactions over a fixed time period.

Approximately forty APAs have been negotiated in the United States and seven in the United Kingdom. Such agreements can provide certainty that the method chosen by the firm will not be contested by the authorities and thus avoid protracted disputes.

The TNC initiates an APA, which may be either: unilateral, with either the home or host country tax authority; bilateral, with both home and one host country tax authority; or multilateral, with home and multiple host country tax authorities. The scope, depth and terms of an APA vary according to each country's tax regulations.

OECD

OECD proposes APAs as one of several administrative approaches for avoiding and resolving transfer pricing disputes. The guidelines are general, suggesting the negotiation of bi- and multi-lateral arrangements whenever possible, the availability of APAs to all TNCs, regardless of size and the use of competent authorities to simplify the administration of the APA programme.

From the OECD's perspective, advantages include collaboration between the TNC and the country's tax authority, possible prevention of lengthy and expensive audits and litigation, and the reduction of uncertainty about the tax treatment of international transfer pricing transactions. Disadvantages include double taxation and corresponding adjustment problems with other countries if an APA is unilateral, an increased demand on both the TNC's and the tax authority's resources to negotiate and finalise the initial APA, the demand for detailed and confidential information from the TNC and an increased risk of audits for unprotected years.

Canada

In February 1995, Revenue Canada issued Information Circular 9404 formalising the APA programme and detailing disclosure procedures and restrictions. These guidelines do not set the actual transfer price, but provide the means to agree upon an appropriate method for setting the price. In any dispute, however, the competent authority (and not the taxing authority, as in the United States) has the final decision on the terms of the negotiated APA.

Germany

TNCs can request advance (binding) rulings or settlements, but these rulings are not common, not specifically restricted to transfer pricing issues and are not guaranteed. Although the programme is informal, there are specific disclosure procedures and restrictions for foreign taxes paid to home-based TNCs. The informal programme is due to lack of demand for a formal APA process by TNCs, whether based in Germany or in other countries.

Japan

The Japanese Pre-Confirmation System (PCS) is most active with United States bank holding companies. In this industry segment, the PCS deals with the appropriate allocations of profits from derivatives between home and host countries. The PCS provides agreement between the NTAA and the TNC on the transfer pricing method to be used, chosen from a list of acceptable methods. It does not, like the United States, consider the arm's length nature of transfer prices and the ranges of those prices.

United Kingdom of Great Britain and Northern Ireland

Inland Revenue employs an informal process to negotiate APAs using the double taxation relief provisions contained in United Kingdom tax treaties with other countries. While no specific procedures or guidelines currently exist, the establishment of a formal programme is being considered. The APAs will be part of a broader advance rulings programme, with the potential for pre-transaction rulings.

United States of America

The APA programme instituted by the IRS in 1991 in Revenue Procedure 91-22 is the most detailed and formalised programme currently implemented. Advance rulings are formalised in the APA process with specific disclosure procedures and restrictions. As of

October 1995, the IRS had completed 41 APAs, had 109 TNCs in the programme at various stages and 56 TNCs actively considering the process at the preliminary discussion stage. The average time to conclude an agreement is currently between ten and fourteen months.

The IRS, in its revised Revenue Procedure 96-53, allows TNCs the option of retroactively applying the APA's terms to a TNC's open years. If a TNC reaches an APA in 1997, the terms can be applied prospectively, i.e. to 1998 and beyond, and retrospectively, requesting a rollback to any years which are still open with the IRS, i.e. have not been audited or closed. This answers the criticisms that APAs "have a potential open year exposure that could be negative and the negotiating process gives companies little control over the information that the IRS has about their financial operations" (DTR 235 9.12.94, p. G-3).

Other countries

Several countries (Australia, Mexico) are in the process of finalising their APA programmes, while Spain may propose a formal APA programme after transfer pricing legislation is enacted. Some countries (Denmark, Italy) have no provisions, formal or informal. France, with no formal procedures for advance rulings on transfer pricing issues, will agree to bilateral agreements using the mutual agreement procedures in its tax treaties. Until the formal APA programme is finalised, Mexico's Secretaria de Hacienda y Credito Publico (SHCP) will grant advance rulings and is considering trilateral agreements with the United States and Canada, using the OECD model. The SHCP is studying the feasibility of APAs with maquiladoras (export production companies on the United States-Mexico border).

Advance agreements for Transfer Pricing Issues

COUNTRY OR TERRITORY	FORMAL OR INFORMAL APA PROGRAMME	ADVANCE RULINGS	DISCLOSURE PROCEDURES, RESTRICTIONS	NO SPECIFIC PROCEDURES	NO ADVANCE RULING OR ACCORD	COMMENTS
Australia	X		X			Finalised version of APA rules expected shortly
Belgium		X	X			Requests must fall within specific categories
Canada	X		X			Competent authority has final say
Denmark					X	
France					X	
Germany	X		X			
Hong Kong		X		X		Related party transaction must fall under anti-avoidance provisions of tax laws
India		X	X			Not available for domestic companies
Ireland		X		X		Possible for related issues, i.e. permanent establishment
Italy					X	
Japan	X		X			May be revised to expand choices on methodology
Korea Republic of					X	Will consider APA requests initiated by foreign government
Mexico	X		X			Formal Programme expected in 1995
Netherlands	X	X	X			Only for bilateral requests involving United States. Advance rulings for unilateral matters
New Zealand		X		X		Government has issued proposal that would provide for APAs
Norway		X		X		Only for oil industry

COUNTRY OR TERRITORY	FORMAL OR INFORMAL APA PROGRAMME	ADVANCE RULINGS	DISCLOSURE PROCEDURES, RESTRICTIONS	NO SPECIFIC PROCEDURES	NO ADVANCE RULING OR ACCORD	COMMENTS
Spain					X	Formal APA programme may be proposed after transfer pricing legislation is enacted
Sweden		X		X		
United Kingdom	X			X		Considering formal programme as part of advance ruling programme
United States	X		X			

Source: Daily Tay Report 72, 14 April 1995 (p. G-3)

C.   Tax treaties

Tax treaties simplify and strengthen co-operation among different national tax authorities and allow similar procedures and conventions to be in place across borders. Such treaties provide procedures for mutual agreement, competent authority, arbitration and information sharing among treaty partners. Tax treaties give a competitive edge to TNCs when home countries have treaties in place with trading partners. Without treaties, TNCs may suffer discriminatory taxes, such as double taxation, non-refundable withholding taxes and no access to foreign tax credits.

The tax treaties of many countries, including Australia, Canada, France, Germany, Japan, the Netherlands and the United Kingdom, are tax sparing. One notable exception is the United States. Tax sparing treaties encourage foreign direct investment by giving TNCs the benefits of tax holidays and lowering the risk of doing business in other countries with whom such treaty provisions exist.

OECD

Articles 9, 25 and 26 of the OECD Model Convention on Income and on Capital (1994) provide the framework for many tax treaties. Article 9 (Associated Enterprises) addresses the double taxation issue. It provides for compensating adjustments so that when transfer pricing adjustments are made, double taxation is avoided. Article 25 (Mutual Agreement Procedure) provides the guidance for competent authorities to settle disputes involving two or more countries. However, neither a settlement nor avoidance of double taxation is guaranteed. Article 26 (Exchange of Information) provides for a confidential exchange of information about TNCs in order to facilitate agreements between competent authorities and to avoid double taxation.

European Union

The Arbitration Convention (on the Elimination of Double Taxation with the Adjustment of Profits of Associated Enterprises) became effective 1 January 1995. This convention eliminates double taxation on transfer pricing adjustments between European Union countries by forcing competent authorities to reach a settlement within two years. If such an agreement is not obtained, the dispute must be settled by independent arbitration within six months.

V.   CURRENT PRACTICES OF TRANSNATIONAL CORPORATIONS

This section presents empirical data on the current methods of 261 TNCs in Canada, Germany, Japan, the United Kingdom and the United States. These data were collected by surveying TNC vice presidents of international operations and/or international taxes. Data include the actual transfer pricing methods used by TNCs, the alternate methods they would use if not subject to country-specific regulations, the factors affecting their choice of a transfer pricing method and the likelihood of entering into an APA with various tax authorities. A comparison of TNC methods with host and home country regulations reveals some significant differences. Such discrepancies may indicate potential problems in the interpretation and application of transfer pricing regulations by both the tax authority and the TNC.

A.   Transfer pricing methods

TNCs choose their transfer pricing methods from methods specified within host and home country regulations. Given the legislative preference for transaction-based methods, it is not surprising that market- and cost-based methods predominate TNC practice, ranging from 89 per cent for Canadian TNCs to 50 per cent for German TNCs. In reality, these percentages are higher because many negotiated methods are transaction-based. If unconstrained by legislation, some TNCs would shift from transaction-based methods to profit-based methods, particularly CPM.

Of thirty-one factors which potentially influence the transfer pricing methods adopted, four were cited as major influences by TNCs, regardless of home country. The ease and cost of implementing the method were considered most important, followed by United States Sec. 482 requirements and the penalties assessed under United States Sec. 6662. The importance of United States regulations to non-United States based TNCs illustrates the influence that the United States tax authority has had on global transfer pricing behaviour and method choice. This is due both to the detailed guidance available for Sec. 482 application and to the willingness of the United States tax authority to aggressively pursue infractions, seek audits and assess penalties.

Many TNCs perceive the transfer pricing methods chosen under the influence of United States transfer pricing regulations and penalties as less than optimal. Therefore, some TNCs implement procedures to nullify the adverse effects of these transfer pricing methods and allow management to better evaluate subsidiary and manager performance.

B.   Advance pricing agreement status

The widespread support of APA programmes expected by various tax authorities has not materialised, even with formalised programmes with written guidance in place in the United States and Canada. The majority of TNCs have no plans to pursue an APA with either host or home countries due to specific objections. In the United States APAs take anywhere between one and two years to negotiate. Some TNCs might feel that they are subject to too much scrutiny during the process and must surrender too much confidential information. In a number of cases managers are motivated to seek an APA solely to avoid penalties.

Current TNC Transfer Pricing Methods for Cross-Border Transactions

	Market-based	Negotiated	Cost-based	Other
Canada	64%	4%	25%	7%
Germany	33%	39%	17%	11%
Japan	41%	38%	18%	3%
United Kingdom	36%	36%	21%	7%
United States	36%	15%	35%	14%

Preferred Transfer Pricing Methods for Cross-Border Transactions

	CUP/CUT	CPM	Cost Plus	Resale Price	Profit Split	Other
Canada	50%	7%	25%	15%	4%	-
Germany	24%	24%	12%	30%	12%	-
Japan	21%	21%	23%	24%	8%	3%
United Kingdom	15%	14%	14%	29%	14%	14%
United States	30%	22%	15%	20%	12%	1%

Measures Taken to Deal with Transfer Pricing Effects

	Two Sets of Books	Approximate Market	Disregard in Analysis	Account for in Budget	Nothing Done
Canada	25%	43%	18%	14%	21%
Germany	18%	35%	12%	12%	35%
Japan	10%	23%	18%	10%	44%
United Kingdom	43%	21%	29%	14%	21%
United States	53%	28%	27%	22%	15%

Advance Pricing Agreements

	WITH UNITED STATES		WITH HOME COUNTRY	
	Have/Plan to Have	No Plans	Have/Plan to Have	No Plans
Canada	7%	93%	11%	89%
Germany	17%	83%	6%	94%
Japan	18%	82%	5%	95%
United Kingdom	29%	71%	21%	79%
United States	10%	90%	-	-

Audit Status

	WITH UNITED STATES		WITH HOME COUNTRY	
	Audit	**No Audit**	**Audit**	**No Audit**
Canada	4%	96%	14%	86%
Germany	11%	89%	6%	94%
Japan	18%	82%	3%	97%
United Kingdom	50%	50%	29%	71%
United States	56%	44%	-	-

Many TNCs did not feel that APAs were necessary in their situation, regardless of host and home countries. Frequently mentioned reasons for not seeking APAs include the perception that the costs of an APA exceed its benefits; the onerous information volume required; and concern about the confidentiality of data provided to the tax authority. Other areas of concern are the perceived difficulty of reaching APAs due both to the variety of products produced by a TNC and to the involvement of multiple country tax authorities; the chance of arbitrary cancellation by the tax authority; the possibility the process could serve as an audit flag; and, the short length of the APA term.

While these reasons have merit, it seems as though TNCs would still embrace APAs as a means of avoiding or decreasing their chances of an audit, given their current audit status. With the exception of Canadian TNCs, a non-United States-based TNC is more likely to be audited by the United States than by its home country tax authority. The United States cannot be viewed as prejudiced against other countries, however; its own TNCs are also audited more often than the others in the survey.

C.   Income manipulation by TNCs

The availability of information about a TNC's transfer pricing activities depends on the TNC's voluntary openness about those activities in their financial reports. Historically this openness has not been forthcoming. There is a concern about the lack of and urgent need for "transparency in the global activities of TNCs ... necessary for informed decision-making by investors, employees, home and host governments" (UNCTAD/DTCI/1, p. iii). This can only be accomplished by increased disclosures about TNC cross-border transactions, particularly those relating to transfer pricing activities. The effects of transfer pricing on, and the manipulation of, subsidiary income are not only tax-related; they also have accounting and reporting implications.

The extent of cross-border income shifting is not easily determined, but evidence exists which demonstrates both its magnitude and its widespread nature. Ernst & Young (1993) reported that in 1992, adjustments of more than USD 1.3 billion were made by the United States IRS to the reported incomes of TNCs domiciled in ten United States trading partner countries, much of which is attributable to income shifting. For the 1989-1993 period, the United States General Accounting Office (1994) reported that the total of individual TNC income adjustments exceeding USD 20 million due to transfer pricing were USD 5.1 billion for non-United States TNCs, and USD 13.9 billion for TNCs domiciled in the United States.

Other evidence is from Japan, which has increased its audits of host and home TNCs suspected of under-reporting and/or shifting income. For the nine years ending June 1995, Price Waterhouse (1995) reports income adjustments by the Japanese NTAA to Japanese TNCs of Y140 billion (approximately USD 1.6 billion). While no figures are available for their audits of non-Japanese TNCs, recent NTAA assessments against United States, German and Swiss-based TNCs for excessive transfer prices and royalty payments have been substantial.

VI. CONSIDERATIONS FOR FUTURE TRANSFER PRICING AND OTHER RELATED REGULATIONS

A. Transfer pricing regulations

Transfer pricing regulations must be flexible and viewed as equitable and practical by both the government and the TNCs. It must be integrated and harmonised with globally accepted policies and practices, supported by an administrative structure and simplified by tax treaty provisions. Any transfer pricing regulations must be developed as part of the country's overall economic structure. For example, if a country's regulation on profit repatriation is strict, TNCs will use a transfer pricing method in order to transfer profits and obviate the law. If foreign currency exchange controls are restrictive, TNCs attempt "to evade exchange control regulations and procedures and to limit exchange risks by importing at higher than fair market prices, particularly where artificial exchange rates exist and where currency devaluations (or revaluations) may be expected" (Lipton 1990). The economic and fiscal systems must support the objectives of the transfer pricing system and vice versa.

The regulations should not discourage foreign direct investment. Based on the findings of Ernst & Young, TNCs choose to invest in developing countries based first on political stability and then on the legal infrastructure, bureaucracy and exchange controls in place. In 1993, a United Nations report suggested that in the design of a tax system, "a Government needs to ensure that it maintains its revenue base while providing a favourable climate for business and investment" (World Investment Report, 1993, UNCTAD, ST/CTC/156, p. 201).

There must be a middle ground between aggressive enforcement of regulations and lack of enforcement of tax compliance requirements. Given the objectives of curtailing tax evasion and avoidance, preventing double taxation, and encouraging investment, regulations should be written for ease of understanding and flexible application, but they must not be ambiguous or vague. Flexibility does not necessarily mean the ability to manipulate transfer pricing results. The experience of the United States, with its extremely stringent rules, sufficient resources, substantial penalties and serious attempts at enforcement, has been that transfer pricing manipulations still occur and profits are shifted.

Reaffirmation of the arm's length principle

Transfer pricing regulations must be based on the arm's length principle in order to maintain consistency and harmony with virtually all other countries' policies. The regulations should not include a ranking by order of preference, but should implement the "best method" rule. This acknowledges the differences between and among TNCs in and across industries, but still restricts method choice to one of the allowable methods.

The transaction-based CUP (CUT for intangible property), resale and cost-plus methods should be equally acceptable, as well as the profit-based profit split method. There is general agreement that these methods provide arm's length results, and are in accordance with most existing regulations. The "best method" should yield a result that is within a given range of acceptable arm's length prices, not an absolute. Given this flexibility in method choice, safe harbours for certain types or sizes of cross-border transactions are not necessary.

Contrary to some countries' regulations, CPM should be eliminated, given the problems associated with its application, widespread disapproval by many tax authorities, and the doubt about whether its results are truly arm's length. The remaining four methods (CUP/CUT, resale, cost-plus and profit split) provide both tax authorities and TNCs with enough choices to find a "best method" for each circumstance. Evidence regarding the appropriateness of TNMM is not yet available to make a decision; it should be used only in extreme conditions.

Factors for determining comparability of transactions include functional analysis, contractual terms, risk analysis, economic circumstances, the specific characteristics of the tangible good or intangible property transferred, and the risks associated with transaction. While the OECD suggests general guidelines for choosing the best method, United States Sec. 482 provides detailed examples of each transfer pricing method, and of the comparative analysis required to apply the best method rule.

Compensating and/or periodic adjustments

The periodic adjustments allowed by the United States under the commensurate with income provisions for intangible property should be restricted. Rather than annual adjustments to match the price of the intangible with the income attributable to that intangible, a periodic assessment at intervals of several years should be done. If there is no significant evidence of profit shifting, there is no need for an adjustment. If profits were shifted, provisions in the tax treaty using the mutual agreement procedures should be adequate to address the imbalance.

Tax authority considerations

The tax authority should be established as a separate governmental unit which collects all data from TNCs, customs, treasury, commerce, and any others with data relevant to assessing transfer pricing methods. They should compare actual TNC performance with the data reported for tax purposes, as well as market prices and/or inexact comparables information.

In developing countries, transfer pricing controls should be part of their existing administrative control systems for customs, imports, exports, etc.. Current customs documentation can serve as the starting point for verification of transfer prices. This will add another level of regulations to administer, adding to the complexity and time of the process, but is necessary to control any TNC manipulation. Eventually, a fairly sophisticated system for data collection, storage and analysis must be developed. The extent to which such a system matures depends on a country's cost/benefit analysis of their specific transfer pricing situation.

The tax authority must be independent, knowledgeable about specific industry practices and pricing, have access and authority to find or calculate arm's length prices, and ability to apply those prices and make adjustments. Given that developing countries will lack records on import and export prices, their tax authorities should use comparables of TNCs in host or other similar countries, co-operation with other tax authorities, and current global prices as references when applicable. Tax treaties should contain OECD Model Convention Article 26 to facilitate the exchange of information between host and home countries about the TNCs involved. Certain tax authorities have dual appointments as customs officials to gain direct access to import and/or export data and guarantee co-ordination of efforts and information-sharing.

Documentation requirements

Contemporaneous documentation of the transfer pricing process must be required to prove a TNC's good faith actions and excuse the TNC from misstatement penalties. The documentation required should include the TNC's transfer pricing methods, company guidelines for application of the methods, any legal agreements among the parent TNC and subsidiaries, functional analyses, lists of comparables, income statements analyses, and corroborating information from the TNC industry to support the methods chosen. This documentation should also be the basis for reaching an APA with a TNC.

B.   Tax treaty provisions

Corresponding adjustments for double taxation

Tax treaties must include OECD Model Convention Article 9 to allow for compensating adjustments so that when transfer pricing adjustments are made, double taxation is avoided. This provision is standard in most existing treaties, and is not controversial.

Mutual agreement procedure and binding arbitration

Article 25 of the OECD Model Convention, as it is written does not guarantee a settlement. It currently details the procedures for competent authorities to reallocate income to avoid double taxation. Currently, most tax treaties only require an attempt by competent authorities to resolve the dispute; failure to do so is acceptable, and arbitration is not obligatory.

Arbitration of unsettled competent authority disputes is usually available in treaty provisions, but is not required. Mandatory arbitration should be required to settle disputes within a reasonable time frame if mutual agreement procedures fail.

When competent authorities fail to settle the dispute, it should be sent to an independent arbitration board whose decision is binding on all participants. The board should consist of transfer pricing, trade law, and tax experts from countries not involved in the particular dispute, or currently involved with one of the parties in another dispute. Board members should not be part of any tax authority or governmental unit. The integrity and independence of the arbitration board must be guaranteed in order for tax authorities and TNCs from the countries involved to accept the board's decision as binding.

If APAs become standardised and more the norm rather than the exception, the procedures could be included in a provision in tax treaties. Currently, APAs are reached in a process which is separate and distinct from the provisions and procedures detailed in tax treaties.

C. Advance pricing agreements

Currently, APAs are more popular with tax authorities than with TNCs. Until APA guidelines are more acceptable to TNCs, they should remain as a longer-term goal of new transfer pricing regulations. APAs can still be reached informally, as is the case with some countries with otherwise sophisticated transfer pricing controls. Although the United States tax authority allow unilateral agreements, such APAs should be discouraged. APAs should be bilateral or multilateral both to avoid double taxation and to discourage TNC favouritism of one tax authority over another. A successful APA programme will save time and money by reducing the number of TNC audits, decrease the cases taken to litigation, and lessen penalties applied. The documentation required should not be much more than the contemporaneous documentation already required for the TNC to prove good faith and avoid penalty assessment.

D. Information exchange provision

Article 26 (Exchange of Information) should also be standard, providing tax authorities access to information about TNCs in order to facilitate competent authority agreements and avoid double taxation. The three ways of exchanging information are "on request (i.e. when a tax administration asks specific questions relating to a particular case); automatic (systematic sending of information concerning specified items of income); (and) spontaneous (e.g. passing on information obtained during examination of a taxpayer's affairs)" (OECD 1996, p. 20).

Other avenues of gathering information include the bilateral Tax Information Exchange Agreements (TIEA) with the United States, or such multilateral agreements as the Nordic Convention on Mutual Assistance, the European Commission's Directive on Mutual Assistance, and the joint Council of Europe/OECD Convention on Mutual Administrative Assistance in Tax Matters. General industry-wide exchanges of information can be set up between the United States IRS and other tax authorities under the Industry Specialisation Programme. Data are limited to a particular industry, rather than specific TNCs.

VII. RECOMMENDATIONS FOR ACCOUNTING DISCLOSURE

A. Current accounting and reporting requirements

Although detailed documentation on transfer pricing methods exists, it is in a format usable by and accessible only to tax authorities. Much of this information should be disclosed for use by other interested parties for analysis and decision-making, and to lessen the incentives for a TNC to engage in cross-border income shifting. Other interested parties include government authorities responsible for anti-monopoly policies, trade union leaders and joint venture partners. In the case of joint venture partners particularly from countries in transition, transfer prices charged by their foreign partners for services have dramatically affected profits and earnings available for distribution. There are many important incentives for engaging in unfair transfer pricing and the users of financial statements must have some assurance that such abuses have not occurred. However, they currently cannot require the necessary information to provide that assurance.

During the 14th session of ISAR, representatives discussed the need for more disclosure. Opinions were divided along north-south lines. The representatives of the Brazil, Morocco, Nigeria and the ICFTU expressed the need for greater disclosure. The representative of the United Kingdom considered that the question of pricing disclosure issues was primarily a matter for special-purpose reports to revenue authorities rather than for general-purpose financial statements. The representatives of Japan, Switzerland and the United Kingdom took the view that the costs and benefits of increased disclosure should be carefully balanced.

Current accounting and reporting requirements do not adequately address, or generally ignore transfer pricing effects, thus providing economic decision makers with an incomplete understanding of TNC operations. As mentioned earlier IAS 24 (Related Party Disclosures) is so general in its transfer pricing reporting requirements that it fails to identify and discourage transfer pricing manipulations which may result in income shifting.

IAS 14 (Reporting Financial Information by Segment) requires specific financial reporting for major business and geographical segments, and will be replaced by Exposure Draft E51 when adopted. Exposure Draft E51, requires TNCs to report detailed information about their primary basis for segment reporting, which is usually by business segment (product and/or service line). Required disclosures about the secondary basis, usually geographical segment, are minimal, limited to the sales revenue, carrying amount of segment assets, and capital expenditures by geographical region.

Some guidance for reporting of segment information is provided in <u>Conclusions on Accounting and Reporting by Transnational Corporations</u> (UNCTAD/DTCI/1) 1994. It recommends that information should be reported by both significant industry segments and geographical areas. The data to be reported are similar to that required by IAS 14, and includes disclosure of the method used for inter-segment (transfer) pricing.

B.   Current documentation requirements

Without increased disclosure, it is difficult for interested parties other than tax authorities to determine segment income and assess segment operations. The OECD (1995) advocates that TNCs provide adequate documentation to tax authorities to support the derivation of transfer prices in accordance with the arm's length principle. This documentation includes how and why the TNC's transfer pricing method was selected. Contemporaneous documentation is not required, however.

The United States IRS requirements include but are not limited to contemporaneous documentation encompassing how and why the transfer pricing method was chosen, why other methods were not used, related party transaction details, economic analyses supporting the current transfer pricing method, subsidiary and consolidated profit and loss statements, ownership and capital structure information, and records of loans, services and other related party transactions.

Given that most TNCs already prepare extensive documentation to comply with tax authority requests (to accompany tax returns, for audit purposes, or to seek an advance pricing agreement), it should not be an onerous task to extract data relevant to economic decision-makers and present it in a usable reporting format.

C. Recommendations for improved reporting

ISAR has provided some guidance, although limited, in its Conclusions on Accounting and Reporting by Transnational Corporations, 1994. Previous guidance on intra-group transactions recommended that:

- the enterprise as a whole should disclose in its financial statements the policies followed with regard to determining the prices for such transactions;
- it should indicate whether such transactions had been made on the basis of market prices or in the absence of such prices, other methods which should be described;
- individual member enterprises in the group should also disclose the volume of such transactions, either as aggregate amounts or in terms of appropriate proportions,
- they should also disclosure the amounts or appropriate proportions of outstanding items in so far as those disclosures are required to present a true and fair view;
- those aspects should be verified by auditors.

Previous conclusions on related party transactions recommended that

- information would usually be most useful if aggregated by transaction and nature of relationship to provide, for example, total sales to related companies or total loans made to directors;
- disclosure on an individual basis might be more informative when there was significant transactions with specific related parties;
- the enterprise as a whole should disclose in its financial statements the policies followed in regard to determining the prices for related party transactions;
- it should indicate whether such transactions had been made on the basis of market price, or in the absence of such prices, other methods which should be described;
- individual enterprises in a group should describe their relationships with related parties and the types of transactions with those parties;
- related party transactions may lead to disclosures by a reporting enterprise in the period which they affect purchases or sales of property and other assets, rendering or receiving of services, agency arrangements, leasing arrangements, transfer of technology, fund transfers, guarantees, collateral;
- the volume of such transactions should be disclosed, either as aggregate amounts or in terms of appropriate proportions, as should the amounts or proportions of outstanding items in so far as those disclosures are required to present a true and fair view.

Additional disclosure, whether through revision of existing accounting and reporting standards or through a special purpose report, is essential. Much of this data can be released to the public without violating TNC confidentiality or exposing trade and business secrets. Much of the following data exist, either internal to the TNC, filed with tax authorities, or shared among tax jurisdictions under Article 26 (Exchange of Information) of the OECD Model Tax Convention The following paragraphs suggest the content of fuller disclosure.

An <u>organisational chart</u> outlining the relationships between the parent TNC and its subsidiaries, divisions, affiliates, joint ventures, etc. is essential. Any relationships between these groups involving intersegment transfers should be summarily identified here. Such disclosure would highlight material cross-border transfers and the countries involved.

The <u>specific transfer pricing methods used</u> by geographic segments or subsidiaries, rather than the single most prevalent method employed by the TNC. Present guidance requires only the prevalent transfer pricing method used, which is insufficient information with which to conduct an economic or financial analysis. Many TNCs use different methods for different subsidiaries, dependent upon the depth and rigor of a given host country's specific tax and transfer pricing environments. Disclosure might deter TNC management from income-shifting if a comparison of methods across countries suggested such behaviour.

<u>Details of related party transactions</u> should be disclosed. Such details should be categorised by transactions between parent TNC and subsidiary, and between TNC subsidiaries, as noted in the organisational chart. Some authorities require revenues to be separated into external sales and inter-segment sales, but no information is required on the costs or any other details associated with inter-segment transfers. The formats for reporting segment information must be modified to more fully address inter-segment activity on a geographical basis;

<u>Profit and loss statements by geographic segment/ subsidiary</u> should be provided, regardless of primary internal reporting class. Some authorities assume internal reporting is driven by either product or service or by geographical area. The proposed accounting standards on segment reporting requires full disclosure only by primary internal reporting class, which is usually product/service. This means that only minimal disclosure is made about the secondary reporting class, which is usually country/geographical area. Full disclosure by both product/service and geographic area are necessary to meet the needs of financial statement users.

<u>Information on tax liabilities, tax payments</u>, and statutory and effective tax rates, by host and home countries. This allows interested parties to analyse individual tax activity, not the consolidated figures presented in the TNC's financial statements. More detailed tax data by geographical segment are necessary for any substantive analysis by economic users and as a deterrent to income-shifting by some TNCs.

<u>All disclosures by segments should be standardised</u> by accounting principles, by presentation, and by profit/loss reporting levels. This creates comparability and consistency across segments, whether by country or by product or service. This will provide immediately relevant and useable information for a variety of segment analyses.

The foregoing disclosures should be required for segments and subsidiaries which engage in significant related party transactions. The threshold for materiality can be determined using criteria set by tax authorities or by the IAS draft (10 per cent). It should be the internal threshold or 10 per cent, whichever is smaller.

Data for these disclosures are currently compiled by TNCs for tax and internal reporting purposes, and must be modified and reformatted for use by other decision-makers. The benefits of such increased disclosure to other users must be weighed against the costs, both real and imagined, of publicly reporting this information:

- increased costs (both financial and time) to the TNC of modifying existing data and providing information in a useable format

- concerns with confidentiality of data which has historically been internally controlled, except for release to tax authorities

- concerns with misuse and misinterpretation of increased disclosures by naive or not fully knowledgeable users

- lack of support from countries which benefit from TNC income shifting and subsequent increased tax revenues

- enforcement of reporting requirements. Should disclosure be mandatory or voluntary?

Given the financial statement user's general lack of information about transfer pricing methods, and their effects on shifting income and tax liabilities, more detailed disclosure as outlined above is essential.

References

Bureau of National Affairs. Daily Tax Reports (DTR). Washington DC: BNA. 1994, 1995.

Coopers and Lybrand. International Transfer Pricing. Oxfordshire: CCH International. 1993.

Ernst & Young. IRS Examination of Foreign Controlled Organizations. Press release, reported in 93 Tax Notes International (TNI) 109-17. 8 June 1993.

_____. Global 1000 Investment in Emerging Markets. London: Ernst & Young International Ltd. 1994.

General Accounting Office. Information on Transfer Pricing (Update). GAO/GGD-94-206R. 15 September 1994.

Harris, D., R. Morck, J. Slemrod and B. Yeung. "Income Shifting in U.S. Multinational Corporations", in Studies in International Taxation, ed. A. Giovannini, R. Hubbard and J. Slemrod. Chicago: University of Chicago Press. 1993.

Internal Revenue Service. Estimates of the Income Tax Gap among Foreign-Controlled Domestic Corporations. Washington DC: Department of the Treasury. 6 June 1994.

International Accounting Standards Committee. IAS 14. Reporting Financial Information by Segment. London: IASC. 1981.

_____. IAS 24: Related Party Disclosures. London: IASC. 1984.

____. Exposure Draft E51: Reporting Financial Information by Segment. London. IASC: December 1995.

Laster, D. and R. McCauley. "Making Sense of the Profits of Foreign Firms in the United States", <u>Federal Reserve Bank of New York Quarterly Review</u>, Summer/Fall 1994, pp. 44-75.

Lipton, C. "Transfer Pricing Protective Provisions in Joint Ventures", in <u>Transfer Pricing and International Taxation</u>, ed. Sylvain Plasschaert, V. 14, UN Library on Transnational Corporations. London/New York: Routledge. 1994.

Organisation for Economic Co-operation and Development. Tax Aspects of Transfer Pricing Within Multinational Enterprises: The United States Proposed Regulations. Paris: OECD. 1993.

____. Model Tax Convention on Income and on Capital. Paris: OECD Committee on Fiscal Affairs. 1994.

____. Transfer Pricing Guidelines for Multinational Enterprises and Tax Administrators, Discussion Draft of Part I: Principles and Methods. Paris: OECD. July 1995.

____. Transfer Pricing Guidelines 1996 Update. Paris: OECD. April 1996.

____. Tax Information Exchange between OECD Member Countries: A Survey of Current Practices. Paris: OECD. 1994c.

____. Transfer Pricing Guidelines for Multinational Enterprises and Tax Administrators, Discussion Draft of Part II: Applications. Paris: OECD. 1 March 1995.

Pagan, J. and J. Wilkie. Transfer Pricing Strategy in a Global Economy. Amsterdam: IBFD Publications. 1993.

Plasschaert, S. "Transfer Pricing in Developing Countries" in <u>Multinationals and Transfer Pricing</u>, ed. A. Rugman & L. Eden. New York: St. Martin's Press. 1985.

Price Waterhouse. International Tax Review. 21(1) January/February 1995.

____. International Tax Review. 21(6) November/ December 1995.

Symons, Terry. "Profit Oriented Versus Transaction Based Methods, Price Waterhouse, London, 1996.

United Nations. World Investment Report, New York: United Nations (ST/CTC/156). 1993.

United Nations. Conclusions on Accounting and Reporting by Transnational Corporations, (UNCTAD/DTCI/1) New York: UNCTAD. 1994.

Van Herksen, Monique and Yi-Wen Hsu. "Avoiding Double Taxation by Way of Advance pricing Agreements and Competent Authority Assistance", Stibbe Simont Monahan Duhot, Amsterdam, 1996

Publications

International Accounting and Reporting Issues:
1999 Review (forthcoming)
1998 Review (Sales No.E.98.II.D.)
1996 Review (Sales No.E.97.II.D.12)
1995 Review (Sales No.E.95.IIA.11)
1994 Review (Sales No.E.II.A.3)
1993 Review (Sales No.E.IIA.16)

Environmental Accounting: *Accounting and Financial Reporting for Environmental Costs and Liabilities* (Sales No.A/C/E/F/R/S.98.II.D.14)

Financial Disclosure by Banks: proceedings of a forum (Sales No. E.98.II.D.13)

Responsibilities and Liabilities of Accountants and Auditors: proceedings of a forum (Sales No. E.95.IIA.10)

Conclusions on Accounting and Reporting by Transnational Corporations: The Intergovernmental Working Group of Experts on International Standards of Accounting and Reporting (Sales No. E.94.II.A.9)

Objectives and Concepts Underlying Financial Statements: the Intergovernmental Working Group of Experts on International Standards of Accounting and Reporting (Sales No. E.98.II.A.18)

Accounting for Sustainable Forestry Management: A case study (sales No. E.94.II.A.17)

Accounting, Valuation and privatization (Sales No. E.94.II.A.3)

Accounting for East-West Joint Ventures (-sales No. E.92.II.A.13)

How to order

United Nations publications may be obtained from bookstores and distributors throughout the world or you may write to:

Sales Section
Room DC2-853
United Nations New York, N.Y 10017
U.S.A.

Or

Sales Section
UN Office at Geneva
Palais des Nations
CH-1211 Geneva 10
SWITZERLAND

For further information write to:

United Nations Conference on Trade and Development
Division on Investment, Technology and Enterprise Development
Enterprise Development Branch
Accounting Section
Palais des Nations
CH-1211 Geneva 10
SWITZERLAND

Telephone: (41) (22) 917 5802 / 917 5601 / 917 5257
Facsimile: (41) (22) 917 0122
e.mail: <Lorraine.Ruffing@unctad.org>   or   <Yoseph.Asmelash@unctad.org>   or
               <Donna.El-murr@unctad.org>